Good Practice in Child Care Cases

THIRD EDITION

D1610859

Other titles available from Law Society Publishing:

Children and Families Act 2014
Noel Arnold

Family Law Arbitration
Dennis Sheridan

Family Law Protocol (4th edn)
The Law Society

Titles from Law Society Publishing can be ordered from all good bookshops or direct (telephone 0370 850 1422, email **lawsociety@prolog.uk.com** or visit our online shop at **bookshop.lawsociety.org.uk**).

GOOD PRACTICE IN CHILD CARE CASES

THIRD EDITION

The Law Society

The Law Society

© The Law Society 2015

Crown copyright material is reproduced with the permission of the Controller of Her Majesty's Stationery Office

ISBN-13: 978-1-78446-020-4

First published in 2004
2nd edition 2010

This third edition published in 2015 by the Law Society
113 Chancery Lane, London WC2A 1PL

Typeset by Columns Design XML Ltd, Reading
Printed by Hobbs the Printers Ltd, Totton, Hants

The paper used for the text pages of this book is FSC® certified. FSC (the Forest Stewardship Council®) is an international network to promote responsible management of the world's forests.

Contents

Foreword to the third edition by the Right Honourable Sir James Munby

Since the publication of the previous edition of this invaluable guide in 2010 there have been many changes in family law, not least, in April 2014, the arrival of the Family Court and the implementation of the revised Public Law Outline.

What has not changed is the need for careful and sensitive handling of the complex issues which arise in public law cases by judges, magistrates, legal practitioners and all the other professionals who come into contact with the child and his or her family. Solicitors acting in these matters have a vital role to play in making sure that cases are dealt with justly and fairly, without delay and with the minimum of distress to the children and others concerned.

I am delighted that the Law Society, with the involvement of the Association of Lawyers for Children and Resolution, has produced an updated edition of this excellent good practice guide. It is an admirable supplement to the fourth edition of the Law Society's *Family Law Protocol* (forthcoming). As with previous editions, it provides practical and welcome guidance to the solicitors who practise in this important, difficult and sensitive field. Its arrival is much to be welcomed. I hope it has a wide and appreciative readership.

James Munby
President of the Family Division
6 July 2015

Preface and acknowledgements

About this book

This book, published here for the third time, is a collection of concise good practice guidelines for all solicitors acting in public law Children Act cases, whether they are acting for a local authority, a parent, a child or another party. Other relevant guidance is appended.

- Part 1 sets out the general principles that need to be considered by all solicitors, whichever party they act for.
- Part 2 includes common issues that need to be considered by all solicitors involved in public law Children Act proceedings.
- Part 3 deals in particular with the role of solicitors acting for local authority clients.
- Part 4 deals with matters to be considered when instructed by children or children's guardians.
- Part 5 outlines the approach to be taken by solicitors when acting for parents and other adult parties.
- Part 6 covers good practice in relation to other aspects of public law children cases, including adoption.
- Part 7 covers issues concerning legal aid and costs.

The first five parts have been written with care order applications in mind, but are intended to be of general assistance with client and professional relationships, and the aspects of conduct covered will also be relevant for other types of specified proceedings.

Since the publication of the second edition a new Part 7 dealing with legal aid and costs issues has been added, and appendices have been updated to include:

- an updated Public Law Outline (in effect from 22 April 2014) contained in Practice Direction 12A – **Appendix 1**;
- a new Child Arrangements Programme (CAP 2014) contained in Practice Direction 12B (in effect from 22 April 2014) – **Appendix 2**; and

- updated useful guidance and directions from the courts and the Official Solicitor relating to children and family proceedings.

Aims of this guide

1. To accompany the Law Society's *Family Law Protocol* (4th edition, forthcoming) which does not cover public law cases involving children in detail.

2. To provide supportive guidance on the conduct of cases and the particular approach required for less experienced practitioners who are not yet members of the Law Society's Children Law Accreditation Scheme, and an *aide mémoire* for more experienced practitioners.

3. To ensure the highest standards of representation for children and their families in public law Children Act proceedings, addressing the needs of the client.

Scope

This book has been drafted by the Law Society's Children Law Sub-Committee with the active and close involvement of the Association of Lawyers for Children, Cafcass, the Official Solicitor and Resolution. The intention is that it should form a benchmark of good practice with which all solicitors practising children law in England and Wales should comply.

Many experienced child care solicitors will undoubtedly find that they already practise to the standard outlined, but even they may find it a helpful guide. For those solicitors who are newly qualified or less experienced, there will be much in this document which will assist them in their professional development in the practice of public law children cases.

It is also hoped that members of the public and the judiciary will find it of assistance in indicating the expected standards to be practised by those representing or appearing before them.

This is the third edition of *Good Practice in Child Care Cases*. The intention is to update the guide regularly to accommodate any changes in law and practice. Users of this guide are encouraged to write to the Law Society at 113 Chancery Lane, London WC2A 1PL or email publishing@lawsociety.org.uk with comments which will be of considerable help in reviewing future editions.

Acknowledgements

Good Practice in Child Care Cases (3rd edition) was drafted by the Children Law Sub-Committee:

- Dorothy Simon, chair
- Noel Arnold
- Jerry Bull
- Valerie Cannon
- Graham Cole
- Mike Hinchliffe
- Lorene Hodkinson
- Robert Hush
- Denise Lester
- VyVy Lewis
- Uma Mehta, CBE
- Vanessa Priddis
- Stuart Smith
- Bill Stone

Thanks are also given to the following for their assistance and contributions:

- Maud Davis and Nicola Jones-King, co-chairs, Association of Lawyers for Children
- Julie Hine, the Office of the Official Solicitor
- Barbara Hopkin
- Nick Denys, Law Society
- David Jockelson
- Vicky Ling
- Janet Noble, Law Society
- Mark Paulson, Law Society
- Rachel Rogers, Head of Policy, Resolution

June 2015

Table of cases

Table of statutes

Table of statutory instruments

Abbreviations

ACA 2002	Adoption and Children Act 2002
CA 1989	Children Act 1989
Cafcass	Children and Family Court Advisory and Support Service
CICA	Criminal Injuries Compensation Authority
ECHR	European Convention on Human Rights and Fundamental Freedoms
ECtHR	European Court of Human Rights
EHC	education health and care plan
FDAC	Family Drug and Alcohol Court
FGC	family group conference
FLA 1996	Family Law Act 1996
FMPO	forced marriage protection order
FPR	Family Procedure Rules 2010, SI 2010/2955
HRA 1998	Human Rights Act 1998
ICO	Information Commissioner's Office
IRO	independent reviewing officer
LAA	Legal Aid Agency
LASPO	Legal Aid, Sentencing and Punishment of Offenders Act 2012
LbP	letter before proceedings
LiP	Litigant in Person
MCA 2005	Mental Capacity Act 2005
NSPCC	National Society for the Prevention of Cruelty to Children
PPM	pre-proceedings meeting
PLO	Public Law Outline
SEND	special educational needs and disability
SRA	Solicitors Regulation Authority
UNCRC	United Nations Convention on the Rights of the Child
VHCC	Very High Cost Case

PART 1

General principles

1.1   CHILD FOCUS

1.1.1   Section 1(1) of the Children Act (CA) 1989 states

> When a court determines any question with respect to –
>
> (a)   the upbringing of a child; or
> (b)   the administration of a child's property or the application of any income arising from it,
>
> the child's welfare shall be the court's paramount consideration.

1.1.2   A focus on the child is essential to good practice and solicitors should ensure that the principle that a child's interests are paramount is reflected in the conduct of the case itself.

1.1.3   All solicitors, whether acting for local authorities, parents and other adult parties, or the child or children's guardian (giving instructions on the child's behalf), have a duty to act on the instructions of their particular client.

1.1.4   Each client may have a different view as to what is in the child's interests. However, all solicitors can, and should, adopt a child-focused approach by ensuring that the presentation of their client's case takes into account the needs of the child throughout and make best efforts to ensure that clients understand that the court's paramount concern is the child's welfare.

1.2   THE 'NON-ADVERSARIAL' APPROACH

1.2.1   Case law and guidance state that public law CA 1989 proceedings should be treated as 'non-adversarial'. However care proceedings, by their nature, are adversarial, since the evidence to satisfy the threshold criteria must be thoroughly tested and issues which relate to disposal are often not agreed, especially when adoption is part of the care plan.

1

1.2.2   In practice, 'non-adversarial' means that solicitors should not behave in an unduly antagonistic, aggressive, or confrontational manner. Child care cases should be approached with a spirit of professional co-operation with due respect to all parties, particularly if any party is unrepresented. See also:

- Resolution's *Guide to Good Practice for Family Lawyers on Working With Litigants in Person* (2014), available to download from: **www.resolution.org.uk**.
- The judiciary's *A Handbook for Litigants in Person* (22 October 2013), available to download from: **www.judiciary.gov.uk**.
- The Bar Council's *Representing Yourself in Court* (2014), available to download from: **www.barcouncil.org.uk**.
- Joint guidelines on dealing with litigants in person (LiPs) published by The Law Society, the Bar Council and CILEx, available to download from: **www.cilex.org.uk/membership/lip_guidelines.aspx**.

1.2.3   Solicitors must therefore:

(a)   Avoid adopting an antagonistic or confrontational attitude in their approach to the case or advocacy that may cause unnecessary acrimony, delay or cost. Solicitors should remember that if one party behaves in such a manner, the other parties may feel forced to respond in kind. All solicitors should resist such an approach, however 'productive' this may appear to be in the short term.

(b)   Ensure that all parties and their legal representatives are treated with respect and that all matters are dealt with in as courteous and cordial a manner as possible while still putting a client's case robustly and challenging the evidence, if necessary (see **1.3**).

1.2.4   It is worth noting that the court is developing a more 'inquisitorial' approach as a result of having to deal with increasing numbers of LiPs – even in public law cases where family members may be parties but legal aid is not available.

1.2.5   Proactive case management is very much connected to the issue of delay. All solicitors, whoever they are representing, should be committed to avoiding delay in the proceedings, both because statute and case law repeatedly emphasise that delay is contrary to the interests of the child and because of the change in procedure which stipulates that care proceedings should conclude within 26 weeks from the date of issue unless the case is exceptional. Please see **1.5** below.

1.2.6   Solicitors have a duty to promote these principles in the interests of children and should bear in mind the following:

(a)   A child's development and stability require prompt and effective decision-making within the child's timescales and using evidence relevant to each child's needs.

(b)   Children and their families are not usually involved in proceedings by choice.

(c)   The effect of proceedings on the child and members of the family can be profound and may impact upon the family members and family dynamics for the long term, particularly if the proceedings are acrimonious or badly managed.

1.2.7   The actions of solicitors can in themselves, therefore, undermine the effectiveness of measures which are ordered by the court, especially if a child is placed within the family network and it is envisaged that a child will have contact with his or her parent.

1.2.8   Solicitors should encourage their clients to work in partnership with local authority professionals, especially in an effort to create a cordial working relationship after the care proceedings conclude in the event that a care order is made and a child resides with foster carers or extended family members for the long term.

1.3   TESTING THE EVIDENCE

1.3.1   Solicitors must ensure that they rigorously test all the evidence and advise their clients to concede issues and/or contest the case as appropriate, in relation to the threshold criteria and all other evidence. Full consideration should always be given to the need to test witness evidence by cross-examination in a thorough but professional and courteous manner.

1.3.2   Clients should be advised that their evidence is dealt with by the court in accordance with prescribed rules and the court has the final decision on which, if any, experts should attend at court to present oral evidence. Likewise, a court will also determine if it is necessary for a separate fact-finding hearing to be held during the course of any Children Act proceeding.

1.4   PROFESSIONAL APPROACH

1.4.1   Solicitors must take care not to become so involved that their personal emotions or own emotional response to the child or any issue which arises in the case adversely affects their judgement. Retaining a professional and objective relationship with the client is crucial. Clients have the right to put their case, subject to the prescribed rules and procedure, and solicitors must be careful not to substitute their own judgement on what is in the child's best welfare interests for that of their client. In acting professionally solicitors should:

(a)   Listen to clients and take instructions throughout.

(b)   Explain and guide clients about the court process and how the court is likely to manage the case to its conclusion.

(c)   Advise clients carefully on the available options and likely outcomes on the basis of the evidence. Solicitors should ensure that they objectively evaluate the evidence, particularly at the early stages so as, for example, to avoid unsuccessful applications for interim orders which serve only to cause unnecessary conflict and costs. As new evidence is presented, solicitors must revise and update their advice to clients.

(d)   Properly exercise professional judgement in advising clients when there are reasonable grounds to contest an issue and when it is appropriate to compromise, seek an agreement or make concessions.

(e)   Advise clients (in writing when possible) on the consequences of their actions, including the consequences of failing to follow advice, undertake court-directed assessments, and/or the failure to provide updating instructions if a client is difficult to contact.

1.4.2   At the conclusion of proceedings, clients should be advised not only of their rights of appeal but of the prospects of success in pursuing an appeal.

1.5   CASE MANAGEMENT, PROCEDURE AND AVOIDING DELAY

1.5.1   Case management and procedure in care proceedings are now tightly prescribed by the revised Public Law Outline (hereinafter referred to as PLO), a comprehensive document which requires detailed consideration by all practitioners in the field (see **Appendix 1**). The PLO details the principles of case management, the case management tools which are available to the court, the various forms and documents (all of which were specifically created for the PLO), and the various stages of the proceedings. Following issue and allocation these are:

(a)   the case management hearing;

(b)   the issues resolution hearing; and

(c)   the final hearing.

It is vital for solicitors to understand the PLO from the pre-proceedings stage all the way until the conclusion of care and placement proceedings.

1.5.2   The Children and Families Act 2014 was implemented on 22 April 2014. On the same date, the revised Family Procedure Rules (FPR) 2010, SI

2010/2955 at Part 12 ('Proceedings relating to children') and the revised Practice Direction for the PLO (PD12A) were brought into effect. The overriding objective set out in FPR Part 1 is to ensure that all cases are dealt with justly and within 26 weeks.

1.5.3   Solicitors have a duty therefore, as the client's representative and as officers of the court, to ensure that all cases are dealt with justly and efficiently. Practitioners are encouraged to keep in mind the overriding objectives of the PLO and of FPR so that the case may be carefully considered by the court and conclude within 26 weeks, unless the case is exceptional and there are grounds for deviating from the usual timescales.

1.5.4   The court will look at each case on a case-by-case basis in order to determine if there are reasonable grounds for the case not concluding within 26 weeks from the date of issue. Solicitors must therefore be proactive in managing their own cases, which in turn will contribute to the court's overall case management function.

1.5.5   There are some exceptional circumstances where the court may decide that the timetable should extend beyond 26 weeks and examples given in case law are cases with:

(a)   international elements;
(b)   separate fact-finding hearings;
(c)   parents who have learning difficulties;
(d)   Family Drug and Alcohol Court (FDAC) proceedings; and
(e)   concurrent pending criminal proceedings.

1.5.6   It is also important to make sure that wherever necessary the court is informed if there is slippage in the timescales and a party does not comply with court orders, especially if such delay will impact upon the date of the final hearing (see in particular *Re W (Children)* [2014] EWFC 22).

1.5.7   Most courts now have a dedicated email address for non-compliance with directions and all parties are under a duty to inform the court of any slippage in timing. Some judges will agree to providing their direct email address and parties can inform the judge of delays and he or she can, if necessary, amend directions or require a formal application to court by the relevant party.

1.5.8   Changes to statutory guidance were made at the same time that the PLO was introduced. The Department for Education's *Children Act 1989: Court Orders and Pre-Proceedings for Local Authorities* (2014), hereinafter referred to as 'Statutory Guidance, Vol. 1', was revised and republished to dovetail with the revised PLO and it can be found at **www.gov.uk/ government/publications/children-act-1989-court-orders–2**.

1.5.9   A previous document was published in 2009 by the Ministry of Justice's Care Proceedings Programme, *Preparing for Care and Supervision Proceedings: A Best Practice Guide for Use by All Professionals Involved with Children and Families Pre-proceedings and in Preparation for Applications Made Under Section 31 of the Children Act 1989* (hereinafter referred to as the 'best practice guide'). The best practice guide remains valid as guidance and this can be found at **Appendix 4**. The route map from the PLO and the best practice guide are reproduced here in **Appendices 1–4**.

1.6   MENTORING

1.6.1   Difficult situations can arise in any child care case. Sources of formal and informal information and support are available. All solicitors should consider seeking advice from other members of the profession in and outside their firm or local authority legal department, including from members of the Children Law Accreditation Scheme. The relevant practitioner associations can assist in finding professional mentors. Their contact details are contained in **Appendix 10**.

1.6.2   In cases where no children's guardian has been allocated for the child, it is a matter for individual solicitors to decide whether or not to accept an appointment as the child's solicitor, taking into account their ability and competence to act and with close regard to the child's best interests as well as their professional duty to the client. All solicitors in this position should consider seeking the advice and support of a mentor or mentors and once appointed, should continue to seek their assistance and guidance until the children's guardian is allocated or an independent social worker is instructed. It is essential that solicitors who act or are likely to act for children in public law CA 1989 proceedings, read the Law Society's Practice Note: Acting in the Absence of a Children's Guardian (21 August 2009), which can be found at **www.lawsociety.org.uk**.

1.7   GOOD PRACTICE GUIDANCE

1.7.1   Solicitors must comply with the rules and principles of conduct contained in the SRA Code of Conduct 2011, published by the Solicitors Regulation Authority (SRA). All references to the 'Code of Conduct' refer to the version available online at the time this book went to print, unless stated otherwise. The online version is accessible at the SRA website:

www.sra.org.uk. See also the family law elements of the new SRA Competence Statement (March 2015) at **www.sra.org.uk/competence**.

1.7.2   The SRA's Professional Ethics helpline can be contacted on 0370 606 2577 between 9 am and 5 pm. The helpline provides guidance concerning issues of professional conduct.

1.7.3   The Law Society's Practice Advice Service also operates a telephone helpline which is staffed by a team of solicitors. The Practice Advice Service can assist with various matters including, for example, costs and anti-money laundering and can be contacted on 0207 320 5675 or by email: practiceadvice@lawsociety.org.uk.

1.7.4   A comprehensive text, *Child Law Handbook: Guide to Good Practice*, edited by Liz Goldthorpe with Pat Monro, was published in 2005 by the Law Society in partnership with the Association of Lawyers for Children.

1.7.5   Chapter 8 of the *Resolution Family Law Handbook* (Greensmith, 2nd edn, Law Society Publishing in partnership with Resolution, 2010) covers children law (both private and public law proceedings).

PART 2

Common issues

2.1   HUMAN RIGHTS

2.1.1   Solicitors must have knowledge of the Human Rights Act (HRA) 1998, relevant Strasbourg jurisprudence from the European Court of Human Rights (ECtHR), and the domestic case law which arises from these authorities, and must keep this knowledge up to date. Solicitors must have particular regard to the European Convention on Human Rights and Fundamental Freedoms (ECHR); particularly Article 6 (right to a fair trial) and Article 8 (right to respect for private and family life) including how this can be balanced against Article 10, the right to freedom of expression, in relation to publishing information about a family case. They should ensure that proceedings are conducted with due regard to such rights, for example in relation to delay, time for preparation, equality of arms, access to documentation and rehabilitation, and that any order sought regarding a child is lawful and proportionate. This means the court should not terminate the relationship between parents and child unless the interests of the child demand it (see *Re C and B (Care Order: Future Harm)* [2001] 1 FLR 611).

2.1.2   Solicitors should not use human rights arguments inappropriately to bolster weak cases or to raise inappropriate points, but they must carefully consider, and keep under review, the general issue as to whether clients' human rights have been breached. If it is considered that there may have been such a breach, solicitors should give advice to clients as to what further action, if any, should be taken. *Northamptonshire County Council* v. *AS* [2015] EWHC 199 (Fam) highlights the increasing willingness of the court to award damages where care proceedings have involved a breach of any of the parties' human rights.

2.1.3   The effects of HRA 1998 are not confined to the court process. Solicitors should be aware of the decisions in *Re M (Care: Challenging Decisions by the Local Authority)* [2001] 2 FLR 1300; *Venema* v. *Netherlands (Application 35731/97)* [2003] 1 FLR 552 (ECtHR); *Re B (Care: Interference with*

Family Life) [2003] EWCA Civ 786, [2003] 2 FLR 813; *R (on the application of B)* v. *Stafford Combined Court* [2006] EWHC 1645 (Admin), [2007] 1 All ER 102); *Re V (A Child) (Care: Pre Birth Actions)* [2004] EWCA Civ 1575; and *Re H (A Child: Breach of Convention Rights: Damages)* [2014] EWFC 38.

2.1.4　　Solicitors must have knowledge of the United Nations Convention on the Rights of the Child (UNCRC), available at **www.ohchr.org/EN/ ProfessionalInterest/Pages/CRC.aspx**. This Convention has been ratified by the UK and all UK government policies and practices must comply with it. The government reports to the United Nations (UN) every five years on the progress which it is making in the implementation of the Convention. Currently it has no direct effect in domestic law in England but it has been implemented in Wales.

2.1.5　　The Convention has been endorsed by both the European and domestic courts and it is endorsed by the Law Society and the authors of this guide. Arguments which rely on the UNCRC will be of persuasive influence on the courts in England and Wales. Particularly so will be arguments or points which rest or rely on articles of the UNCRC and are accepted in judgments of the ECtHR. That jurisprudence is binding on domestic courts and the UNCRC is now commonly referred to in case decisions as international standards become increasingly important.

2.1.6　　Solicitors should observe the content of the *President's Direction (Human Rights Act 1998)* [2004] 2 FLR 429 of 24 July 2004 when considering raising human rights points in family cases. Practitioners will need to note particularly HRA 1998, s.7 which discusses forum and form (free-standing application or application within proceedings). The solicitor will also need to consider the impact of the statutory charge on any damages received. Close observation of s.7(5) is needed as this deals with limitation periods. In addition, some procedural guidance is offered in FPR rule 29.5.

2.1.7　　It is important for solicitors to consider whether Brussels II, the Hague Convention on Child Protection 1996, the EU Service Regulation, and the EU Evidence Regulation are relevant to a client's case in the event that any international issues exist. If issues with international aspects exist within a case (e.g. extended family members who are being assessed as an alternative carer for a subject child, forced marriage, immigration issues, etc.) then practitioners are encouraged to seek information from colleagues and to undertake legal research in order to determine whether the court should be invited to focus on these international aspects and to make directions in order for the case to be progressed. Cases with international aspects may be considered 'exceptional' and may be grounds for a case not to conclude within 26 weeks from the time of issue.

2.2   DIVERSITY ISSUES

2.2.1   Solicitors should be sensitive to any diversity issues such as ethnicity, language, religion, culture, gender (including transgender), sexual orientation, disability, capacity, age and vulnerability, in relation to the child, their dealings with clients and the issues in each case.

2.2.2   Solicitors should consider whether there is any information which a court will need so that it may address diverse cultural contexts. Local authority solicitors should seek to ensure that applications clearly identify at an early stage any diversity issues that exist, including but not limited to the family's race, language, culture, and religion. It is important, in addition to providing the descriptive information, to bring to the court's attention the substantive relevance and significance (if any) of the cultural context in each particular case. Solicitors for all the parties should consider what directions are necessary to ensure that relevant evidence on any diversity issue is available to the court.

2.2.3   Solicitors should be sensitive to the services which are needed by both children and adults in terms of diversity. For example:

(a)   Consider in advance access to the courtroom.

(b)   Consider additional services that might be offered in the context of the care plan and whether venues for therapeutic services are accessible by the child and their parents/carers.

(c)   Check that contact venues are suitable for both the child and adults involved.

(d)   Consider the use of court-appointed interpreters, particularly in forced marriage or so-called honour based violence cases, and be aware of the possibility of their unsuitability because of links with the extended family of any parties.

(e)   Consider safety planning, for example in the case of vulnerable clients in the context of domestic abuse. It is important for a practitioner to consider the layout of the court and to formulate a plan so that the client may enter and leave a courthouse without being unnecessarily exposed to the alleged perpetrator of violence whilst present at court. Early liaison with court security staff is essential in such cases.

2.2.4   The Mental Capacity Act (MCA) 2005 applies to people aged 16 years and older, and under that Act there is a presumption of capacity to make decisions post-16 years of age. Solicitors need to be aware of this if there are proceedings concerning a child approaching 16. They also need to be aware of the provisions of MCA 2005 in considering whether family proceedings should transfer to the Court of Protection.

2.2.5 Any perceived need for special facilities (e.g. use of a prayer room) should be made known to the court as soon as possible.

2.2.6 The Law Society has some helpful guidance and advice on diversity issues and invites firms to sign up to its Diversity and Inclusion Charter (see 'Practice Support' at **www.lawsociety.org.uk**).

2.3 COMMUNICATION WITH OTHER PARTIES AND WITH CLIENTS

2.3.1 Solicitors must show courtesy and be professional in all communications with other solicitors and parties. Solicitors should not give personal opinions or comments within correspondence. Solicitors are referred to Resolution's *Guide to Good Practice on Correspondence* (2012), which can be downloaded from **www.resolution.org.uk**.

2.3.2 Where there are current proceedings with the local authority's solicitors on the record, solicitors for non-local authority parties should not contact members of children's services departments directly without the consent of the relevant local authority legal department unless there are exceptional circumstances (SRA Code of Conduct 2011, indicative behaviour 11.4), or in accordance with any relevant local authority policy. It is good practice for a solicitor not to communicate directly with any party who is legally represented. It is good practice to obtain prior permission from the legal department before contacting the children's services department directly (irrespective of whether there are pending court proceedings) and to copy in both departments with any written queries or correspondence directed to social services. It is also preferable for solicitors not to engage in communications with any court in respect of cases without informing the other parties. It is good practice to copy all legal representatives into all correspondence to and from a court in respect of cases.

2.3.3 Where the solicitor for the child intends to visit the child in a local authority placement (for example, to take instructions from an older child), or where the child is not yet allocated a children's guardian, it is good practice to inform the local authority's legal department, and as a matter of courtesy to liaise with the social worker, so that arrangements can be made with the extended family, foster carer or children's home. Local authority solicitors should encourage a facilitative approach in order to enable solicitors to visit children who are placed in local authority placements.

2.3.4 It is good practice for a child's solicitor who is considering a visit to the child at home (where the child is still living at home) to contact the solicitor for the resident parent(s) as a matter of courtesy, and to discuss whether arrangements should be made with the parent(s) direct or through their solicitor. Legal representatives for the parent(s) should explain the reasons for the home visit and encourage the parent(s) to allow the child(ren) to meet with the solicitor and/or children's guardian separately to ensure privacy.

2.3.5   Communications should focus on identification of issues and their resolution and be clear and free of jargon. It is preferable for communications to be expressed in 'plain English' when possible. Protracted, unnecessary, hostile and inflammatory exchanges and 'trial by correspondence' should be avoided. The effect of correspondence upon clients and other family members should be considered so that correspondence which is sent by solicitors does not further inflame emotions, antagonise and/or offend. When acting for children, solicitors should be particularly vigilant to maintain even-handedness in correspondence with adult parties and their solicitors and the local authority.

2.3.6   The impact of any correspondence upon its readers and in particular the parties, including the child, must always be considered. It is desirable that solicitors or parties do not raise irrelevant issues nor unreasonably cause other parties or their own clients to adopt an entrenched, polarised, or hostile position.

2.3.7   When writing to unrepresented adult parties, solicitors should recommend that they seek independent legal advice from a specialist children public law solicitor (preferably a Law Society Children Law Accreditation Scheme member) and enclose a second copy of the letter to be passed to any solicitor instructed. It is helpful to provide the unrepresented person with the contact details for the Law Society so that they may make enquiries, if necessary, in an attempt to obtain legal representation.

2.3.8   Email is a normal means of correspondence, unless a party objects, but solicitors should take steps to protect the transmission of sensitive personal data.

2.3.9   Use of email or text message may be appropriate for communicating some matters to child clients if the child has access to these mediums and would like this method of communication to be used. However, the child must know that this might be used as a means of communication and be warned of the security risk. A written record should be kept by their solicitor of all communications which are sent and received.

2.4 DATA PROTECTION

2.4.1 It is good practice not to leave case-related documents such as position statements on the usher's desk at the courthouse and practitioners should bear in mind that the unintentional disclosure of documents may result in the punishment of a fine. The Information Commissioner's Office (ICO) can impose a monetary penalty of up to £500,000 for a serious breach of the Data Protection Act 1998 provided the incident had the potential to cause substantial damage or substantial distress to affected individuals.

2.4.2 Solicitors are generally classed as data controllers and are therefore legally responsible for the personal information they process. The ICO has published some guidance to assist solicitors with the handling of personal client information so that best efforts may be made to keep this material secure. See the ICO's *Guide to Data Protection* (2015), which can be downloaded from **ico.org.uk**.

2.4.3 It is suggested practitioners bear in mind the following:

- Solicitors must ensure that any email with confidential documents attached goes to the correct recipient(s) at the correct address(es). When sending personal information by email consider whether the information and any documents which are attached need to be encrypted or password protected.
- Avoid the pitfalls of sending an email message which contains confidential documents to the wrong person by using auto-complete.
- Double-check to make sure that the email address where you are sending the information is correct.
- Most local authorities and Cafcass use secure email systems. It is often the case that a request to 'recall' an email message does not work and the email message will be sent out in any event. It is also essential not to inadvertently send out confidential information on discussion groups.
- Many local authorities and Cafcass are now using the Egress Switch secure email system to send documents. Unfortunately the courts are not set up to accept and to receive e-documents by any secure email system at the time of this publication.
- It is best practice to keep hard copies of paper records secure by not leaving hard copies of files in a car overnight. Papers should also be locked away when not in use.
- Practitioners should make best efforts to implement data minimisation techniques in order to ensure that only information which is essential to the task in hand is exposed to unintended disclosure (i.e. do not carry documents with you unnecessarily).

- Where possible, store personal information on an encrypted memory stick or portable device which is password protected. If the information is properly encrypted then it will be difficult for others to access it, even if the device is lost or stolen. It is imperative for practitioners to ensure that any technical device, or the sensitive information which is stored on any device, is appropriately encrypted and safeguarded by way of password protection.
- Only keep information for as long as is necessary. Delete or dispose of information securely if it is no longer needed.
- When disposing of an old computer or other device ensure that all of the information that is held on the device is permanently deleted before disposal. There are methods to ensure that hard drives are wiped prior to their destruction which may be found through usual internet searches. Businesses exist which offer services for the secure destruction of hard drives and firms should have policies in place which address the destruction of confidential data (both the paper versions and electronic versions).

2.4.4   Overall, a practitioner who holds personal client information is regarded as a 'data controller' under the Act and therefore has a duty to comply with the data protection principles in relation to all personal data.

2.5   DOMESTIC ABUSE

2.5.1   Solicitors must be aware of the possible consequences to the welfare of the child and other family members wherever the issue of domestic abuse is raised. See the Home Office Guidance on Domestic Violence and Abuse (**www.gov.uk/domestic-violence-and-abuse**) for the new cross-definition of domestic abuse which lists the various areas in broad terms and provides further elaboration. This may be useful to show to clients so that they have a greater understanding of this area, how they may be affected and also how their children and family life may be affected.

2.5.2   Applicants for orders under CA 1989 and respondents to such applications (save for applications for care and supervision orders) are given the opportunity to indicate at the outset whether or not they believe that the subject child has either suffered or is at risk of suffering harm from, *inter alia*, any form of domestic abuse. A positive answer will require further information to be set out in Supplemental Form C1A. Solicitors should be alert to the possibility of such circumstances and to the general practice that it is in a client's best interests to state any allegations of domestic abuse as early as possible if this results in protective action being taken in relation to the client and the child. This may need to be the case if there is local authority involvement pre-proceedings. This approach will go towards the parent protecting their own safety and the child's welfare and it will avoid accusations that allegations have been raised late in the proceedings to perhaps bolster the client's position or damage that of another party. There may also be the need for assessments of parents who are involved in this within the context of public law proceedings regarding their parenting capacity, ability to protect their children and capacity to change. Parents should co-operate with such assessments if considered necessary or appropriate by the court or other parties.

2.5.3   Domestic abuse is often a significant factor in child protection cases. Solicitors are referred to Part 3 of the *Family Law Protocol* (4th edn, Law Society Publishing, 2015) for guidance, for example on screening for domestic abuse and safety planning, including keeping parties' whereabouts confidential and preparing for safety issues within the court building. Local authority solicitors should be mindful of any need to keep a party's whereabouts confidential from another party on preparing the application. Form C8 (Confidential Contact Details) should be lodged with the court and the client's address and contact details should not be included in the application form (which will be served upon the other parties).

2.5.4   Solicitors for adult parties should advise their clients, as appropriate, about the making of applications under the Family Law Act (FLA) 1996, Part IV during the course of public law proceedings. Solicitors must remain alert to safety issues for their client and any other children before and after removal of a child from the home.

2.5.5   Solicitors are reminded of the court's power to include an exclusion requirement in an interim care order under CA 1989, s.38A. The court also has a power under FLA 1996, s.42(2)(b) to make a non-molestation order in any family proceedings against a party for the benefit of any other party to the proceedings or a relevant child, even if an application is not made.

2.5.6   Alternative carers may sometimes come forward seeking orders in their own right to care permanently for the child. These extended family members and 'connected persons' may be joined as a party to the proceedings. The involvement of such other persons may give rise to issues of domestic abuse which were previously not present or not in issue. Solicitors should also keep in mind that any person who is joined as a party to proceedings will be entitled to see all of the papers in respect of the proceedings. It is therefore important to keep in mind whether there are any documents which contain information about a client that the client would like to keep private. If so, an application for redaction may be made to the court at or prior to the time when papers are set to be disclosed to the person who is joined as a party. Solicitors should also consider with a client if any of these extended family members have been involved in domestic abuse which may have resulted in criminal involvement which would mean that they would not necessarily be assessed positively by the local authority who could ask for consent to run police checks.

2.5.7   It is worth noting the careful guidance which is provided in the *Practice Direction: Residence and Contact Orders: Domestic Violence and Harm* [2009] 2 FLR 1400 (issued by the President of the Family Division on 14 January 2009). This can be downloaded at **www.hmcourts-service.gov.uk**. Whilst its focus is exclusively private law CA 1989 proceedings, it offers a useful prod that

> a fact-finding hearing is part of the process of trying a case and is not a separate exercise and that where the case is then adjourned for further hearing it remains part heard.

Paragraphs 21–23 in particular serve to explain the very notion of the fact-finding hearing and how it should be conducted. Practitioners may also wish to note Practice Direction 12J, Child Arrangements & Contact Order: Domestic Violence and Harm (22 April 2014) which incorporates and supersedes the President's Guidance in Relation to Split Hearings (May 2010) and can be downloaded from **www.justice.gov.uk**.

There are a number of agencies that can help with issues of domestic abuse. See **www.resolution.org.uk** for a list and for their helpful Domestic Abuse Toolkit.

2.6   FORCED MARRIAGE AND HONOUR BASED VIOLENCE

2.6.1   Forced marriage is a specific form of domestic abuse and practitioners should be aware of it and screen for it as part of the initial interview. The Forced Marriage (Civil Protection) Act 2007 came into force on 25 November 2008 and forced marriage protection orders (FMPOs) made pursuant to FLA 1986, Part 4A to protect a person from being forced into a marriage, or from any attempt to be so forced, or to protect a person who has been forced into a marriage. From 1 November 2009, a local authority is designated as a relevant third party which allows it to apply for a FMPO on behalf of a person who needs to be protected. Solicitors who represent local authorities may wish to understand the provisions in greater detail since local authorities may need to be advised on whether to apply for FMPOs on behalf of children within pending public law proceedings. For further information see *The Right to Choose: Multi-Agency Statutory Guidance for Dealing with Forced Marriage* (HM Government, June 2014) at **www.gov.uk**.

2.6.2   In more recent years, professionals who are involved in child care cases and family law in general have become more aware of issues which relate to so-called honour based violence or killings. Such issues may be raised in public law CA 1989 proceedings and of course could, in some cases, be the very reason for protective measures having been taken by the local authority. It is important that solicitors have an understanding of the cultural sensitivities that are involved so that they are able to effectively represent their client. This extends to care in the use of interpreters who may know the family. Enhanced safety planning (in relation to taking instructions and for security arrangements at court) may be required for vulnerable subjects of such applications. If the practitioner does not have the expertise to deal with the issue of forced marriage/honour based violence they should refer the client to a specialist practitioner who can assist.

2.6.3   Practitioners should consider *Family Law Protocol* (4th edn, Law Society Publishing, 2015) for further guidance on forced marriage and honour based violence.

2.6.4   The Resolution website (**www.resolution.org.uk**) has a useful Forced Marriages and Honour Based Violence Toolkit which is essential reading for any practitioner in this area.

2.7   HUMAN TRAFFICKING

2.7.1   Solicitors should also consider whether a client or other parties have been a victim of human trafficking. A local authority may issue care proceedings when an undocumented child is located within the borough. Children who are found in the United Kingdom without identification and/or without identified families are often placed in foster care after care proceedings are issued because no parent and/or guardian can be located to give consent for the child's placement in care. Local authorities may request that a child's age be determined by forensic testing in order to determine if the subject child is a 'child' under the 'looked-after children' or 'child in need' definition which imposes a duty upon a local authority to provide for this child. Solicitors are referred to: the Home Office guidance, *Victims of Human Trafficking – Competent Authority Guidance* (which can be found at **www.gov.uk/government/publications**); and to the Law Society's Practice Note: Criminal Prosecutions of Victims of Trafficking (6 October 2011) (which can be found at **www.lawsociety.org.uk**), regarding their own duties and the general position regarding human trafficking.

17

2.8   SECTION 20 AGREEMENTS

2.8.1   Solicitors are encouraged to familiarise themselves with the definitions of 'looked-after children' and 'children in need' in order to better understand local authority duties to children who are located in their boroughs. These issues are also relevant to a child's placement at the pre-proceedings stage especially when a child is placed with an extended family member with a parent's consent. However, the principal actor in the child's move outside the family home is a local authority.

2.8.2   Solicitors are encouraged to consider section 20 of the Children Act 1989 and related case law at the pre-proceedings stage if any designated authority issues arise within care proceedings. Further guidance on the issue of designated authority is outside the scope of this guide.

2.8.3   Care proceedings are sometimes issued after a child has been placed in foster care under a section 20 agreement for a considerable amount of time. Often local authorities do not have an incentive to issue care proceedings if a child is placed in foster care under a voluntary agreement, especially if a parent has not requested that a child be returned home. Local authorities will usually indicate that assessments of parents will be undertaken outside the court arena in order to determine if the local authority would agree to the plan for a child to return to his or her parents' care. However these assessments may take quite some time without judicial scrutiny and there is usually no letter of instruction sent to the assessor during the pre-proceedings stage. Parents are not always legally represented during this stage and they may not be aware that they have a right to revoke the agreement for their child to remain placed in foster care. There is no children's guardian or solicitor and children have no independent voice, although there have been pilot projects in which Cafcass has been involved at the pre-proceedings stage.

2.8.4   Practitioners need to be mindful that sometimes it benefits a child and a parent client for the local authority to be forced into issuing care proceedings by revoking the section 20 consent for a child to remain placed in foster care. Clients need to be informed that a children's guardian will be appointed to represent a child's best interests, the child will have his or her solicitor, and the court will have oversight of the case if care proceedings are instigated.

2.8.5   Practitioners and their clients will need to consider carefully whether there is merit to a client revoking a section 20 agreement at any particular time. A balancing exercise will need to be undertaken in weighing the benefit of court proceedings being instigated versus the child remaining in foster care under a section 20 agreement with the local authority being solely responsible for timescales and the facilitation of assessments.

2.8.6   It is however good practice to ensure that clients are aware that a revocation of the section 20 agreement will likely result in the local authority issuing care proceedings and it does not mean that a child will be returned home. It is suggested that practitioners, with authorisation from their parent clients, give the local authority notice in writing of at least 10 working days that the section 20 agreement will be revoked on a specified time/date. The provision of such notice will enable the local authority to have sufficient time to lodge an application for a care order along with the documents in support of the application with the court.

2.8.7   Some local authorities use section 20 placements as an alternative to issuing care proceedings. Some authorities will strongly suggest to parents that a child should reside with an extended family member under a section 20 agreement and mention that if the family does not agree with these proposals then the local authority may issue care proceedings and adoption may be a possible outcome in that situation. The local authority would then usually request that the extended family members lodge an application for either a child arrangements order or a special guardianship order which the local authority would fund.

2.8.8   Unfortunately most parents would not qualify for legal aid to be represented on such a private law application and a child's placement may change due to the actions of a local authority in this situation. There have been concerns voiced by some advocates on behalf of parents about the potential violation of a parent's human rights (e.g. the right to family life) in this scenario since they are not entitled to legal aid under these circumstances (see *Re W (Parental Agreement with Local Authority)* [2014] EWCA Civ 1065). As the checks and balances provided by the appointment of a children's guardian and a solicitor for the children are absent, children are deprived of a voice (contrary to UNCRC, Art.12, as well as ECHR, Art.6) and there is no independent scrutiny of the local authority's actions, including planning for the child's future.

2.9   LOCAL AUTHORITY CHILDREN ACT MEETINGS

2.9.1   Solicitors should read and observe the guidance issued by the Law Society's Children Law Sub-Committee in consultation with the SRA in its Practice Note: Attendance of Solicitors at Local Authority Children Act Meetings (9 January 2013) (this can be found at **www.lawsociety.org.uk**).

2.9.2   Child protection procedures, including the conduct of the child protection conference, are the responsibility of the local authority's Local Safeguarding Children Board acting in accordance with the Department for Education Guidance, *Working Together to Safeguard Children* (2015). It is available at **www.gov.uk/government/publications/ working-together-to-safeguard-children–2**.

2.10   FAMILY GROUP CONFERENCES/FAMILY MEETINGS

2.10.1   Solicitors should be aware of non-court based processes which may assist them to run the case, particularly the role of family group conferences (FGCs) and family meetings. The FGC is a growing area of social work practice, which can be a useful tool to avoid the issue of proceedings, or be directed by the court to take place during the course of proceedings, where appropriate. These are considered in more detail in Statutory Guidance, Vol. 1.

2.10.2   FGCs are decision-making forums that focus on the welfare of the child. At a FGC, the wider family (this can include friends) meets and is given information by the relevant agencies on the needs of the child and the reasons why a FGC is necessary. Members of the wider family are given time on their own to engage in discussions about safeguards which may be put into place in order to secure the child's welfare. In care proceedings, FGCs may be helpful:

(a)   in identifying family and community supports which are available so that it would be safe for a child to remain living with his or her parent(s) or to be rehabilitated into their care;

(b)   in identifying a placement and possible sources of support in the wider family network, if the child cannot live with his or her parent(s);

(c)   where a kinship placement is not possible, allowing the wider family to support the plan for the child and to discuss and formulate a contact schedule.

2.10.3   Solicitors should invite the court to direct the local authority to facilitate and hold a FGC by a specified date and to serve the notes/minutes of the FGC within 10 days of the FGC being held. Further information on the process is available from the Family Rights Group at **www.frg.org.uk**.

2.10.4   Adult clients should be strongly advised and encouraged to provide information about the identity and the current contact details of any persons who should attend the FGC, information which should be provided to the FGC, and to attend any FGC. Solicitors should make best efforts to obtain information about any extended family members or family friends who have not been invited yet who may have something to contribute and to provide the FGC facilitator or the local authority with information about such persons.

2.10.5   It is unusual for solicitors to attend FGCs. If a legal representative or any staff from a law firm were to attend the FGC it would be likely that this person would attend solely as an observer and in a supportive capacity to the client. It would be appropriate to discuss the possibility of a legal representative attending a FGC and to seek approval for such attendance with the local authority and any legal representatives for the other parties prior to the date of the FGC.

2.11   IDENTIFYING ALTERNATIVE CARERS

2.11.1   Solicitors for children should make requests for local authorities to undertake investigations (if possible) to identify potential alternative carers at the commencement of care proceedings, in order to avoid potential delay. It is often the case that respondent parents in care proceedings do not have close relationships with extended family members and they therefore do not disclose much information about the children and/or their lives to the family network.

2.11.2   Many parents are also unable to contemplate a potential situation where their child(ren) will be placed outside the family network for the long term. They are therefore unable or unwilling to approach extended family members to request assistance and to request that viability assessments be undertaken in respect of family members, since they are not able to appreciate the need for such an assessment to be undertaken during the early stages of care proceedings.

2.11.3   They may indeed be alienated from members of their families who could offer a suitable placement for the child(ren). Those family members may not even be aware that proceedings are underway.

2.11.4   In some cases the court may direct the local authority or the solicitor for the child to instruct an enquiry agent to locate such members of the wider family, with the local authority paying the fee which is often modest and sometimes on a 'no find, no fee' basis. Suitable agents can be found in the *Law Society Gazette* or online.

2.11.5   It is often the case that extended family members are reluctant to become involved with the proceedings or to come forward as alternative carers, at least until the court has reached the stage of excluding the parents as potential carers for the child(ren). Extended family members may fear that a parent may interpret their willingness to be assessed as a carer for the child(ren) as 'competition' or view it as the instigation of a 'custody battle' for the child(ren). It is therefore vital for information about potential alternative carers to be obtained by the local authority and/or the children's guardian in addition to this information being provided by a respondent parent when possible. Parents and their families also need a careful explanation of parallel planning. That may not alleviate their anxieties, but the framework can be set out so that everyone has a chance to understand that 'fallback' plans are needed, and assessments must take place at the same time (and not sequentially) to avoid delay.

2.12 EXPERTS

2.12.1 The court will only allow additional expert evidence to be filed and served if this accords with the requirements of s.13(6) of the Children and Families Act 2014 and it is necessary to assist the court to resolve the proceedings justly. The key issues for solicitors to consider in readiness for the case management hearing are:

(a) what evidence is necessary and what gaps might exist;

(b) whether additional evidence to that usually filed by the parties is necessary;

(c) which party or parties should seek the evidence;

(d) who should provide the evidence; and

(e) how the cost is to be funded, including how it is to be split between the parties.

2.12.2 Solicitors must observe the requirements set out in FPR Part 25 and Practice Directions 25A–F (see **www.justice.gov.uk/courts/ procedure-rules/family/rules_pd_menu**). Please refer to **Appendix 5** for details in relation to the use of experts, including questions to experts and experts' meetings.

2.12.3 All solicitors should be prepared to justify whether anyone who is involved in the case already has the necessary appropriate expertise to assist the court. The court will likely consider whether the children's social worker or the children's guardian has the requisite expertise to make recommendations in lieu of the instruction of an expert. The court will only grant leave for an expert to be instructed if the court finds that such an instruction is 'necessary'. The court will usually direct the instruction of an expert to be a joint instruction and for the costs of the instruction to be equally shared between the local authority and the public funding certificates of the respondent parents and the subject child. The court order should indicate that the court finds the instruction of the expert necessary and record the finding that the costs which relate to the instruction of the expert are reasonable, necessary, and proportionate disbursements on the public funding certificates of the publicly funded parties. Such wording on a court order may assist the solicitors if any difficulties arise with the Legal Aid Agency (LAA) during the costing phase of the case in respect of the costs of the expert's instruction. See the LAA's *Guidance on the Remuneration of Expert Witnesses* (2015) (**www.gov.uk/government/uploads/system/ uploads/attachment_data/file/420106/expert-witnesses-fees- guidance.pdf**) and Practice Direction 25C, Children Proceedings: the Use of Single Joint Experts (**Appendix 5**) and *Re TG (A Child)* [2013] EWCA Civ 5 (which can be found at **www.bailii.org**).

2.12.4   All solicitors should therefore ask themselves the following key questions before an expert is instructed:

(a)   Is an expert necessary? If so, why?

(b)   What type of expert is required?

(c)   What are the issues which this proposed expert will address?

(d)   Can the allocated social worker and/or children's guardian assess and prepare a report in respect of these issues?

(e)   What are the timescales? What are the costs in respect of the instruction of an expert?

2.12.5   For further guidance see the standards for expert witnesses in PD25B (**www.justice.gov.uk/courts/procedure-rules/family/ practice_directions**). In addition, the Law Society has produced useful template letters for instructing experts in children and family proceedings, which can be found at **www.lawsociety.org.uk/support-services/ family-court-resources/family-law–templates-for-instructing- experts**.

2.12.6   It is vital to give early consideration to the need for expert evidence in relation to whether an adult party lacks capacity (within the meaning of MCA 2005) to conduct the proceedings and is therefore a protected party who will require a litigation friend pursuant to FPR rule 15.2.

2.12.7   Appropriate expert evidence will usually be needed to enable the court to determine whether a party is a protected party within the meaning of the rules. It is best practice for solicitors to request leave of the court to instruct an appropriate expert (for mental health issues this may be an adult psychiatrist while for an adult with learning disabilities a psychologist may be appropriate, but their identity will depend upon the circumstances) to assess and to complete a certificate of capacity in respect of a client if concerns arise regarding whether that person has the capacity to conduct the proceedings. Information from the Official Solicitor's office is available at **www.gov.uk/government/publications/ certificate-as-to-capacity-to-conduct-proceedings**.

2.12.8   The Official Solicitor's acceptance criteria remain:

1.   uncontested evidence of lack of capacity to conduct these proceedings or a finding of the court that the party is a protected party within the meaning of FPR rule 2.3;

2.   security for costs of the protected party's legal representation;

3.   confirmation that there is no one else suitable and willing to act as litigation friend.

2.12.9   To avoid delay in public law proceedings the electronic referral form should be completed (see **www.gov.uk/government/publications/ official-solicitor-referral-form-for-children-act-public-law- proceedings**) and used together with the litigation friend checklist (see **Appendix 6**). See also the Official Solicitor's Practice Note at **Appendix 7**.

2.12.10   Solicitors are reminded to observe the SRA Code of Conduct 2011. The Code of Conduct may be found at **www.sra.org.uk/solicitors/handbook/ code/content.page**.

2.13   PROFESSIONALS' MEETINGS

2.13.1   There are many types of professionals' meetings with which solicitors may be involved in the course of public law children work.

2.13.2   Solicitors must be clear about the nature and purpose of any meeting and their role at that meeting. A 'professionals' meeting' is a generic term and may mean different things to different professionals. Meetings include:

(a)   an initial child protection conference;

(b)   a child protection conference to review a child protection plan;

(c)   other local authority Children Act meetings (see guidance referred to at **2.9**);

(d)   an experts' discussion (meeting) in accordance with Practice Direction 25A, Experts and Assessors in Family Proceedings;

(e)   a professionals' meeting as envisaged by the Practice Direction: between the local authority and named professionals (probably non-lawyer professionals), for the purpose of assisting with local authority planning;

(f)   meeting as a case management tool to ascertain whether there is possible agreement on threshold, what the outstanding issues are, and the expert and other witnesses needed to give live evidence to the court.

2.13.3   Where there is any preliminary meeting between the expert(s), social worker, and children's guardian, solicitors should insist that this meeting be minuted and the minutes disclosed to all parties (with attendees having an opportunity to agree the minutes prior to circulation).

2.13.4   The PLO and FPR Part 25 both provide information about experts and provide a strict timetable for when experts' meetings should be held. Any relevant dates in respect of experts should be included in the case management order.

2.13.5   Solicitors should consider the use of telephone or video conferences if professionals and/or experts are not available to attend meetings in person. The solicitor for the child is the person who usually chairs professionals' meetings and is responsible for preparing the agenda and minutes. Local authority solicitors usually chair the professionals' meetings if guardians and solicitors for children do not attend.

2.13.6   If possible, it is helpful for a professional transcript company such as BT to be instructed to provide a transcript of the professionals' meeting if one attendee attends the meeting by telephone. The services of companies that offer minute taking may also be employed. It is best practice to request the court to include a direction in the court order which orders that the costs which relate to obtaining a transcript of the professionals' meeting be equally shared and a finding that such costs are reasonable and necessary expenses upon the public funding certificates of the publicly funded parties.

2.13.7   However, note that there are no codified rates for transcription fees and therefore any assessment will be based on whether it was reasonable to incur the costs and whether the costs are reasonable. A copy of the court order requesting the transcription should be provided. See further the LAA's *Guidance on the Remuneration of Expert Witnesses* (2015) at **www.gov.uk/government/publications**.

2.13.8   The cost of transcribing a professionals' meeting may be seen by the LAA as an overhead, and part of the costs the solicitor has to bear.

2.14 CONTINUITY OF CONDUCT OF CASE

2.14.1 Clients must be given details of who is responsible for the conduct of their case at the law firm or organisation in accordance with the SRA Code of Conduct 2011, indicative behaviour 1.3. It is also important to provide clients with information in writing about anyone else who will be involved in the day-to-day running of the case, the identity and contact details of the solicitor's supervisor and also information about the firm's complaints policy.

2.14.2 It is desirable for the same solicitor to retain conduct of the case, wherever possible, particularly in relation to meetings with the client, and including advocacy at court hearings where appropriate. Full and careful consideration should be given as to who will be the best advocate, in terms of serving the best interests of the client, to present the case at each case management hearing and at the final hearing (see outcomes 1.2 and 1.4 of the SRA Code of Conduct 2011).

2.14.3 Consistency of representation for the child is particularly important. All members of the Children Law Accreditation Scheme are reminded of their undertaking to attend at court hearings when possible in order to represent the child. Please refer to **www.lawsociety.org.uk/support-services/ accreditation/children-law** for details.

2.15 THE USE OF COUNSEL OR SOLICITOR ADVOCATE

2.15.1 Where counsel or another solicitor advocate is involved, they must be adequately instructed. Briefs and instructions should include all material information which will need to be considered by the court.

2.15.2 If counsel is instructed to attend a hearing then they should have appropriate expertise in child care law. If another solicitor is instructed to undertake advocacy they should be a member of the Children Law Accreditation Scheme and approved as a children representative if representing the child, save in exceptional circumstances (see Children Law Accreditation Scheme Guidance, which can be found at the link given in **2.14.3**).

2.15.3 Solicitors should request that the same advocate is present for all court hearings when possible to ensure continuity of representation at court. It is good practice to obtain undertakings from the advocate that they will take all reasonable steps to ensure that (so far as practicable) a conflicting professional arrangement does not arise that would stop them attending hearings which are listed. Again, Children Law Accreditation Scheme solicitors are reminded of the terms of their undertaking to attend all court hearings when possible and to instruct another advocate only when necessary or it is in the client's best interests to do so.

2.15.4   Whenever another advocate is to appear on behalf of the client, the client should be made aware, save in exceptional circumstances, of the identity of the advocate concerned prior to the date of the listed hearing. The solicitor conducting the case should discuss with the client the arrangements for attendance by a responsible representative of the solicitor with that advocate and the client. Solicitors must observe the SRA Code of Conduct 2011 (Chapter 5) on attending advocates at court.

2.16   APPROACH TO ADVOCACY

2.16.1   In any court hearing, solicitors should be careful about their approach to other advocates and be even-handed in their approach to them and their clients. It is important during the duration of the case, and especially examination in chief and cross-examination, that advocacy is conducted in language which is understood by the client (if present in court) when it is possible to do so. Cross-examination should not be aggressive and should be limited to the pertinent issues a court will need to address in order to make a determination at the conclusion of the proceedings. At the time of publication, it is relatively rare for it to be necessary for children to give evidence although this may change in future. Practitioners should note the current leading case on the subject: *Re W (Children)* [2010] UKSC 12. Should children be required to give evidence, solicitors must be alert to the natural anxiety of children to do so. Solicitors may also wish to note the publication *Measuring Up? Evaluating Implementation of Government Commitments to Young Witnesses in Criminal Proceedings* (Plotnikoff and Woolfson, NSPCC, 2009), available to download from: **www.nspcc.org.uk/globalassets/documents/research-reports/ measuring-up-report.pdf**, as this offers valuable guidance regarding young witnesses, albeit from the criminal sphere.

2.16.2   Every effort should be made to keep the hearing strictly to the issues and as short as practicable. If there are any vulnerable witnesses giving evidence, early consideration and preparation by the court and parties are necessary to avoid delay. For further advice on vulnerable witnesses see the Report of the Children & Vulnerable Witnesses Working Group (**www.judiciary.gov.uk/wp-content/uploads/2015/03/ vwcwg-report-march-2015.pdf**) which proposes further guidance and the need for specialist training and skills. The Advocate's Gateway Toolkits (**www.theadvocatesgateway.org/toolkits**) are useful aids for setting out common problems encountered when examining vulnerable witnesses and defendants, together with suggested solutions. Further guidance is also given at **4.13**.

2.17 DISCLOSURE

2.17.1 From the outset, the solicitors for all parties should consider how they can be satisfied that all relevant information is available and that only the necessary information is filed with the court. A core index to bundle should be agreed and the agreed court bundle will be lodged with the court prior to the date of the listed hearings. Not all documents that solicitors receive will be included in the court bundle and filed with the court (e.g. it is likely that not all contact notes, police disclosure, medical records, and foster carer notes will be filed with the court). The President of the Family Division has reiterated very clearly the need to observe PD27A, with regard to the contents of the bundle; see *In the matter of L (A Child)* [2015] EWFC 15 and Practice Direction 27A, Family Proceedings: Court Bundles (Universal Practice to be Applied in the High Court and Family Court) at **www.judiciary.gov.uk/wp-content/uploads/2013/02/ presidents-bundles-practice-direction-pd27a.pdf**.

2.17.2 The solicitors for all parties must be satisfied in readiness for each hearing that the necessary information has been provided to them and included in the core bundle which is filed with the court.

2.17.3 Solicitors must have knowledge of the implications of the common law duty of confidentiality, the statutory schemes in relation to children, the Data Protection Act 1998, and the Human Rights Act 1998. A guide to data protection of personal information held by children's services is included in the ICO's *Guide to Data Protection* (see **ico.org.uk/for-organisations/ guide-to-data-protection**).

2.17.4 Reports should be read and redacted as necessary before service and disclosure to other parties. Solicitors for local authorities should particularly be mindful and ensure to redact any information about a child's address from documents which will be provided to the lay parties if a child is placed in foster care. It is important that information about a child's foster home is not inadvertently disclosed to parents and family members if information about a child's foster home is not available to the lay parties and family members. Solicitors should always read documents before sending them out and consider whether to meet the client to discuss the contents of the document before giving him or her a copy (for instance if the client is vulnerable, and/or the document contains information likely to distress the client). If a solicitor is uncertain as to whether a particular document should be disclosed, particularly to a child client, directions from the court should be sought.

2.17.5 Solicitors should obtain instructions from clients about whether clients prefer for documents to be sent by way of email and/or post. It is important to ensure that all documents which are sent to clients by post are securely sent to an address where the client will definitely receive the documents (not, for example, to a common hallway shared with other tenants of a building) since the documents for care proceedings will almost certainly contain very private and confidential information. Documents sent by post should be sent special delivery to ensure they are received by the intended recipient only.

Transparency

2.17.6 In April 2013 the President of the Family Division issued a statement, *View from the President's Chambers: the Process of Reform* [2013] Fam Law 548, in which he identified transparency as one of the three strands in the reforms which the family justice system is currently undergoing. The President said:

> I am determined to take steps to improve access to and reporting of family proceedings. I am determined that the new Family Court should not be saddled, as the family courts are at present, with the charge that we are a system of secret and unaccountable justice. Work, commenced by my predecessor, is well underway. I hope to be in a position to make important announcements in the near future.

2.17.7 The issues of transparency and openness in the family courts are therefore relevant issues to consider at the time of writing. The need for family courts to be 'private' to prevent intimate details of family life being published is criticised by many as 'secrecy' which prevents important and relevant information from being provided to the public in a democratic society where there is freedom of press.

2.17.8 There is a trend is towards greater openness in the family courts but there are still quite significant limitations on what one can disclose about care proceedings and who is allowed into the courtroom during hearings for care proceedings.

2.17.9 Proponents of transparency claim that we can rely on efficient anonymisation and improved public accountability. Some people would assert that there is a need for improving transparency of process for the child and the family as much as for the wider public.

2.17.10   Opponents of transparency have concerns about the operation and commercial imperatives of the mainstream press and broadcast media, of the wider publication of information about cases as well as the effect on children (including their willingness to speak to professionals and experts if no guarantee of privacy can be given) (see the NYAS/ALC Report, *Safeguarding, Privacy and Respect for Children and Young People and the Next Steps in Media Access to Family Courts*: **www.nyas.net/wp-content/ uploads/2014/07/nyas-alc-report-children-safeguarding-and-next- steps-media-access-to-family-courts-final-7.pdf**).

2.17.11   'Jigsaw' identification is an issue, with regard to how various pieces of information from a case – possibly insignificant in isolation – could, if put together, lead to children and families being identified, particularly in their own neighbourhoods.

2.17.12   It may be necessary ask the court to consider parties' rights under Articles 6 (right to a fair trial) and 8 (right to respect for private and family life), as against Article 10 (right to freedom of expression – for individuals as well as the media), if publication becomes an issue in a case.

2.17.13   It is important for practitioners to advise children and families about the rights of the media to attend court, and what they can publish, in addition to the duty of confidentiality.

2.17.14   Practitioners should also be aware that the Court of Appeal conducts its hearings in open court, which are open to public observation and reporting (although the identification of any children concerned is not permitted). Reporting restrictions should be applied for as necessary (for instance, under the Children and Young Persons Act 1933, s.39 or under the Contempt of Court Act 1981, s.4). This needs to be considered from the outset, so that the case title, for example, does not reveal (directly or indirectly) any children's identities.

2.17.15   For further details refer to the Family Division's Practice Guidance, *Transparency in the Family Courts* (2014), which may be found at **Appendix 8**.

2.18   CONCURRENT CRIMINAL PROCEEDINGS

2.18.1   A solicitor should give very careful consideration to the question of whether to act for a client in both criminal and care proceedings in accordance with professional rules. Representing a client in concurrent care and criminal proceedings can raise complex issues. It is generally advisable for a solicitor to decline to take instructions in the criminal proceedings if he or she is likely to be invited to act later in related CA 1989 proceedings. However, it is not unusual for a firm of solicitors to represent a client for both care and criminal proceedings if the firm undertakes work in both fields.

2.18.2 Possible difficulties which relate to acting in both care and criminal proceedings for a client include:

(a) receiving conflicting instructions from the client;

(b) advising in relation to outcomes in both proceedings; and

(c) having constructive knowledge of an expert report or other evidence adverse to the client's interests which may be required to be disclosed.

2.18.3 Solicitors should remember that the children's guardian is not automatically entitled to experts' reports which are filed in criminal proceedings. A request for police disclosure will need to be made by the local authority according to the police protocol.

2.18.4 Solicitors should be familiar with any procedures or arrangements in place in their area of practice for joint directions in respect of concurrent criminal and care proceedings. It is suggested that solicitors familiarise themselves with the following documents:

(a) 2013 Protocol and Good Practice Model: Disclosure of Information in Cases of Alleged Child Abuse and Linked Criminal and Care Directions Hearings (can be found at **www.cps.gov.uk/ publications/agencies/index.html**); and

(b) FPR Part 12, Chapter 7 and Practice Direction 12G (can be found at **www.legislation.gov.uk**).

2.18.5 Courts should be invited to consider whether there is a judge who has both a Family ticket and a Crime ticket who may be willing/able to hear both the criminal matter and the care proceedings so that the two cases could be linked.

2.19 COURT SECURITY

2.19.1 Solicitors should bring court safety issues to the attention of the court and other parties as early as possible in the proceedings. Any safety issues within the confines of the court building should be discussed with the court and security staff in advance.

2.19.2 Solicitors should consider the use of available video links for the presentation of evidence, if appropriate. Courts have procedures in place which may be implemented in order to request the use of video conferencing facilities.

It is best practice to approach a court sooner rather than later with a request for the use of the video conferencing facilities because more often than not the court will need to test out the video conferencing connection with the organisation which is setting up the video link on the other side. Most courts will only link up to a video conferencing line which is secure and meets the court requirements so there may be a chance that it will not be possible for a client and/or witness to attend a hearing by way of a video conference link. In the alternative, if a video link is not available the court may be requested to provide a telephone link so that a client or witness may attend the hearing by telephone.

2.19.3   There are also occasions when the court will agree to the use of screens to allow witnesses to give live evidence either anonymously or in a way that prevents intimidation.

PART 3

Local authority solicitors

3.1 INTRODUCTION

3.1.1 This part of the good practice guidance takes into account (in so far as it is still current) *Arrangements for Handling Child Care Cases* (revised 2005); this is the guidance published by the Association of Council Secretaries and Solicitors and Solicitors in Local Government Child Care Law Joint Liaison Group (now known as the Lawyers in Local Government Child Care Lawyers Group). See **Appendix 9**. It does not overlap with the guidance set out in this document. However, it will set out important guidance on other issues relevant to local authority solicitors, and Children Law Accreditation Scheme solicitors in private practice handling child care cases on behalf of local authority legal services, with which those practitioners should be familiar.

3.1.2 The primary role of solicitors acting for local authorities is as follows:

(a) to ensure the proper conduct of cases;

(b) to ensure scrutiny of the local authority's case;

(c) to safeguard the integrity of the local authority before the court: for example, to ensure through appropriate preparation and presentation that all relevant information is before the court and other parties; and

(d) to assist the court in its investigation and undertake all necessary steps to allow the court to arrive at an appropriate result which meets the paramount interests of the welfare of the child.

3.1.3 No solicitor should represent a local authority in contested child care cases without an up-to-date working knowledge of child care law and the Public Law Outline, appropriate training in those areas not covered by experience in practice, and recent significant practical experience of conducting child care proceedings. All child care solicitors should have adequate supervision arrangements in place. It is desirable for all local authority solicitors to seek accreditation to the Children Law Accreditation Scheme (see **www.lawsociety.org.uk**).

3.1.4 Local authority solicitors should be aware of the role and responsibility of their Local Safeguarding Children Boards. Solicitors should be aware of the different agencies which now have a statutory duty to co-operate to safeguard and promote the welfare of children. They should also be aware of any protocols and procedures between those agencies and children's social care that exist in order to enhance working together to safeguard children and to improve the quality of child protection work. Local authority solicitors should consider specifically arrangements in place under the statutory assessment framework provided by the Department for Education's *Working Together to Safeguard Children* (2015), which can be found at **www.gov.uk/government/publications**. This may include either a multi-agency support team/or a 'team around the child' in accordance with integrated practice. If this has led to the use of child protection procedures, local authority solicitors must also consult their Local Safeguarding Children Board child protection procedures. Local authority solicitors should have regard to the importance of encouraging co-operation between services within the local authority such as children's social care, education, adult services and housing services.

3.2 RELATIONSHIP AND COMMUNICATION WITH CLIENT

3.2.1 The local authority solicitor's 'client' is the council itself, but the day-to-day working relationship is with the Director of Children's Services, acting through managers and social workers. Solicitors should be familiar with the local authority's decision-making procedure on taking legal proceedings. In this connection, solicitors should be aware of the following:

(a) Local authority solicitors have a duty as officers of the court to ensure that cases are dealt with appropriately, and this role transcends their duty to the client department. Coupled with the fact that the local authority solicitor's client is the council itself, this means that many authorities will have in place a protocol or other agreement between the legal department and children's social care, to regulate their working relationship and to deal with any disputes that might arise in the conduct of case work.

(b) Connected to (a) above is the role of the local authority monitoring officer. Every local authority has to appoint a monitoring officer under the Local Government and Housing Act 1989, s.5. The role of the monitoring officer is to ensure that the authority acts at all times within the law and observes due process. The monitoring officer has statutory powers that can be exercised if he or she considers any proposed action of the authority to be unlawful.

3.2.2 Clients should be advised that if they are contacted by solicitors for other parties during proceedings, those solicitors should be referred to the local authority's legal services.

3.2.3 Special care should be taken when a decision is required on commencing proceedings in respect of a child. Decisions about the welfare and protection of a child should be taken within children's social care, which is where the necessary statutory duty to exercise this function is to be found. Solicitors should not take decisions on matters that are within the province of children's social care.

3.2.4 Local authority solicitors should give advice to their client about the legal strengths, weaknesses and complexities of their case before proceedings, before pre-proceedings steps or when and after proceedings are commenced. They should always be mindful of their duty to act in the best interests of the council (see **3.2.1**).

3.2.5 The steps involved in deciding whether or not a child should be made subject to care proceedings will inevitably be a complex process, requiring in-depth and regular consultation and discussion between lawyer and social worker. Their respective roles are significantly different, but when it comes to making a decision, there will be similar factors for both to consider, albeit from different perspectives.

3.2.6 Local authority solicitors should create and maintain a professional relationship with the local authority and its children's social care services which will preserve fully their independent judgement.

3.3 BEFORE ISSUE OF PROCEEDINGS

3.3.1 Changes to statutory guidance were made at the same time that the PLO was introduced. The Department for Education's *Children Act 1989: Court Orders and Pre-Proceedings for Local Authorities* (2014), hereinafter referred to as 'Statutory Guidance, Vol. 1', was revised and republished to dovetail with the revised PLO and it can be found at **www.gov.uk/government/publications**. A previous document was published in 2009 by the Ministry of Justice's Care Proceedings Programme, *Preparing for Care and Supervision Proceedings: A Best Practice Guide for Use by All Professionals Involved with Children and Families Pre-proceedings and in Preparation for Applications Made Under Section 31 of the Children Act 1989* (hereinafter referred to as the 'best practice guide'). The best practice guide remains valid as guidance and this can be found at **Appendix 4**. A pre-proceedings flowchart is set out in Annex A to the Statutory Guidance, Vol. 1.

3.3.2   Prior to consideration of care proceedings and in accordance with the requirements of Chapter 2 of Statutory Guidance, Vol. 1 (see **1.5.1**) the local authority solicitor will be asked to advise at a legal planning meeting on whether a decision should be made in principle about whether the threshold criteria have been met. The local authority should then decide, based on a robust analysis of the level of assessed risk, whether it is in the best interests of the child to provide a further period of support for the family with the aim of avoiding proceedings, or whether proceedings should be initiated immediately. The legal planning meeting should also identify any evidential gaps, clarify whether additional assessments will be required, and consider what would be a suitable draft care plan for the child (see **1.5.1**).

3.3.3   The local authority solicitor should be prepared to give advice on:

(a)   whether, in the circumstances of the case, and having regard to the CA 1989, s.1(3) checklist (the 'welfare checklist'), the court is likely to be satisfied, first, that the CA 1989, s.31(2) criteria are satisfied (threshold for significant harm) and second, that there is a need for an order under CA 1989, s.1(5) ('no order' principle);

(b)   the implications of another party to the proceedings opposing the application and applying for a s.8 order instead;

(c)   whether the evidence in the case satisfies the grounds for an interim care/supervision order, having regard to the paramountcy principle, the welfare checklist and the 'no order' principle. Consideration then needs to be given to whether the welfare of the child demands immediate separation from their carers; to the desired length of any interim order and whether this should be sought until the cessation of proceedings;

(d)   what are the parallel plans for permanency within the wider family under CA 1989, s.8 (child arrangements orders), s.14A (special guardianship orders) or adoption; or adoption outside the wider family, having regard to the 'adoption welfare checklist' as set out in Adoption and Children Act 2002, s.1(4);

(e)   local authority documents to be filed and served in compliance with the requirements under the PLO;

(f)   the case management issues and directions likely to be considered at the case management hearing in accordance with the PLO (see **Appendix 1**);

(g)   the alternative disposals available to the court as appropriate alternatives to a care order, for example: a family assistance order, a supervision order, a child arrangements order or a special guardianship order;

(h)   consideration of parents' litigation capacity and requirement to consider an assessment of litigation capacity.

3.3.4 It should be seen as in the local authority's interests for parents to have legal advice and representation from as early a stage as possible. Local authority solicitors have a role in reminding their social worker clients to be alert as to whether the family members have access to legal advice and of the role of their legal representatives. They should be advised to give information to family members on how to access legal advice, including the list of local Children Law Accreditation Scheme solicitors (see **www.lawsociety.org.uk/support-services/accreditation/children-law**).

3.3.5 In accordance with Statutory Guidance, Vol. 1, children's social care should be encouraged to request early legal planning meetings with legal services. Where children's social care is making a request for a legal planning meeting to consider proceedings, the timing of a legal planning meeting should be considered in the light of urgency versus readiness. The purpose is to advise the social worker client on the case and whether to take pre-proceedings steps or to issue immediately. No emergency legal action should be taken by children's social care without first obtaining legal advice. The checklist contained in Form C110A should be considered with the client and especially the following:

(a) the application;

(b) whether the client has fully reviewed the history of the case: that is, whether they have reviewed all the files;

(c) whether a running chronology has been kept at the top of the social work file and the updating of the running chronology as necessary;

(d) whether there is a complete set of all previous assessments of the family, minutes of statutory reviews and child protection conferences;

(e) the evidential weight of the social work and assessments carried out to date, and whether further assessments will be required;

(f) whether written information has been obtained from all other involved agencies and third parties on whom the local authority wishes to rely;

(g) the interim care plan and whether the plan takes into account the outcome of the child protection conferences and plans, and requirements for parallel planning; and

(h) whether there is complete information on the wider family and friendship networks for the purposes of permanency planning.

3.3.6 If the legal planning meeting agrees that pre-proceedings steps should be taken then in accordance with the PLO this decision must immediately be notified to the parents and others with parental responsibility for the child, using language and methods of communication (both in writing and orally) that will be understood by them. This is effected by sending out a letter before proceedings (LbP).

37

3.3.7   Statutory Guidance, Vol. 1 provides that the local authority should send parents and persons with parental responsibility a letter before proceedings (LbP) stating its intention to issue an application for a care or supervision order if the family is to be given one last chance to protect their child's welfare. The letter should act as a warning that the child's situation is deemed to be seriously wanting, matters must change and that now is effectively the last opportunity before formal proceedings will be initiated. The LbP will invite recipients to a pre-proceedings meeting (PPM) where the issues can be discussed and hopefully resolved. If not completely resolved then it is hoped that certain issues will be resolved. If, having completed its pre-proceedings work, the local authority continues to have concerns, it will make an application to the court and there will be 'no surprises' on the part of the family if this is the eventuality.

3.3.8   The parents (and any others with parental responsibility for the child), on receipt of the local authority's LbP, are entitled to non-means/non-merits tested publicly funded legal advice and assistance, Family Help (Lower), which covers liaison and negotiations with the local authority, including the solicitor's attendance at the PPM (see **5.3.3** and **Part 7**). See also a helpful governmental guide, If Your Child Is Taken into Care, which provides information for parents on care proceedings (**www.gov.uk/ if-your-child-is-taken-into-care**).

3.3.9   If the local authority considers that the level of risk requires an immediate application to court then a letter of issue should be provided instead.

3.3.10   With the exception of those cases where urgent court action, including emergency protection proceedings, is needed to safeguard the child, the local authority should then liaise with the parents (and those with parental responsibility) with a view to considering what steps, if any, can be taken to avoid proceedings, including by improving parental engagement with the local authority (where this is in the interests of the child), by further explaining the local authority's position and concerns and, where proceedings cannot be avoided, by narrowing the issues at the PPM. Communication with the parent has to be appropriate and adequate (e.g. writing to someone who is illiterate is probably not helpful).

3.3.11   At or immediately after the PPM with the parents (and their legal representatives) the local authority should provide in writing any revised plan for the child, setting out what the parents and the local authority are to do to safeguard the child, timescales for action and the steps that the local authority will take if this action is not effective in safeguarding the child. The outcome of the meeting should also be explained orally to the parents by the local authority.

3.3.12   Crucially paras. 2.39 and 2.40 of Statutory Guidance, Vol. 1 provide that in some cases, the level of concern about a child's welfare may require rapid and sometimes immediate recourse to the courts. There may not be time for a PPM and the collation of all documentation as would otherwise be required by the PLO. A lack of documentation should never prevent a local authority from bringing a case to court quickly where it believes this is essential to protect the child's welfare.

3.3.13   Reasonable but robust efforts should be made at an early stage to locate both parents, notably non-resident parents, and to identify members of the extended family. The primary carer's interpretation as to who is significant to the child should not necessarily be relied upon.

3.4   THE CONDUCT OF CASES

3.4.1   Local authority solicitors must ensure the case presented to the court and the other parties is clear and comprehensive. Any procedural irregularity must be drawn to the attention of the court and other parties by any of the solicitors involved, in accordance with the SRA Code of Conduct 2011.

3.4.2   The solicitor is responsible for ensuring the integrity of the local authority's case before the court. Their duty is to consider all the evidence and to make the local authority's case, submitting balanced evidence that is true to the facts, fair and complete, full and frank. All relevant information should be shared with the court and other parties, including evidence favourable to the other parties.

3.4.3   Bearing in mind that proceedings affect the continuing relationship with the family, solicitors should seek to achieve a constructive solution to the child's best interests, without prejudicing the best interests of the child.

3.4.4   All local authority solicitors should adhere to the guidance set out in Chapter 4, 'The local authority legal adviser', in the handbook *Reporting to Court Under the Children Act* (Plotnikoff and Woolfson, HMSO, 1996), the principles of which still remain valid.

3.4.5   They should ensure that full co-operation is given to the children's guardian in the performance of his or her duties. Such co-operation should include advising children's social care to provide access to the appropriate case files in accordance with CA 1989, s.42.

3.4.6   The client must be kept informed throughout the case by regular written updates. The solicitor with responsibility for the case should keep social workers and other professionals (as appropriate) informed of the state and stage of the proceedings and the reasons for and implications of any changes in plan or delays.

3.4.7   The solicitor with responsibility for the case should ensure that social workers understand what will be expected of them and of all others involved in the proceedings. When they attend court, they should be advised of court etiquette and reminded to ensure they have access to the relevant records at meetings and hearings.

3.4.8   All correspondence in child care cases should be dealt with promptly and copies sent to the social workers and/or others as necessary.

3.4.9   The Data Protection Act 1998 principles must be complied with at all times to ensure security of correspondence. See the *Guide to Data Protection* by the Information Commissioner's Office (can be downloaded from **ico.org.uk/media/for-organisations**).

3.4.10   It is the duty of the local authority solicitor to comply fully with the requirements of the Practice Direction on bundles (PD27A, available to download from **www.justice.gov.uk/courts/procedure-rules/family/ practice_directions**). There are regional variations and local practice directions and directions given by the court but these are not intended to vary substantively from PD27A. This will ensure up-to-date accurate bundles are available to the court when required and that a copy of the current index is provided to all other parties.

3.4.11   At the conclusion of the proceedings, the local authority solicitor must ensure that all appropriate directions for disclosure of papers are obtained for the purposes of further planning, including placement for adoption and ongoing work with the child and relevant family members.

3.5   CARE PLANS DURING THE COURSE OF PROCEEDINGS

3.5.1   Local authority solicitors must be familiar with Statutory Guidance, Vol. 1 (see paras. 17–20) and Local Authority Circular LAC 99 (29). There is now detailed guidance in respect of care planning in Chapter 2 of Volume 2 of the Statutory Guidance, *Children Act 1989: Care Planning, Placement and Case Review* (see **www.gov.uk/government/publications/ children-act-1989-care-planning-placement-and-case-review**). These documents were issued under the Local Authority Social Services Act 1970, s.7, which places a duty on the local authority to act under the general guidance of the Secretary of State in the exercise of its social services functions.

3.5.2   All parties should recognise that a successful outcome for the child may require flexibility. Local authority solicitors should ensure that the care plan before the court accurately reflects the situation of the child and any significant change in circumstances. Where proceedings are before the court (except in cases of emergency) the local authority solicitor must advise the client that there should be no significant change in the child's circumstances without prior consultation with the children's guardian and without taking into account the wishes and feelings of the parents and any other relevant person, as well as the necessary decision-making processes.

3.5.3   Regard should be had to the contents of, and changes to, other local authority plans which may overlap with the care plan, for example pathway plans for children who are entitled to leaving and after-care services, personal education plans and health assessments for looked-after children.

3.5.4   For children who have special educational needs there will be, from 1 September 2014, an Education Health and Care Plan (EHC) up to the age of 25 years in accordance with the statutory Special Educational Needs and Disability (SEND) system for children and young people aged 0 to 25 for which there is a statutory SEND code of practice. See **www.gov.uk/government/publications/send-code-of-practice-0-to-25**.

3.6   EXPERTS

3.6.1   Use of experts will only be directed if the court has decided this is necessary. If an expert is instructed pre-proceedings but it is intended that their report will be used in later proceedings then their instruction must comply with FPR Part 25 (**www.justice.gov.uk/courts/procedure-rules/family/parts/part_25**) and the Practice Directions 25A–F.

3.7   THE USE OF COUNSEL

3.7.1   Solicitors should be aware of their local authority's general policy with regard to the instruction of counsel.

3.7.2   It is the duty of all local authority solicitors to give counsel clear written instructions, including their expectations of them. The local authority solicitor must ensure that any counsel instructed has an up-to-date working knowledge of child care law and appropriate experience in conducting child care proceedings.

3.8   AFTER CONCLUSION OF PROCEEDINGS

3.8.1   See **6.7.2–5** where the local authority solicitor's role post-proceedings is covered in full.

PART 4

Solicitors instructed by children or children's guardians

4.1   INTRODUCTION

4.1.1   Solicitors instructed by children's guardians or directly by children in public law CA 1989 proceedings should be members of the Law Society's Children Law Accreditation Scheme (formerly the Children Panel). For details see **www.lawsociety.org.uk/support-services/accreditation/children-law**. See also Cafcass' *Guidance to Children's Guardians on Appointing a Solicitor for the Child* (2013) at **www.cafcass.gov.uk**. It is important to build a good working relationship with the guardian and to bear in mind the different roles played by those representing the child. Consider the experience and views of the guardian when providing advice (see checklist below).

4.1.2   In those cases where a solicitor is instructed on behalf of a child in cases in Wales, CAFCASS Cymru requires that advice be provided by the children's solicitor to the guardian prior to the case management hearing. This would be good practice in any event, regardless of region. That advice is intended to assist the guardian in formulating the guardian's case analysis document for the court. The solicitor for the child should make it clear when preparing any written advice to the children's guardian that the guardian understands that the advice document itself is by its nature privileged. It should not form a part of the case analysis document and it may be considered good practice to mark any written advice as being privileged.

4.1.3   Matters that should be included in the advice are as follows:

    1.   What documents have been received from the local authority in line with the PLO pre-proceedings checklist columns 1 and 2?

    2.   Are documents missing that impede the work of the children's guardian?

3. The solicitor should consider whether an early application is required.

4. What specific documents have been seen (i.e. birth certificates, immigration status, etc.)?

5. Are there any specific issues such as unresolved DNA issues based on medical or forensic issues or immigration matters that should be considered?

6. Have the parents and other parties been served with notice of proceedings?

7. Have they had access to legal advice and assistance including a pre-proceedings meeting?

8. Are there any diversity issues? For example, relating to the use of the Welsh language, is an interpreter required for any meetings?

9. Should anyone who is not already a party be made a party at this stage?

10. Is there a need for expert assessment on a specific issue taking into account the timetable for the child and also the requirements of FPR Part 25?

11. Are any interim orders required at this stage, if there is a plan of removal? Is the test for immediate removal satisfied?

12. Are there any disclosure issues such as previous or linked proceedings?

4.1.4 A children's guardian appointed in public law cases has a duty to advise the court of what is in the child's best interests from their professional point of view and to communicate the child's wishes to the court. The children's guardian will appoint a solicitor whose client is the child although occasionally the court will appoint a solicitor and the guardian will be allocated to the case some time after.

4.1.5 The solicitor takes instructions from the children's guardian when the child is not sufficiently competent to instruct directly, or when the child is sufficiently competent and his or her instructions do not conflict with the children's guardian's views. The competent child who is in conflict with the children's guardian will give instructions directly to his or her solicitor, and the child's instructions must be followed (as with any other client), even if contrary to the client's interests as perceived by the solicitor. See *Mabon* v. *Mabon* [2005] EWCA Civ 634 and *Re K and H* [2006] EWCA Civ 1898.

4.1.6 It is important to distinguish between a situation in which the solicitor is taking instructions from the children's guardian and one in which the solicitor is taking instructions directly from the child. The distinction should be borne in mind when following this guidance on the relationship between solicitor and child.

4.2   ROLE OF SOLICITOR WHERE NO CHILDREN'S GUARDIAN IS ALLOCATED

4.2.1   In circumstances when a solicitor is appointed for a child who is not competent to give instructions, and no children's guardian has been appointed, it is the solicitor's professional duty to act in the child's best interests. All solicitors acting for children should be familiar with the Law Society's Practice Note: Acting in the Absence of a Children's Guardian (see **1.6.2**), which should be read in conjunction with the Public Law Outline (see **Appendix 1**).

4.2.2   Solicitors should contact the local authority's legal department for further papers available.

4.2.3   Pending the allocation of a children's guardian, solicitors should keep the relevant Cafcass office informed of prioritisation needs and the court timetable so that these can be taken into account when allocating a children's guardian. It is good practice to provide a written report to Cafcass after the first appointment and to respond promptly to requests for information from Cafcass.

4.2.4   A variety of materials are available to assist children and young people who are the subject of care proceedings to understand the court process and the different roles of the professionals involved. Solicitors may wish to distribute to children the relevant Cafcass information leaflets, if there is to be delay in the allocation of a children's guardian. The leaflets include factsheets for older and younger children, and are available in different languages. They can be downloaded from **www.cafcass.gov.uk**.

4.2.5   Solicitors should consider carefully whether to meet or interview a child before the appointment of a guardian as any direct disclosures could compromise the position of the solicitor. Age and competency may be factors in reaching a decision. Each situation should be carefully evaluated and advice can be sought from the SRA's Professional Ethics team (see **Appendix 10**).

4.3   WORKING RELATIONSHIPS WITH CHILDREN'S GUARDIANS

4.3.1   Solicitors should read and observe the *Guidance to Children's Guardians on Appointing a Solicitor for the Child* (Cafcass, 2013) on the working relationship between Children Law Accreditation Scheme solicitors and children's guardians (this can be found at **www.cafcass.gov.uk**). Solicitors should make themselves aware of current local practice relating to duty Cafcass officers.

4.3.2   Solicitors and children's guardians need to be, and to be seen as, even-handed towards the parties throughout. Children's guardians have to file initial analysis and recommendation reports in time for the first hearing and therefore may form and share their view at an early stage in the case (i.e. when it is necessary to meet the needs of the child in relation to the issue of immediate removal or the instruction of an expert and with a strong focus on the timescales for making long-term decisions for the child). Those representing the child should be alert to the impact of this on the parents and ensure that parents are aware that this may be no more than a preliminary view on the basis of limited, partial evidence, which will be open to regular review. Part of the initial analysis of the guardian will be to establish what further evidence, if any, is required. The independence of the children's guardian and child's solicitor can often be used to reduce conflict and broker agreements throughout, and therefore must not be compromised. However if the guardian is of the view that no further evidence is necessary then the view taken may be more robust and lead to a early timetabling of the final hearing.

4.3.3   Solicitors have a duty to not mislead the court. Whilst it is important for the solicitor as an advocate to represent the child's case on the instructions of the children's guardian or the child, it is also part of that solicitor's duty to ensure that any relevant but unclear issue is rigorously explored and evidence clarified.

4.3.4   There are differing opinions as to the role of the children's guardian and the solicitor at fact-finding hearings. This issue requires careful consideration. The child's solicitor should consider raising at case management hearings at an early stage the issue of planning for the fact-finding hearing, including the role (if any) of the children's guardian and attendance of the children's guardian at that hearing. If the court decides that the children's guardian's attendance is not required, the child's solicitor should still seek to attend and, whenever possible, make arrangements with the children's guardian for the taking of instructions, if necessary (see *Islington London Borough Council* v. *Al Alas* [2012] EWHC 865 (Fam)). The role of the children's guardian can include drawing to the court's attention all relevant matters to assist in the fact-finding exercise (see *Lancashire County Council* v. *D and E* [2008] EWHC 832 (Fam), [2010] 2 FLR 196 at [19]).

4.3.5   It is often appropriate for the children's guardian to hear evidence from lay parties at the fact-finding hearing. However, given the resource implications for Cafcass it is advisable to obtain a direction from the court that the children's guardian attend parts of the hearing, if appropriate.

4.3.6   Since the President's Guidance (see **2.5.7**), split hearings have become increasingly rare in the public law arena. In the past split hearings were regularly used in order to allow the court to conduct a fact-finding exercise prior to the court determining welfare issues and disposal at a later, final hearing. The guidance makes clear that a split hearing should only be ordered in the event that the court decides that the case cannot properly be decided without such a hearing. However, even if this is the case, then it does not follow that such a hearing needs to be separated from the substantive hearing; the guidance is very clear that the preference would be for a 'composite' final hearing where facts related to threshold and welfare could be dealt with together. See also *S (A Child)* [2014] EWCA Civ 25 where Lord Justice Ryder sets out further guidance as to the circumstances in which separate fact-finding exercises are necessary. See also Practice Direction 12J, Child Arrangements & Contact Order: Domestic Violence and Harm.

4.4   SEEING THE CHILD

4.4.1   As a general principle, the solicitor should always meet the child, whether taking instructions from the children's guardian or directly from the child. In cases involving young children, or those under a profound disability, solicitors should not assume that they do not have to see their clients. Consideration should be given to the most appropriate setting and style for such meetings. The length and venue of interviews should be appropriate to the child's needs and the interview should be taken at the child's pace. Once seen, the child will continue to be valued as an individual client throughout the proceedings. Clearly the number of visits will depend on the level of the child's understanding of his or her current situation. The solicitor should not assume that it will be sufficient to see the child only once.

4.4.2   When making arrangements to see the child, it is advisable to bear in mind the child's age and familiarity with meetings. Consultation with the child's social worker and the children's guardian may assist, and the children's guardian may introduce the solicitor to the child. However, even if a children's guardian is yet to be appointed, it may be appropriate and/or advisable for the solicitor to see the child, particularly prior to a court hearing. A child or young person who has had a long history of being looked after may be experienced in attending meetings. For such a young person, a meeting in the office may not present such difficulties as may be faced by a less experienced child of any age. Consideration should be given as to whether, for example, the child's home, foster home or school will provide a sensitive and safe environment to meet the child.

4.4.3   Solicitors should be alert to issues of safety for both the solicitor and the child, and the possible vulnerability of the child. It may be necessary for solicitors to consider whether to see a child alone or not. Again, consultation with the child's social worker and children's guardian may assist. Solicitors should record where they see the child and why.

4.4.4   Solicitors should be alert to confidentiality issues for both the parents and the child when seeing the child at home.

4.4.5   It is important when taking instructions from a child or young person that sufficient time is allowed to ensure instructions can be given in a relaxed and unhurried manner.

4.5   ASSESSING UNDERSTANDING/COMPETENCE TO GIVE INSTRUCTIONS

4.5.1   From the outset, and throughout the case, the solicitor should be alert to the child's level of understanding and capacity to give instructions about the case. This should be kept under regular review.

4.5.2   In practice, the decision on the child's capacity and ability to give instructions will only become relevant where a conflict arises or is likely to arise between the child and the children's guardian.

4.5.3   This can be assessed on the basis of the child's age and ability to understand the nature of the proceedings and to have an appreciation of the possible consequences of the applications before the court, both in the long term and in the short term (see FPR rule 16.3).

4.5.4   Philip King and Ian Young in *The Child as Client* (Family Law, 1992) provide a useful checklist:

> To be competent, the child should understand [. . .] the following [which should not be regarded as exhaustive]:
>
> - the solicitor's role
> - the nature of the proceedings in respect of which the child is subject
> - the reasons for the proceedings
> - what takes place at court
> - what other professionals think is best for the child
> - what the child's parents and other parties to proceedings think is best for the child
> - the analysis of the children's guardian

- the threshold criteria which must be proved before a care order can be made

4.5.5 A solicitor alert to a potential or clear conflict should notify the children's guardian of the child's wishes and feelings with the child's consent, and discuss with him or her the issue of separate representation for the child and the children's guardian.

4.5.6 A child with capacity to give instructions, who has a contrary view to that of the children's guardian, may not wish to give their own instructions, however. In such a case, the solicitor should make clear to both the child and the children's guardian that the child has the right not to advance a case, and advise the children's guardian to explain to the child and the other parties (having informed the child of their intention of doing so) that the child's view is contrary to the children's guardian's instructions.

4.5.7 In the first instance, it is the duty of the solicitor, not that of the children's guardian, to assess a child's understanding, although advice can be sought from the children's guardian. If there is conflict on the issue of competence the court will make the final judgement, and it may be necessary to produce evidence where the court is minded to make a different judgement to the solicitor. It is important for the child to understand that the solicitor's judgement as to his or her capacity may be overruled by the court. The solicitor should discuss this with the children's guardian who should inform the child of any court decision, as appropriate.

4.5.8 Where in a solicitor's judgement there is a conflict between the child and the children's guardian, and the child has capacity to give instructions, the solicitor should formally notify the children's guardian that he or she can no longer be represented by the solicitor, and all parties and the court should be notified of the solicitor's position. Instructions should be taken directly from the child unless, and until, the court rules otherwise. In these circumstances it is for the children's guardian to make an application for leave for separate legal representation, if he or she requires it.

4.5.9 If the solicitor is in doubt as to the child's capacity to give instructions, and what the child says is in conflict with the children's guardian, the solicitor should seek the advice of one of the other professionals involved in the case, such as a child psychiatrist, social worker or teacher, or should approach an independent expert (for example, a child psychiatrist/ psychologist). When making these consultations solicitors should remain sensitive to the duty of confidentiality to the child. Ultimately, if the solicitor cannot decide on the child's level of understanding, an application can be made to the court.

4.5.10   As the proceedings progress, the solicitor will need to explain to the child giving direct instructions, and the child will need to understand, such factors as what parents and other parties want for the child, and what the children's guardian and other experts recommend for the child.

4.5.11   If the child loses capacity to give instructions, the court should be informed and where instructions are withdrawn by the child, the court must be informed. If it appears that the child's decision-making ability has become impaired, the solicitor should reassess the child's capacity and consult with the children's guardian, or other professionals involved, being careful not to breach the child's confidentiality or prejudice the child's case. If need be, an application may be made to the court (on notice) for the leave to instruct a solicitor directly to be rescinded, or for other suitable directions. Consideration should be given to the Mental Capacity Act 2005 as to whether to request the appointment of the Official Solicitor by the child (see **5.2.2**).

4.5.12   Where a child approaches a solicitor direct and where no proceedings are issued or pending, the solicitor should meet the child to establish a preliminary view as to the child's understanding or maturity. Even if the child is not sufficiently competent to give instructions for the purposes of proceedings, the solicitor may judge the child as sufficiently mature and competent to receive independent advice, under the legal aid scheme. It should be established whether the child's parents, and/or the local authority in the case of a looked-after child, know that the child is seeking advice, and the child should be encouraged to agree that they be notified of the same. If the child insists that they not be notified, the solicitor's duty of confidentiality must be observed subject to an exception applying (SRA Code of Conduct 2011, Chapter 4).

4.6   RELATIONSHIP AND COMMUNICATION WITH CHILD

4.6.1   The solicitor should be alert to the particular needs of the individual child, for example for interpretation and translation services, whether taking instructions from the children's guardian or directly from the child. It is not the role of the solicitor to act as interpreter between the child and other professionals involved in the case, even if able to speak the child's first language.

4.6.2   Solicitors should not take direct instructions from a child when they do not speak the language of the child and no interpreter is available.

4.6.3   When receiving instructions directly from the child, the solicitor should keep the child informed in an appropriate manner, as with any other client. The solicitor should carefully consider whether to write to the child on particular matters or perhaps at all, and the solicitor should record in writing the reasons for decisions. Solicitors should bear in mind that many young people may prefer to communicate by way of text message, Skype, FaceTime or email and that all communications should be recorded, whatever the format. In this case it may be reasonable to use colloquialisms to communicate more effectively with a child.

4.6.4   When solicitors receive instructions from a children's guardian, the extent of their communication with the child and provision of information to the child about the case will be a matter of judgement to be considered with the children's guardian in each case. In any event, solicitors should also consider writing to the child before the final hearing.

4.6.5   Whoever gives the instructions, the child is always a party to the proceedings and the solicitor's client. It is therefore important for the child to have continuing contact with their solicitor by visits and/or letters and for the solicitor to build a relationship with the child, although the frequency of contact will depend on the circumstances of the case and the child. The solicitor should consider the importance for the child of a written record about the proceedings in the future. The UNCRC, in particular Art.12, states:

> Parties shall assure to the child who is capable of forming his or her own views the right to express those views freely in all matters affecting the child, the views of the child being given due weight in accordance with the age and maturity of the child.

4.7   CONFIDENTIALITY

4.7.1   When acting for any child, the duty of confidentiality exists as it does for the adult client. This duty always exists save in the exceptional circumstances summarised below.

4.7.2   The child client should be made aware of the duty of confidentiality and when and how the solicitor's duty of confidentiality may be breached in appropriate circumstances. This should also be explained, if possible, to any younger, less mature child in an appropriate way and according to his or her level of understanding, after consultation with the children's guardian.

4.7.3   Where a children's guardian is appointed, it is important for solicitors to ensure that the mature child consents to information being given to the children's guardian (who is not a client). Even if no potential conflict exists, consent should still be obtained.

4.7.4   What any child tells his or her solicitor is subject to the solicitor's duty of confidentiality. The child should be advised, as appropriate (in practice this is likely to apply to the mature child), that if he or she wants a discussion to be confidential it should be with his or her solicitor, subject to the exceptions below applying. What the child tells the children's guardian is not confidential. However, if, for example, the child will only tell the solicitor with whom he or she wants to live, and asks for this not to be disclosed, the solicitor should explain to the child that the child's views will not be known if he or she insists on confidentiality.

4.7.5   If the child's solicitor finds himself or herself to be in conflict with the children's guardian, the duty of confidentiality is owed to the client (the child). No information should be disclosed to the children's guardian (or any other person) without the child's consent, unless an exception to the solicitor's duty of confidentiality applies.

4.7.6   It may be necessary to breach confidentiality in relation to a child against the child client's wishes:

  (a)   Where the child reveals information which indicates continuing sexual or other physical abuse, but refuses to allow disclosure of such information, the solicitor must consider whether the threat to the child's life or health (both mental and physical) is sufficiently serious to justify a breach of the duty of confidentiality (SRA Code of Conduct 2011, Chapter 4).

  (b)   There is a duty to disclose experts' reports obtained in the course of proceedings even if adverse (SRA Code of Conduct 2011, Chapter 4).

  (c)   In relation to disclosure of adverse material not obtained within the course of proceedings, in exceptional cases to do otherwise would breach the solicitor's duty not to mislead the court (SRA Code of Conduct 2011, Chapter 5).

  (d)   Where the solicitor is summoned as a witness or subpoenaed, the court may direct the solicitor to disclose documentation or divulge information.

4.7.7   If there is media interest in a particular case, and publication is an issue, children need to know that what they say may not only be reported back to the court and the other parties, but also that professionals cannot promise that details of the case will not be published (see also **6.6**).

4.7.8   However, solicitors should always bear in mind that they owe a duty of confidentiality to their clients and may have to justify any breach of that duty to their professional body. It is always advisable to seek advice from the SRA's Professional Ethics helpline (see **1.7.2**), mentors, other members of the profession, partners in the firm and/or professional insurers.

4.8   CONFLICTS OF INTEREST BETWEEN CHILDREN

4.8.1   Where the solicitor is representing more than one child in the proceedings, he or she must be aware of the possibility of a conflict arising not only between a child and the children's guardian, but also between the children. It will be necessary to determine how many of the children are of sufficient understanding to instruct the solicitor direct.

4.8.2   If there is a conflict, either between two or more mature children, or between a mature child and the children's guardian in relation to other children, solicitors must consider whether they can continue to act for any of the children involved in the light of information received at the time. It is impossible for an advocate both to support the care plan and at the same time challenge that plan on behalf of one dissenting child. Where solicitors take the view that they must cease acting for all or some of the children, they should inform the children, the children's guardian and the court of the position, so that separate representation can be arranged. Solicitors must decide which children (if any) they will continue to represent and should help the mature children seek alternative representation.

4.8.3   In such situations, consultation with the children's guardian is essential and guidance from the court by way of directions may have to be sought. Whatever the decision, solicitors must be mindful of the existing and continuing duty of confidentiality to the child.

4.8.4   When a solicitor is acting for several children and the extent of access to the evidence afforded varies, solicitors should warn children to whom documents are disclosed, that such documents are strictly confidential and should not be shown to those who are not entitled to see them.

4.9   THE CONDUCT OF CASES

4.9.1   Solicitors representing a child should ensure that all the other professionals involved are informed of their involvement and all other relevant details.

4.9.2   Care and caution should be taken when acting on a child's direct instructions in terms of testing and evaluating the parents' contribution to significant harm. The solicitor should clarify the facts, bring inaccuracies to the court's attention and set out the child's story, without making judgements about the parents. However, the child may specifically wish for his or her perception of the parents' contribution to significant harm, for example, in cases of physical and sexual abuse, to be expressed to the court.

4.9.3   A solicitor should ensure that a child giving direct instructions as the client has sufficient information to be able to make informed decisions. However, solicitors should be aware that the client may feel under pressure to agree to a course of action in a wish to please and later regret such a decision. It is important to proceed at the child's pace and allow the child to change course or ultimately withdraw. It is easy for solicitors effectively to take over a case and solicitors should be sensitive to this risk. The obligation to take instructions and give robust advice is the same as applies in relation to an adult client, save that the advice must always be given in terms that the child can understand. The child must be helped to understand that although the court will know of the child's wishes, it will make its decision based on that which it perceives to be in the child's best interests.

4.9.4   Any statement by the child must represent the child's evidence as to fact, the child's views on the issues and their wishes and, in so far as is possible, must be in the child's own words. The statement should indicate that the child understands it is his or her duty to speak the truth and that it is a declaration as required by FPR Part 17. If a child makes a statement the child needs to understand that he or she can be cross-examined on it; the solicitor should consider whether this is the best way to present the evidence.

4.10   EXPERTS

4.10.1   Solicitors must be aware of the need to advise any child client of sufficient understanding to make an informed decision of his or her statutory right to refuse consent to medical or psychiatric assessment or treatment. The child should be warned that in certain circumstances, the court may override his or her decision. Instruction of experts is dealt with by Practice Direction 25A: Experts and Assessors in Family Proceedings (which can be found at **www.justice.gov.uk/courts/procedure-rules/family/ practice_directions**).

4.10.2   In CA 1989 proceedings, solicitors are under a duty to disclose expert reports commissioned in the course of proceedings. Before instructing an expert, the child giving instructions should be warned like any other client of the risks involved in seeking reports which may contain adverse information or opinion (see **4.7.6(b)**). The child client needs to be warned that a solicitor is an officer of the court, and an advocate cannot mislead the court by act or omission, therefore such documents may have to be disclosed even if adverse. Where the children's guardian has given the instructions, the solicitor should discuss this with him or her.

4.10.3 Careful consideration should be given by the solicitor before discussing with the child the selection of the expert and the letter of instruction. The child or the children's guardian should be reminded that any expert instructed should be unbiased. If the child is to be seen or examined by the expert, the solicitor will need to seek the leave of the court.

4.10.4 Where chairing an experts' meeting or other professionals' meeting, the child's solicitor must be mindful of the issues and the need for an unpartisan view (see also **2.13**).

4.11   CHILD'S ACCESS TO DOCUMENTS

4.11.1 The solicitor is generally under a duty to allow all clients, including child clients, unfettered access to any relevant documentary evidence which the solicitor holds, save where such evidence would adversely affect the client's physical or mental condition (see SRA Code of Conduct 2011, Chapter 4 and **5.7.15**). Generally, as a matter of good practice, there may be exceptional cases such as serious child sexual abuse when the nature of the document is such that it would be inappropriate for clients to be sent a copy of the document. When representing a child, solicitors should be particularly careful about showing documents to their client. Where solicitors are instructed by a children's guardian, they should discuss sending any documentation, and requests for documentation made by the child, with the children's guardian. If in any doubt as to whether a document should be disclosed to a child giving direct instructions, the solicitor should seek the opinion of the children's guardian or another professional involved in the case. Speaking to a senior colleague or another Children Law Accreditation Scheme solicitor may also be of help. Ultimately, directions can be sought from the court as to non-disclosure.

4.11.2 Care should be exercised before copies of documents are given to child clients to keep. It is likely to be inappropriate to send a child client copies of documentation through the post. It is likely to be more appropriate to visit the child and talk them through the documentation.

4.11.3 Solicitors acting for a child should be aware that if a local authority holds personal information about their client, the child has a right of access to that information unless an exception applies. The parties should ensure therefore that due consideration is given to what documents a child should see and other parties must be warned of this possibility. There are similar regulations that give a right of access to education and health records.

4.11.4   The children's guardian may also wish to go through documents with the child and a joint visit should be considered as it may be appropriate.

4.12   IN COURT

4.12.1   The solicitor should consider the options for the child's attendance at court, whether taking instructions from the children's guardian or directly from the child, and discuss matters with the children's guardian or the child. The solicitor should consider whether the child might:

(a)   never go to the court;

(b)   visit the court before a substantive hearing as part of understanding what is happening, whether or not the child will come to the hearing;

(c)   attend the hearing but not give evidence and either sit in or outside the hearing; or

(d)   attend the hearing for the purposes of giving evidence (see **2.16.2**).

4.12.2   There is currently much discussion on creative ways to involve children in the decision-making process and to ensure that their voice is heard. Solicitors should keep themselves informed of practice developments in this area. A working group set up by the President of the Family Division reviewed the existing Family Justice Council's *Guidelines for Judges Meeting Children Who Are Subject to Family Proceedings* (2010), following the Court of Appeal's decision in the case of *Re KP* [2014] EWCA Civ 554. The final report and recommendations can be found in the Report of the Vulnerable Witnesses & Children Working Group (February 2015) (see **www.judiciary.gov.uk/publications**).

4.12.3   The child can attend court hearings if he or she wishes to do so, but this should be discussed with the child who should be warned that he or she may be excluded by the judge from the court. It may be helpful to discuss the issue of the child's attendance at court with the other professionals involved in the case. The solicitor should be sensitive to the fact that the child may not wish to be in close physical proximity to certain parties in and outside the court.

4.12.4   If the child attends the hearing, the solicitor should warn the child that they may hear evidence which may be upsetting and the solicitor should be sensitive to the child's emotional state throughout the hearing.

4.12.5   The solicitor should offer to show the child the courtroom and make sure that there are arrangements for the child if the child asks to leave the hearing. Suitable arrangements should be made for someone to sit with the child.

4.12.6 It is generally highly unusual for the child to meet the magistrates or judge either before or after the court makes its decision, but this may depend on local practice (taking into account the FJC Guidelines referred to at **4.12.2**). In some cases the judge or magistrates may suggest a private meeting. The solicitor should ensure that the child and whoever accompanies the child is comfortable with the proposals, and be clear about the basis on which any meeting takes place, with a note to be taken (usually by the child's solicitor, and agreed with the judge or magistrates) of what was said in the meeting.

4.12.7 Solicitors should take whatever steps they can, as appropriate, to facilitate a meeting where a child expresses a wish to meet the judge or magistrates, but should liaise with the children's guardian, be careful not to raise the child's expectations and be clear about the basis on which any meeting takes place. This is not, for instance, an opportunity for the child to give evidence, or otherwise try to persuade the judge or magistrates to make a particular decision. Rather, it is

> an opportunity [for children] to satisfy themselves that the judge has understood their wishes and feelings and to understand the nature of the judge's task[, the primary purpose being] to benefit the child

> FJC Guidelines, page 1

4.12.8 Before any meeting, the child should be made aware that the conversation will not be confidential.

4.12.9 The solicitor may wish to consider with the child whether the child would like to write a letter to the judge or magistrates, which could be read in court and could also consider other methods of getting a view across such as a short DVD. The use of technology could be useful and should be explored.

4.13 THE CHILD AS WITNESS

4.13.1 The child's evidence may be given if the court considers that the child understands the duty to speak the truth and that he or she has sufficient understanding to justify the giving of evidence (CA 1989, s.96(1) and (2)). It is noted above at **2.16.1** that whilst children giving evidence is currently rare, that may well change in the future.

4.13.2 Whether or not a mature child should give evidence in court is a matter which will have to be considered carefully by the solicitor with the child, after full discussions with the children's guardian where they are giving instructions. The child's evidence can be given by a third party relying on the rule that hearsay evidence is admissible in family proceedings under the Children (Admissibility of Hearsay Evidence) Order 1993, SI 1993/621.

However, where the child's evidence is particularly relevant to the issues in the case, the fact that hearsay evidence is not as cogent as real evidence will need to be borne in mind when considering with the child whether he or she will give evidence.

4.13.3   In any consideration of whether or not the child should give evidence, the solicitor should ensure that it is the child who decides. If the child files a statement, the child should be warned he or she may have to give evidence and be cross-examined. The child should also be informed of the possibility of being forced to give evidence if he or she has made allegations which a party wishes to challenge.

4.13.4   Solicitors should bear in mind that there will be limited instances where, if the evidence is relevant and the child wants to give evidence, it may be therapeutic or enabling for the child to have the opportunity to give evidence.

4.13.5   The solicitor should consider and advise upon the likelihood of the child giving evidence before the hearing. The child is likely to be worried about speaking in court and needs to know if this is likely. In relation to the substantive evidence to be given by a child, it is important not to coach the child, but it would be acceptable to give him or her an idea of the kind of questions which will be asked. The child should know that it is all right to say that he or she cannot remember (if this is the case) or does not understand the question. Generally the more information the child can be given about what is likely to happen, the easier it will be for the child to give evidence in a relaxed manner, with the minimum of trauma. Opening evidence in chief should be by way of gentle questions dealing with non-contentious issues, to enable the child to relax.

4.13.6   If the child is to give evidence, he or she should be reassured about the privacy of the proceedings (subject to any issues as to media interest, as noted at **4.7.7** and **4.13.7**) but told of the other people who will be in the courtroom. This includes court staff, particularly ushers who may be wearing black gowns and in respect of whom the child may have wholly unrealistic ideas. The solicitor should arrange a visit to the court on a day before the hearing takes place. Provided the courtroom is not in use, ushers and staff are always willing to facilitate such visits. It is the solicitor's duty to check what arrangements are made for the child to give evidence (for example, behind a screen) if it is appropriate in the circumstances of the case. The solicitor may need to seek directions at an early stage in the proceedings. The solicitor should establish with other advocates whether or not they anticipate extensive cross-examination, and encourage them to consider the child's natural anxiety about giving evidence and to limit their cross-examination to the pertinent issues.

4.13.7   Solicitors should also do all they can to minimise the time the child has to wait outside the court, as this naturally increases the child's anxiety. Arrangements should be made to use the care room or children's suite at the court (if the court is so equipped). The child should also be advised there is a possibility the press may be present and consideration should be given to how this can best be managed.

4.14   AFTER CONCLUSION OF PROCEEDINGS

4.14.1   See **6.7.6–10** where the child's solicitor's role post-proceedings is covered in full.

PART 5

Solicitors instructed by parents and other adult parties

5.1 INTRODUCTION

5.1.1 Much of this guidance will apply to both solicitors who act for parents and those who act for other adult parties. It is the role of such solicitors:

(a) to ensure the proper conduct of cases;

(b) to test the case of the children's guardian and local authority on behalf of their client;

(c) to present their client's case to the court and all others who are involved in the case in an appropriate manner.

Clients should be advised that the court will decide the case on the basis of what is in the child's best interests and therefore it is recommended that they adopt a child-centred approach. Nevertheless, solicitors must follow their client's instructions and advocate their case in court, even if those instructions are not, in the solicitor's view, in the client's or the child's best interests.

5.1.2 No solicitor should represent an adult party in child care proceedings unless that solicitor is competent to do so. Solicitors should be familiar with their duties under the SRA Code of Conduct 2011, particularly the various outcomes set out in its first chapter. It is desirable for solicitors to seek accreditation to the Law Society's Children Law Accreditation Scheme (previously and sometimes still known as the 'Children Panel') – see **www.lawsociety.org.uk** for details.

5.2 PROTECTED PARTIES

5.2.1 Solicitors must bear in mind that they cannot be retained by clients incapable of giving instructions but should not assume that a client who has a disability is incapable of giving instructions. Solicitors must be aware of the provisions of the Mental Capacity Act 2005. Care should be taken when assessing the litigation capacity of those under 18 years of age or those, for example, who have learning disabilities, mental health problems, cognitive impairments, or any combination of these characteristics.

5.2.2   A solicitor who is consulted by a client who cannot conduct the proceedings (the 'protected party') must identify a willing and suitable litigation friend to conduct any litigation (FPR rule 15.2). The Official Solicitor will act as a litigation friend in the absence of anyone else who is willing and suitable to act. However, the Official Solicitor will usually not consent to act in proceedings unless there is security for the costs of the legal representation of the protected party. The funding of the Official Solicitor is usually secured by legal aid or provided by the protected party's own private funds (if the protected party has financial capacity or there are Court of Protection orders in place permitting the Official Solicitor to recover costs from the protected party's funds). See the Official Solicitor's Practice Note, *The Official Solicitor to the Senior Courts: Appointment in Family Proceedings and Proceedings Under the Inherent Jurisdiction in Relation to Adults* [2013] Fam Law 744, 1 March 2013, reproduced at **Appendix 7**.

5.2.3   The Official Solicitor will only consent to act when his three acceptance criteria have been fulfilled, and it is the solicitor's responsibility to ensure that confirmation of this is sent to the Official Solicitor as soon as possible to avoid delay.

5.2.4   Note that a Cafcass officer cannot act as a litigation friend on behalf of an adult protected party.

5.2.5   If a solicitor is in any doubt about whether a client (or the other party) is a protected party for the purposes of the FPR then a certificate which is prepared by the person's treating doctor or another relevant expert may be provided to the court. The pro forma can be found here: **www.justice.gov.uk/downloads/forms/ospt/civil-capacity-cert.doc**. Time will naturally be of the essence in dealing with such practical aspects.

5.2.6   Bear in mind that the client has the right to challenge the evidence that they lack capacity to conduct the proceedings, so the evidence of incapacity must be discussed with them. If the client does not accept an opinion of lack of litigation capacity then the matter must be put before the court to decide whether the client is a protected party before anyone can be appointed to act as a litigation friend.

5.2.7   If the Official Solicitor is invited to act in public law proceedings, both the Referral Form to the Official Solicitor and Litigation Friend Checklist should be completed. These online documents can be found at **www.gov.uk/government/publications**.

5.2.8   Capacity is issue specific and the client's capacity to conduct the litigation must be kept under review and updating evidence should be obtained if there is any change, such that the solicitor thinks that the client has regained capacity to conduct these proceedings.

5.3   RELATIONSHIP AND COMMUNICATION WITH CLIENT

5.3.1   Regardless of whether or not there are pending court proceedings, or if the child is already a looked-after child, the client should be encouraged, if possible, to bring to the first meeting all documentation in their possession, including the minutes and reports in respect of any child protection conferences or statutory reviews of the child's case (if the child is a looked-after child these reviews are sometimes called 'LAC reviews'). In particular, if the local authority provided the client with a letter before proceedings (LbP) or a letter of issue then the solicitor will need that document as it will set out the concerns the local authority has in respect of the client's ability to provide 'good enough' parenting to the child(ren). The client (if a parent or a person with parental responsibility) will automatically be entitled to non-means, non-merits tested legal advice and assistance under Family Help (Lower) Public Law (Form CW1 PL) after receiving these letters from a local authority. See also **Part 7**.

5.3.2   Clients often do not realise the significance of documentation sent to them by children's services and other agencies. Solicitors should advise clients to keep possession of all documentation received at any stage in relation to the children, whether they are looked-after children or not. Solicitors should request copies of any documentation from the local authority legal department, which the clients should have but which may not be immediately available.

5.3.3   Adult clients should be advised and encouraged to attend any family group conference, any pre-proceedings meeting (see also **3.3.5**) and all child protection conferences, review conferences and core group meetings. If the client is unclear about the concerns of the local authority and what he or she is expected to do to overcome these, then the solicitor should write to the local authority and ask for the concerns to be set out in writing. Whenever possible the solicitor or other appropriate representative of the firm should accompany and represent the client at the pre-proceedings meeting. Attendance is covered by the relevant legal aid scheme: means and merits tested Family Help (Lower) Public Law (see **3.3.8** and **7.3**).

5.3.4   At the commencement of every case, solicitors should send clients a letter of retainer confirming the client's instructions, the extent of the retainer, and any limits placed upon them by clients. They should try and ensure that the client verifies that the letter accurately reflects the instructions given and understands the effects of the instructions and the limitations. The letter should normally be sent to the client as soon as possible following the first meeting.

5.3.5   At the end of the first meeting, or as soon as practicable, solicitors should outline the possible and likely outcomes to the client in writing as far as this is practical with the information available. Advice should also be given about how the case is likely to proceed (including information about timescales and costs) and how the law applies to the case. It is important that clients are not given unrealistic expectations of what can be achieved or unrealistic expectations of the time a matter may take to resolve. If the client is unable to read (or unable to read English), arrangements should be made to provide this information in person (with an interpreter, as necessary – see **5.3.8**) with a careful note being taken of what has been discussed with the client.

5.3.6   If, at any time during the conduct of a case, the client decides to ignore advice given by a solicitor, or to act in a way that the solicitor considers to be unreasonable, unwise, and/or detrimental to that client's interests, the solicitor must write to the client expressing these concerns and the potential consequences of such action which is proposed by the client, including any potential impact on eligibility for legal aid (see **3.3.8** and **Part 7**). In practice, in light of the nature of the proceedings and the human rights implications of a parent or person with parental responsibility being unrepresented, the legal aid consequences are only likely to be an issue where solicitors are without instructions. It is a requirement of legal aid that a solicitor must notify the Legal Aid Agency (LAA) if that solicitor believes that the client is acting unreasonably. Acting 'unreasonably' is not the same as acting unwisely or against their own interests and should be carefully distinguished. The grounds for withdrawal of legal aid during the pendency of care and supervision proceedings is an unusual step if a client remains in contact and continues to provide instructions since there are significant human rights implications (for the reasons set out above). The solicitor is under a duty to provide the LAA with information about any concerns in a timely manner. Ultimately, however, a decision about whether a client's legal aid certificate should be discharged is a decision which rests with the LAA.

5.3.7   Solicitors are advised to confirm the mailing address for a client in order to establish whether it is appropriate to send any sensitive materials to that address. If the client does not have a secure mailing address where documents may be sent then the client should be asked to come into the office to collect documents or provide an alternative mailing address where the documents can be sent. If clients have access to email then e-documents can be sent if security measures are in place (e.g. a password for documents or using a secure email site). Materials that involve sensitive issues such as allegations of child sex abuse should not be sent by post if there is a risk that they will be passed to someone who is not the intended recipient. There is a particular risk of this unintended disclosure if the client is detained in prison, sectioned in hospital, or held at an immigration detention/removal centre. In some cases undertakings have to be given by the solicitor in order to receive certain sensitive material and that solicitor should ensure that they comply with all the requirements of that undertaking as to storage and any possible onward transmission of such material.

5.3.8   Solicitors should be alert to the particular needs of individual clients, for example, interpretation and translation services. Where English is not the client's first language, solicitors should always consider whether an interpreter should be present throughout an interview and whether it is necessary for any documents to be translated. Solicitors should not obtain instructions from a client when they do not speak the language of the client fluently and no interpreter is available. Professional interpreters should be used wherever possible. Solicitors should also note that interpreters are often part of various ethnic communities, and therefore may not always be independent (for instance, they may have links with family members). There is a chance, particularly in smaller communities, that information about families may be leaked by way of interpreters into the community. Solicitors should also be alert to an interpreter not interpreting word for word but providing a general synopsis of the advice given by the solicitor to a client and engaging in conversations and discussions with the client. Solicitors should sternly and clearly remind the interpreter who engages in the above actions of the terms of their instructions and request that each and every word expressed is translated not summarised.

5.3.9   Ideally, the client would have every document translated into their native language but the LAA will likely not pay for all of the documents to be translated (see *In the Matter of L (A Child)* [2015] EWFC 15). Prior to proceedings, the local authority should be asked to have all significant documents translated. Once court proceedings commence the solicitor should request the court to direct the local authority to translate any documents specifically identified by a certain date. It is likely that the issue in respect of the costs of translation will be a subject of some debate and argument. The solicitor will need to be aware of the limitations that the LAA will impose in relation to the translation of documents and will need to consider whether summaries of important documents can be produced which can then be translated in order to minimise costs. Solicitors for parents should also consider whether an application for prior authority should be submitted to the LAA if court proceedings have been instigated so that relevant documents may be translated in the event that the local authority refuses to provide funding for the translation of documents.

5.3.10   Solicitors should allow sufficient time for the taking of instructions at every stage of the proceedings, particularly where clients are non-English speaking or have other communication difficulties. Clients may need to be taken through various documents, including their own statements and the statements of other parties, more than once. It also needs to be borne in mind that some clients have difficulties in concentrating for long periods of time, so there may need to be a series of short appointments rather than fewer longer ones. Solicitors must avoid 'giving instructions' to vulnerable clients even when it may seem clear to that solicitor what is in that particular client's best interests. Solicitors must ensure that they only give advice and allow the client time and space to be able to consider, reflect, and then give instructions. Similarly the solicitor should do their best to ensure that the client is not simply 'parroting' instructions given by a person with influence over them.

5.3.11   Solicitors should seek to ensure that, as far as possible, the client is given the opportunity to fully participate in and be fully informed of what is happening in the case, even if there is a lack of documentation at any stage. It is best to keep the client updated on a regular basis in order to avoid the risk of the client feeling uninvolved in the process.

5.3.12   It is important for solicitors to bear in mind and to emphasise to clients, throughout the case and as appropriate at the conclusion, the continuing nature of the relationship between the family and the local authority.

5.3.13   Where the client's instructions are to oppose the local authority's case, solicitors must ensure that they rigorously test the validity of that case and all the evidence, and that they advise their clients appropriately on what evidence can be challenged and/or what will be difficult to challenge successfully. This will be the case when considering the threshold criteria, the evidence after assessments are completed, and the proposed care plan. It also applies when an application for an emergency protection order is made, or on the first application for an interim care order (see *Re A (A Child)* [2015] EWFC 11).

5.3.14   The draconian nature of the removal of a child from the family home has been emphasised in decisions which were made after the Human Rights Act 1998 came into force (see generally **2.1**), for example: *Re M (Care Proceedings: Judicial Review)* [2003] EWHC 850 (Admin), [2003] 2 FLR 171; *Re V (A Child) (Care Proceedings; Human Rights Claims)* [2004]

EWCA Civ 54; and *Re H (A Child: Breach of Convention Rights: Damages)* [2014] EWFC 38. The guiding principles in relation to emergency protection orders are set out in the judgment of Munby J (as he then was) in *X v. B (Emergency Protection Orders)* [2004] EWHC 2015 (Fam), [2005] 1 FLR 341 and the judgment of McFarlane J in *Re X (Emergency Protection Orders)* [2006] EWHC 510 (Fam), [2006] 2 FLR 701. See also *Re L (Care Proceedings: Removal of a Child)* [2008] 1 FLR 575; *Re L-A (Care: Chronic Neglect)* [2009] EWCA Civ 822; and *Re S (Minors)* [2010] EWCA Civ 421.

5.3.15 Solicitors are reminded that it is their responsibility to advise clients if, in their professional view, the court is likely to find that the threshold criteria are clearly established by the evidence. It is therefore important for the child, as well as the parents, that the parents work with the court and the other parties in order to make any appropriate, timely and constructive concession(s).

5.3.16 Where the threshold criteria are conceded or established, solicitors should be mindful when advising their clients about the importance of moving on in an open, constructive and co-operative way. For example, clients should be encouraged to co-operate with any assessment which is designed to test their ability to change or to provide 'good enough' parenting, and/or any other psychological/psychiatric assessment.

5.3.17 Clients should generally be encouraged to be open and frank in their disclosure of information. They should be advised to 'reveal all' on the basis that matters will probably emerge in any event, and in order to enhance their chances of retaining care of or reunification with the child. Where appropriate, parents should be advised that acknowledging difficulties can often be the first step towards resolving a situation. At the same time, with the introduction of a 26-week timetable, there is remarkably little time for the parent to make all necessary changes and so there need to be early and significant discussions with the parent client as to whether they accept the need for change and how they will seek to achieve the requisite changes. Solicitors should also be mindful of CA 1989, s.98, and associated case law on the relationship between criminal and care proceedings, and advise their clients accordingly (see **2.18**).

5.3.18 Interim orders are now usually made to remain in effect until the conclusion of the proceedings so there is no need for them to be renewed every 28 days (as was the previous procedure). Rather than requesting the court to list a hearing to consider whether the interim care order should be renewed, the party who believes that the interim order should not continue will need to lodge an application for the interim order to be discharged. For a challenge to be successful, the court will need to hear information about whether there has been a significant change of circumstances since the interim order was made; for example, new information that an undesirable relationship is clearly over or that an alleged violent perpetrator who poses a significant risk of harm to a child has been sentenced to a long term of imprisonment. These may be considered significant changes of circumstance, which may support the grounds for an interim order to be discharged.

5.3.19 Parents and other significant adults may have different views from those of the local authority, children's guardian, and/or the court about what is in the child's best interests on disposal of the case. If this is the case, it is appropriate that full representations are made. However, solicitors must advise their clients that the court will approach disposal of the case from the viewpoint of what is best for the child, and that this can override views and wishes of the local authority, the client and/or the child. The welfare of the child is the court's paramount concern.

5.3.20 Solicitors should use their best efforts to dissuade clients from making wholly unmeritorious applications that are unsupported by evidence, which may be clearly motivated by intentions other than consideration for the child's welfare, and/or from opposing applications where the evidence is overwhelmingly not in their favour. Potential consequences should also be appropriately explained to the client. Solicitors should generally lodge a request to the LAA for a client's legal aid certificate to be discharged, having regard to the nature of the proceedings and the human rights implications of the client being unrepresented if legal aid is withdrawn because the client is acting unreasonably. It is not, however, the place of a solicitor ultimately to dissuade parents from seeking to oppose an order relating to their own child, if that is their instruction.

5.4 SEPARATE REPRESENTATION

5.4.1 Solicitors should be alert to whether separate representation of the adult party (non-parent or person with parental responsibility) can be justified in each case. Solicitors should generally consider whether their client's case can be adequately put to the court or if there is good reason for them to be joined as a party. For example, a parent may wish for a relative who would not otherwise be entitled to legal aid to look after their child and it may be possible for that relative to be a witness for the client rather than having to be a separate party to the proceedings. The solicitor in this situation will need to be careful that there really is no conflict of interest before taking this option. Joinder and co-representation can sometimes be complex within care proceedings since family dynamics and relationships are often not straightforward. The SRA's Professional Ethics helpline may be able to assist (see **1.7.2** and **Appendix 10** for contact details).

5.5 CONFLICTS OF INTEREST

5.5.1 Solicitors should be alert to one or both of the parents presenting themselves as a family unit and not recognising that issues exist between them which may require separate representation. Conflicts of interest are a matter of professional conduct and are dealt with in Chapter 3 of the SRA Code of Conduct 2011.

5.5.2 Conversely, over-representation where there is no conflict should be avoided (see the references at **5.4.1** in relation to professional assistance). Solicitors are reminded of their duty to safeguard public funds and to ensure that such funds are not wasted.

5.6 CONFIDENTIALITY

5.6.1 Solicitors should be aware of, and, in appropriate circumstances, must make clients aware of, the effect of Chapter 4 of the SRA Code of Conduct 2011. Chapter 4 sets out the exceptional circumstances in which solicitors should consider revealing confidential information to an appropriate authority. See outcome 4.1 and indicative behaviours 4.2 and 4.3.

5.6.2 However, solicitors should always bear in mind that they owe a duty of confidentiality to their clients and may have to justify any breach of that duty to their professional body. It is always advisable to seek advice from the SRA's Professional Ethics helpline (see **1.7.2**), mentors, other members of the profession, partners in the firm, and/or professional insurers.

5.6.3 Clients should be advised of the greater chances of their case being reported by the press. There is a move to open up the family courts to the press and to allow cases to be reported in an anonymised fashion. In particular, anonymised judgments are increasingly being made public. While it is fair to say that the vast majority of cases do not attract the attention of the press the solicitor needs to be aware of this possibility and the rules that apply to press reporting (see also **6.6**).

5.6.4 Clients should also be advised as to their own duties of confidentiality and the fact that no documents produced for proceedings relating to children, including any expert reports and the report of the children's guardian, may be disclosed to individuals who are not parties to the proceedings without prior permission of the court or as permitted by the relevant court rule.

Some clients will wish to involve the press or their MP and they will need to be advised as to how the rules of confidentiality apply to them and the consequences of breaching those rules. See FPR Part 12, Chapter 7 regarding communication of information in children proceedings.

5.7   THE CONDUCT OF CASES

5.7.1   Solicitors for parents and others should ensure that the client and the professionals who are involved are informed of their involvement and all other relevant details.

5.7.2   Clients should be kept informed throughout the case of the state and stage of the proceedings, and the reasons for and implications of any changes in the local authority's plans or delays.

5.7.3   Solicitors should advise the client about the possibility of parallel (i.e. concurrent/twin-track) planning, as appropriate. It is essential to provide the client with information about the local authority's duty from the outset to consider and assess alternative carers in the event that the children cannot live at home in the future, and to reassure the client as appropriate. A preferable outcome may be for the child to be placed with extended family members if the client finds that he or she is not able to care for the child for the long term. Clients must be asked from the outset to provide information about extended family members as soon as possible in order to assist the local authority and the children's guardian in investigating alternative placements for the child within the family and friends network. They should also be advised of the consequences of not providing the contact details for extended family members upon the instigation of proceedings in light of the 26-week time frame for care cases (i.e., a court may deny an application for an extended family member to be assessed as a child's alternative carer at a later stage within the proceedings). The PLO now includes a requirement for parents in care proceedings to identify extended family members who may be able to care for the child in the initial directions upon issue of proceedings. Solicitors should also explain to their clients that it is the local authority's obligation to investigate potential long-term placements for the child(ren), which may include adoption.

5.7.4   Solicitors should bring to the attention of the court and other parties, as early as possible in the proceedings, issues which relate to language and communication difficulties, including requests for interpretation facilities and other 'special measures' to meet the client's particular needs in giving and listening to evidence.

5.7.5 Solicitors should advise clients on the need (if any) for witnesses, and should discourage clients from offering a proliferation of witnesses who add nothing to the case. In particular a succession of friends who will simply attest that the client is a 'good parent' is unlikely to assist the court unless they can give specific examples which may help to rebut specific allegations or are directly relevant to a significant issue which needs to be litigated during the court process prior to the finalisation of any care plan.

5.7.6 Solicitors should not interview children who are the subject of any case in which they are advising unless they are acting for the child who is a separate party to the proceedings. Parents who come to give instructions often have no one else to care for their children. Solicitors must be aware that it is usually highly inappropriate for instructions to be given in front of children who understand what is being said. Solicitors should err on the side of caution as to whether a child is able to understand. Solicitors should take into account that clients often get upset when discussing sensitive issues, may find it difficult to discuss those issues in front of their child (even when that child does not understand what is being said), and may find it difficult to give the meeting their full attention when their child is also in the room.

5.7.7 Solicitors should draft statements using the client's own words, where possible, but should avoid using emotive and/or inflammatory language, and/or expressing subjective opinions. That said, they should ensure that statements which are drafted reflect the client's instructions. The solicitor should ensure that they are familiar with all the court papers before allowing a client to sign a statement so as to avoid any inherent contradiction of evidence which has not properly been explored with the client. For example, it may be recorded in a police interview that a client has accepted that something had happened which that client now denies has happened. That contradiction needs to be explored in the client's statement and the reason for the change should be set out and clarified in the statement. Failure to address any discrepancies or contradictory information contained in the client's statement and the documents which have been filed with the court may result in an allegation that the client is misleading the court. It has to be remembered that the client's statement is of huge importance to the client's case. Proper time must be given to its preparation in spite of pressure from the court and the pressures associated with managing the solicitor's existing workload. If there is not enough time to cover all aspects of the case in the first statement because of the pressure to produce a document in a very short time then it is advisable to make it clear in the client's statement that additional time is required and detailed information will be contained in a further statement. Do not risk harming the client's case by allowing a statement to be filed which has not considered all the evidence. The solicitor should ensure that sufficient time is available before meeting with the client so that the solicitor will have time to prepare for that meeting. It is vital for there to be sufficient time during the meeting with the client so that the most important issues are covered in the time which is available.

5.7.8　　Clients will need to be provided with explanations of the roles of the other parties and professionals who are involved in the case, for example the role of the children's guardian and of the judge/magistrates. Cafcass offices and the courts have supplies of explanatory leaflets. It is likely that some firms will have prepared standard letters to cover these aspects.

5.7.9　　Solicitors should also ensure that clients understand what will happen when they attend court and provide the client with the identity of the person who will represent him or her at court. Before every hearing, the solicitor should try and discuss with the client whether the client is required, or whether it would be desirable for him or her to attend the hearing. In care cases the court will generally expect the client to attend every hearing, and leave would normally need to be sought if the client is not able to attend due to other commitments (e.g. work commitments, medical appointment, assessment meeting, contact, etc.). Solicitors should check their client's arrangements for getting to court and assist them in making arrangements as necessary. Giving evidence can be a very challenging experience. Time must be taken to explain to the client what is involved without actually rehearsing the evidence to be given. Solicitors should be aware of the court's facilities for separate waiting areas where there is or has been conflict between the parties, particularly where there are concerns about domestic violence. Arrangements may have to be made, in advance, with court and security staff.

5.7.10　　Solicitors should be aware of the importance of identifying early in pro-ceedings whether a client is a vulnerable witness and that expert evidence may be required on the client's competency to give oral evidence. It may be that special measures are required in some circumstances (see **4.5**).

5.7.11　　Solicitors should seek to ensure that full co-operation is given to the children's guardian in the performance of his or her duties. Clients should be advised of the role of the children's guardian in the decision-making process, and the importance of his or her report. Solicitors should encour-age clients to co-operate with the children's guardian and advise them that failure to do so could prejudice their case.

5.7.12　　Solicitors should consider which documents, if any, provided by the client to the solicitor are relevant and should be disclosed to the court and the parties. It is best practice to append any documents which the client provides to a client's statement as an exhibit unless there is a specific order from the court directing the solicitor to file and serve a specific document (in which case that specific document should be filed/served upon receipt).

5.7.13　Solicitors should advise their clients that the children's guardian (or a child's solicitor where the child is directly instructing the solicitor or where no children's guardian is available) may wish to meet with the child. If the child is living with the client they should be advised that the children's guardian (or indeed the child's solicitor) is likely to wish to see the child alone and the importance of them having privacy during such a meeting. The client should be encouraged not to 'coach' their child before such meetings. The client should also be advised to encourage the child to meet with the children's guardian and/or the child's solicitor and to reassure the child that this meeting is approved by the client.

5.7.14　All correspondence in child care cases should be dealt with promptly.

5.7.15　Solicitors should have regard to indicative behaviour 4.4 of Chapter 4 of the SRA Code of Conduct 2011 in relation to their duty to disclose all relevant information to their client unless an exception to that general 'rule' applies. This is a matter of professional judgement in each case. Speaking to a senior colleague or the SRA Professional Ethics helpline may be of help.

5.7.16　Solicitors should always consider the most appropriate method of communicating sensitive or distressing information to their clients. For example, it may be appropriate to ask clients to come into the office to discuss the contents of a report, rather than forwarding it to their address without preparation or advice. In any event, the solicitor should try and summarise a report to the client if it contains difficult or complex language or concepts.

5.7.17　At the conclusion of proceedings, solicitors should consider seeking permission for disclosure of materials filed in the proceedings (e.g. an outstanding complaint under CA 1989, s.25 or a client's psychiatric or psychological report to medical service providers and/or therapists). Documentation may also be relevant for the purposes of treatment of an adult party, or to assist other relatives now caring for the child. In this regard, consideration should be given to FPR Part 12, Chapter 7 regarding the communication of information in children proceedings.

5.7.18　Solicitors should be aware that the timing of when complaints are made under CA 1989, s.26 can affect the conduct of the case. It will be difficult for children's services to respond where proceedings and a complaint investigation are underway at the same time. It is good practice to put the local authority on notice that a CA 1989, s.26 complaint is anticipated, and to air matters as appropriate within the proceedings. However, a complaint is more likely to be resolved after the conclusion of court proceedings. The client needs to be advised that it is unusual for a local authority to replace a social worker who is allocated to the child simply because a parent complains about them. Such complaints are common in care proceedings and are often to do with the fact the social worker is the face of the local authority rather than the conduct of the individual social worker. Similarly, the client should be informed that it is unusual for a children's guardian to be removed from a case. However, a solicitor needs to be aware of those few times when a complaint may actually be needed.

5.8   EXPERTS

5.8.1   In proceedings under CA 1989, solicitors are under a duty to disclose expert and other reports commissioned in the course of proceedings. It is usual practice for experts to be jointly instructed in care proceedings. The client should therefore be warned before instructing an expert of the risks involved in seeking reports which may contain adverse information or opinion. The client needs to be warned that a solicitor is an officer of the court, and an advocate cannot mislead the court by act or omission, and that therefore such documents may have to be disclosed even if the conclusions and recommendations of such reports are adverse to the client. Where all parties agree to jointly instruct an expert, no specific permission is required from the court to disclose the papers to that expert. Under FPR Part 25, no expert can be instructed without a formal application to the court and the court deciding that such an expert report is necessary. It is essential to be familiar with the Practice Directions on experts and the LAA guidance on the use of experts and when to seek prior authority. The Law Society has produced a series of standard letters and terms which it is strongly recommended are followed in preparing the letter of instruction to the expert. See **www.lawsociety.org.uk/support-services/family-court-resources**.

5.8.2   Solicitors should ensure that the right type of expert to assess an adult is appointed (e.g. whether an adult psychiatrist as opposed to an adult psychologist should be instructed). It is important for solicitors to be able to clearly articulate the reasons why the proposed assessment of a client is necessary and to provide the court with information about the timescales in respect of the filing and service of the proposed report by the expert and its impact on the time frame. The court will bear in mind that there is pressure for care proceedings to conclude within 26 weeks from the date of issuance when possible. Cases will however be considered on a case-by-case basis.

5.8.3   Parent clients can be reluctant to share their medical records with experts, fearing that their past medical history will damage their case. Solicitors must remember their duty not to mislead the court. They should be prepared to advise clients that their concerns can be overcome where appropriate, and that the sharing of information can be of benefit to their case. In some cases, only the expert (and not the court, the parties, and the legal representatives) needs to see the medical records. The client should be advised of the likely view to be taken by the court if the client does not agree to disclosure and the fact that an adverse inference can be drawn.

5.9   AFTER CONCLUSION OF PROCEEDINGS

5.9.1   Please refer to **6.7.11–20**, where the role of the parent's solicitor in the context of post-proceedings is covered in full.

PART 6

Other important aspects of public law Children Act cases

6.1 TRANSFER OF PROCEEDINGS

6.1.1 When considering whether to transfer an application for a care order for a child over the age of 16 (under the Children Act 1989) to the Court of Protection (to be dealt with under the Mental Capacity Act 2005), solicitors need to consider whether the young person's welfare will be better safeguarded within the Court of Protection. The Mental Capacity Act 2005 (Transfer of Proceedings) Order 2007 (SI 2007/1899) outlines the procedure that practitioners need to be aware of so that cases transfer in an orderly and timely way into the other jurisdiction (see also *Re AM; B (A Local Authority)* v. *RM* [2010] EWHC 3802 (Fam)).

6.2 SECURE ACCOMMODATION

6.2.1 The court cannot make a secure accommodation order unless the child's solicitor has had the opportunity of taking instructions from the child and the child has been granted the minimum rights contained in ECHR, Art.6(3) (see *Re AS (Secure Accommodation Order)* [1999] 1 FLR 103 and *Re C (Secure Accommodation Order: Representation)* [2001] 2 FLR 169). Solicitors must also have regard to ECHR, Art.5 (right to liberty and security).

6.2.2 It is essential that all solicitors dealing with a secure accommodation application have regard to: CA 1989, s.25; Chapter 4, paras. 39–51 of the Statutory Guidance, Vol. 1; the Children (Secure Accommodation) Regulations 1991 (SI 1991/1505); the Children (Secure Accommodation) (No.2) Regulations 1991 (SI 1991/2034); and Annex B of the Department for Education's *Guide to the Children's Homes Regulations Including the Quality Standards* (2015), which can be downloaded from **www.gov.uk/ government/publications/childrens-homes-regulations-including-quality-standards-guide**. The welfare checklist applies but the child's welfare, although relevant, is not paramount in these proceedings (see *Re M (A Minor) (Secure Accommodation Order)* [1995] 1 FLR 418; *Re W (A Minor) (Secure Accommodation Order)* [1993] 1 FLR 692; *Re B (A Minor)* [1994] 2 FLR 707; and *C* v. *Humberside County Council* [1994] 2 FLR 759).

6.2.3   Solicitors will probably only have a few hours' notice of an appointment to act for a child on a secure accommodation application. Solicitors should consider how instructions will be obtained and confirm the arrangements for the child's attendance at court. Solicitors should try to ensure the child is brought to court as early as possible in order to allow time for the taking of instructions, and through liaison with the court ensure that the matter is heard promptly to avoid unnecessary waiting time, particularly if the court facilities are inadequate. Although most young people facing a secure order wish to be brought to court, some do not and as it is their choice the solicitor needs to confirm this with them and explain what it entails. This includes the option of giving evidence. They should be given the option of writing a letter to the judge instead of or as well as attending court.

6.2.4   Solicitors should check in advance with the court and the secure unit to ensure that children will not be kept in cells before the hearing, nor be admitted to the court through the cells, and make representations as necessary. Only on very rare occasions can it be justified for a young person to be handcuffed even on their way into court and almost never once they are in court. This is not only humiliating but extremely prejudicial.

6.2.5   It is possible that the solicitor's first meeting with the child will be at court although this should be avoided except in the rarest of circumstances. The solicitor for the child should assess initially whether the child is of suffi-cient age and understanding to give instructions. It will be very rare for a child in these circumstances not to be competent in view of the fact that most applications involve older children. The issue of separate representa-tion for the child and the children's guardian will almost inevitably arise as in almost every case the local authority will only have brought the applica-tion where it has no alternative way of providing accommodation that ensures the child's safety. The solicitor will therefore separate from the guardian and represent the competent child in the same way that they would represent any other party.

6.2.6   The evidence should be rigorously tested by all the parties since the serious issue of the child's liberty is at stake. Continuity of representation for all parties is preferable in secure accommodation applications but for the child it is vital as they will invariably be in a crisis situation and very slow to trust anyone in authority. It is likely that more than one order will be made as the duration for the first order is limited to three months and thereafter further orders may be made for up to six months. There is often a real prospect of negotiation with the local authority to reduce the length of the order it is asking for. This could be seen by the child as a partial victory and they may feel more listened to but they must always be reminded that the local authority can apply for another order at any time.

6.2.7   Solicitors should also have regard to the age of the child. Where the child is under 13, secure accommodation proceedings should not be commenced without the permission of the Secretary of State. This should be confirmed with the local authority. If an accommodated child over 16 seeks to discharge himself or herself from secure accommodation, consideration should be given to making an application for a care order. Bear in mind that no such order can be granted in respect of a child who is 17 or over, so if a care order is being considered the court may need to expedite a hearing.

6.3   CONTACT WITH LOOKED-AFTER CHILDREN

6.3.1   Early consideration should be given to the issue of contact, including sibling contact as well as contact between the child and parents and any other significant person in the child's life. Local authorities must take account of the statutory guidance on arranging for looked-after children to maintain sibling contact, which is a part of detailed statutory guidance in respect of care planning (see **3.5.1**).

6.3.2   Interim and final care plans should address these contact issues. Solicitors for the other parties must be alert as to whether the issue of contact has been addressed.

6.3.3   Any contact centres used should be suitable to meet the safety needs of the child and family.

6.3.4   Solicitors should ensure that in all cases where contact is suspended under CA 1989, s.34(6), either contact is reinstated or an application is made for an order under CA 1989, s.34(4).

6.3.5   During care proceedings if an application is made for a placement order the local authority must consider whether or not there is to be contact and whether or not an order under Adoption and Children Act (ACA) 2002, s.26 should be made. Contact with family members should also be considered where a special guardianship order is being made

6.3.6   After the making of a final care order, if any departure from the plan in relation to contact is proposed at any stage, the local authority solicitor should remind the social worker to discuss this with the parties. If the parents or family are concerned that the plan in relation to contact is not being followed, attempts should be made to discuss and settle this with the local authority. It may be helpful for the local authority to be the party making any necessary application to the court. Legal aid will be means and merits tested and parents are more likely to be granted legal aid as respondents to an application than as applicants. Changes or proposed changes of this nature are serious and should be brought to the immediate attention of the child's independent reviewing officer (IRO), who will wish to consider convening a looked-after child review in order to discuss such changes or proposed changes. Again, solicitors will need to be familiar with the detailed statutory guidance on care planning (see **3.5.1** and Chapter 2 of Statutory Guidance, Vol. 2).

6.4 ADOPTION

6.4.1 The law is to be found in ACA 2002 (as amended by the Children and Families Act 2014) and in the draft statutory adoption guidance issued in July 2014, which can be downloaded from **www.gov.uk/government/ uploads/system/uploads/attachment_data/file/321968/ Adoption_Statutory_Guidance_2014.pdf**.

6.4.2 Parallel planning should be used where adoption is under consideration. This is the process by which, as the name implies, other options are actively considered and if the plan is still for adoption a further set of proceedings are issued (for placement for adoption) to run alongside the care proceedings. It is an important part of the process in avoiding delay. However, before reaching a decision that adoption should be the principal placement aim of the care plan, the local authority must be satisfied that sufficient assessment has taken place to rule out reunification or placement with alternative carers including family and friends, for example, under a child arrangements order or special guardianship order. It is vital that solicitors ensure that parents are aware of the possible implications at the outset where adoption is being considered. There has to be analysis of the realistic care options in compliance with *Re B-S* [2013] EWCA Civ 1146, recognising that adoption will only be appropriate 'when nothing else will do'.

6.4.3 Where adoption is the probable option, the court will need to be advised of the key steps and estimated timescales to implement such a plan. Lack of such information could result in serious delay before placement, and is detrimental to the child's welfare. Such information will naturally form part of the timetable for the child under the PLO.

6.4.4 It is not appropriate before the final hearing in the care proceedings for there to have been introductions between the child and the prospective adopters, or for the agency decision-maker to have confirmed the panel's recommendation of any proposed match between a child and prospective adopters.

6.4.5   In certain circumstances the local authority may have placed a child with prospective adopters who are approved as connected person foster carers, or foster carers may be seeking to adopt in accordance with the statutory guidance on care planning and in particular on early permanence placements and approval of prospective adopters as foster carers. In all other circumstances it is not appropriate.

6.4.6   If a final care order is made with an adoption care plan but no placement order has been made, the local authority solicitor must ask the court for a direction that papers in the care proceedings be released to any prospective adopters.

The court should consider which documents should be released for any subsequent adoption proceedings.

6.4.7   The findings of fact made in the care proceedings are often of importance in later adoption proceedings. Accordingly, if the judgment or reasons are not given in writing, consideration should also be given to whether a transcript should be obtained and who should pay for it. If a transcript is not made available, at the very least the advocates should agree a note of the findings of fact in the care proceedings.

6.4.8   If the parent has been given permission to oppose the final adoption proceedings, it is usual for the local authority to fund the prospective adopters' legal costs for advice and representation.

6.5   DISCHARGE AND VARIATION OF CARE/SUPERVISION ORDERS

6.5.1   Local authority solicitors should be mindful of the need for their client to be aware of the continuing need for review of whether a care order remains necessary.

6.5.2   Where a care order is no longer necessary and proportionate, for example because the care plan has been changed, the local authority should apply for discharge of the care order in a timely manner, not wait for the adult parties or the child to make an application.

6.5.3   Where another party is considering applying for discharge of the care order, initially this should be discussed, if possible, with the local authority. It may be possible to reach agreement before referral back to the court. This also gives an opportunity for the parties to consider whether it would be better if the local authority made the application.

6.5.4   When considering an application for discharge of a care order, consideration should be given as to whether the issue of the leaving care needs assessment and pathway plan for eligible children has been adequately addressed, including the question of a referral to adult services for the child for when they reach 18.

6.5.5   When discharging a care order the court may substitute a supervision order and it is not necessary for the threshold still to be met for such an order to be granted.

6.5.6   An application to extend a supervision order should be made no less than three months prior to its expiry. This application is made under CA 1989, Sched.3 and can only be made prior to the expiry of the supervision order.

6.6   PUBLICITY IN FAMILY PROCEEDINGS

6.6.1   In *Re J (A Child)* [2013] EWHC 2694 (Fam) (a case where a father was extensively publicising information about care proceedings), Sir James Munby summarised the legislative provisions which restrain publicity in respect of children. He started by pointing out the 'automatic restraints' – that is, the statutory restraints – on publicity. CA 1989, s.97 prohibits publication, but only till the conclusion of proceedings (*Clayton* v. *Clayton* [2006] EWCA Civ 878, [2006] 1 FLR 11); Administration of Justice Act 1960, s.12 is limited to 'proceedings in private', including family proceedings, except those proceedings in relation to children; and Children and Young Persons Act 1933, s.39 applies only to children who are directly involved in court proceedings, e.g. as parties, witnesses, etc.

6.6.2   The Practice Direction on the attendance of media representatives at hearings in family proceedings (PD27B) provides further guidance on the issue of media representatives' right to attend hearings.

6.6.3   Solicitors need to advise parents that the press have the right to attend proceedings and that there are limited opportunities for seeking to prevent this. Representations can be made to exclude the media but the court must identify the risk to which the application is directed, namely whether it arises from:

(a)   the mere fact of media presence at the particular hearing;

(b)   the subject of the application;

(c) health risks (the court may identify the need to protect the welfare of a child or vulnerable adult who is unrepresented).

The court will also consider whether the risk can be adequately addressed by exclusion of the media from part of the hearing only.

6.6.4 PD27B goes on to state that:

> Reasons of administrative inconvenience are not sufficient. Examples of circumstances where the impact on justice of continued attendance might be sufficient to necessitate exclusion may include –
>
> (a) a hearing relating to the parties' finances where the information being considered includes price sensitive information (such as confidential information which could affect the share price of a publicly quoted company); or
> (b) any hearing at which a witness (other than a party) states for credible reasons that he or she will not give evidence in front of media representatives, or where there appears to the court to be a significant risk that a witness will not give full or frank evidence in the presence of media representatives.

6.6.5 There are likely to be only limited circumstances in which the press will be excluded from the court. That, of course, is different from the press being entitled to report what was said in court.

6.6.6 Solicitors should also be aware that the Law Society's press office can provide useful assistance on media handling, including out of hours contact. It is also worth noting that in most cases the press are only really interested in 'celebrity' cases either where there was a notorious murder or abuse, some other salacious details in the case, or if it involves the offspring of someone famous, so this is unlikely to arise very often.

6.6.7 However, all parties and their representatives need to be aware that most newspapers publish digitally (i.e. are 'digital first'); and/or publication may be by individuals through social media (as was the case in *Re J*). Thus, information about a case is likely to remain available online for decades after a case concludes. This can have serious implications for children and their families, and should be considered if publication is either likely or has already happened.

6.7   AFTER PROCEEDINGS

6.7.1 It goes without saying that all parties should be advised by their respective lawyers about any routes of appeal in relation to final court decisions which a party finds to be unsatisfactory. It will be important to consider the prospects of success when so advising, and any funding implications (see also **1.4.2**).

Immediately after proceedings – the role of local authority solicitor

6.7.2   The local authority solicitor should remind the social worker of the significance and importance of the main provisions of the final care plan as approved by the court. A complete copy of the final care plan must be provided to the child's IRO to keep a copy of that plan in its entirety on the child's social care file, to form the basis for future care planning.

6.7.3   The local authority solicitor should advise the social worker that if any significant departure from the final care plan is planned at any stage, it must be discussed (as far as possible) in a timely manner with the child, the child's parents, any other person with parental responsibility, and any other person deemed relevant including the IRO who may, in turn, wish to convene a looked-after child review in order to discuss the proposed changes to the care plan. It may also be the case that legal advice will need to be given to the allocated social worker (at the time) who is dealing with changes or proposed changes to the care plan.

6.7.4   Social workers should be reminded of the need to consider an application on behalf of a child subject to a care order to the Criminal Injuries Compensation Authority (CICA) and should be aware of relevant time limitations concerning such applications. Again legal advice about this issue may be required should there be any need for a serious case review.

6.7.5   Where proceedings conclude with a supervision order being made, it may be the case that the children's services department will wish to apply for it to be extended before it expires. The local authority solicitor will wish to advise the social worker when a final supervision order is made about the options for the order to be extended.

Immediately after proceedings – the role of the solicitor acting for the child

6.7.6   When the children's guardian is giving instructions, the solicitor and guardian should discuss and agree the best way of advising the child of the outcome of the proceedings. The way in which this will be done will depend on factors such as the child's age, and the child's relationship with the guardian and/or solicitor. In any event, the child should be informed, in person, of the outcome at the earliest possible opportunity with confirmation being given, in age appropriate language, by way of a follow-up letter.

6.7.7   When the child instructs the solicitor direct, the solicitor must inform the child in person of the outcome and confirm this by way of a follow-up letter. The solicitor should ensure that he or she remains accessible to the child and is sympathetic and professional, yet over-dependence should be discouraged. Although some children may wish to keep in touch with their solicitor from time to time, care should always be exercised in such a situation because the solicitor–client relationship has ended, the child's public funding certificate will have been or will shortly be discharged and continued communication might compromise the solicitor's future representation of that child in any future or subsequent proceedings. This, however, does need to be balanced with the need for the solicitor to remain accessible to the child once he or she is in care to ensure that, should issues arise for that child, he or she has a means, through the solicitor, of accessing advice.

6.7.8   It is important that the solicitor prepares the child for the end of the relationship and begins telling the child, before the end of the case, that the solicitor's role will shortly be over.

6.7.9   When the solicitor's role is over, solicitors should ensure, through the children's guardian if more appropriate, that the child:

(a)   has access to information in writing about the local authority's responsibilities to him or her;

(b)   is aware of the right to complain (with the support of an advocate) about matters concerning his or her welfare in care, if appropriate, and may make further applications to the court; and

(c)   is given details of local and national advocacy and other children's rights organisations which may be able to assist the child if issues arise whilst he or she is in care (for details see **Appendix 10**).

6.7.10   Although there is no explicit guidance from the SRA or the Law Society, case papers should be kept until six years after the child's 18th birthday (see **6.7.20**).

Immediately after proceedings – the role of the solicitor acting for parents

6.7.11   Solicitors must write to clients confirming the outcome of proceedings and return, where available, any original documents which clients have provided.

6.7.12   Solicitors must remind clients of the continuing confidential nature of the proceedings and any relevant documents.

6.7.13   Solicitors should explain to clients what contact they will have with the child. They should be advised to contact their solicitor if contact is not offered as provided for in the care plan, or if changes are made in relation to contact.

6.7.14   Solicitors should consider the need for making a CICA claim where the child is placed with their client (see further **6.7.4**).

6.7.15   Solicitors should be aware of any support and specialist services which should be made available to clients in relation to problems underlying the causes of removal of the child, and removal itself, including counselling.

6.7.16   Solicitors should advise the client of the local authority's future responsibilities to them and the child. These will vary depending on whether the outcome was a care order, a supervision order, a s.8 order, a s.14A order, an adoption order or no order. The child may remain a child in need within the meaning of CA 1989, s.17. Solicitors should advise as to:

(a)   the importance of the child's final care plan;
(b)   the parent's right to be invited to meetings that seek to make fundamental changes to the care plan where the child is subject to a final care order;
(c)   where appropriate, the documentation and information on the child which the parent should expect to receive; and
(d)   the statutory review process and the parent's right to participate in that process.

6.7.17   Parents should be advised to attend every six-monthly review (or any other reviews, if the local authority remains involved, e.g. if there is a 'child in need' plan) and of the proposed dates, if already fixed by the local authority. This will assist in the mechanism for reviewing and spotting 'breaches' of the care plan. Parents should be advised to expect issues of contact and discharge of the care order to be covered at every review and should raise any omission of these items at the review itself. Parents should also be informed of the existence of organisations listed in **Appendix 10** which promote the child's voice when he or she is in care. The role of the IRO should be explained to the parent and parents should be advised to raise concerns with the child's IRO as the IRO's role is, *inter alia*, to challenge (on behalf of the child) issues of concern with the local authority and ultimately to refer the matter to Cafcass if issues cannot be resolved satisfactorily with the local authority.

6.7.18   Solicitors should advise clients to retain all future documentation and information on the child received, which may be of importance in the future and to any future proceedings.

6.7.19   The importance of the care plan should be emphasised to clients. Solicitors should advise on the mechanism for reviewing the court's decisions and the circumstances in which it would be appropriate to apply for discharge of a care order or for variation of contact, as appropriate. Solicitors should advise as to the steps the local authority will take in considering whether to apply to extend a supervision order on its expiry.

6.7.20   The SRA Code of Conduct 2011 only gives brief mention to the safekeeping of documents in indicative behaviour 1.7. Therefore, regard should be had to the Law Society's Practice Note, File Retention: Wills and Probate (6 October 2011), which can be found at **www.lawsociety.org.uk**. Particularly useful is Part 5 of the Practice Note which discusses limitation periods.

The representation of children in care

6.7.21   Solicitors may be contacted directly by children facing potential legal issues concerning the local authority's exercise of or failure to exercise its statutory duties towards children in care. As well as assessing at first instance the child's capacity to instruct him or her direct, the solicitor should be aware of the local authority complaints mechanisms plus other methods of dispute resolution which may be available to the child, including seeking to involve the child's IRO.

6.7.22   The solicitor will need to assess whether the issue is one he or she can deal with or whether it should be referred on to a different practitioner for potential challenge. For example:

- a child facing a change of placement may need to challenge a local authority by way of judicial review;
- a child who has lost contact, contrary to the care plan, with siblings may need to challenge by way of application under CA 1989, s.34(2); or
- a child accommodated under CA 1989, s.20 may need their welfare to be safeguarded by means of court action, e.g. under CA 1989, s.8, or recourse to the inherent jurisdiction.

6.7.23   Solicitors will also need to be aware of issues arising for young people wanting to be accommodated under CA 1989, s.20 (see **2.8**). For example, the overlaps/gaps created between housing and social care legislation concerning homeless 16–17 year olds.

The representation of children leaving care

6.7.24   Solicitors should have knowledge of the Children (Leaving Care) Act 2000 which, *inter alia*, amends CA 1989, ss.23–24. Solicitors should also be aware of Volume 3 of the Statutory Guidance, *Children Act 1989: Planning Transition to Adulthood for Care Leavers* (which can be found at **www.gov.uk/government/publications**). This is now updated by the requirements of the Children and Families Act 2014 to include local authority statutory guidance on accommodation for care leavers with former foster carers ('staying put' arrangements). Volume 3 should be read in conjunction with Volume 2 of the Statutory Guidance, which includes detailed guidance on care planning (see **3.5.1**).

6.7.25   Solicitors should be aware, in particular, of the following:

- the different categories of young people leaving care and the services to be provided to each; and
- the mechanisms for challenge if issues arise under this statutory framework.

PART 7

Legal aid and costs information

7.1 AVAILABILITY OF LEGAL AID

7.1.1 Solicitors must advise clients on the availability of legal aid where clients may be entitled to it (SRA Code of Conduct 2011, Chapter 1, indicative behaviours 1.16–1.18). From 1 April 2013, the availability of legal aid has been governed by the Legal Aid, Sentencing and Punishment of Offenders Act 2012 (LASPO) and the subject matter of a case must ordinarily be listed in Schedule 1 to the Act to be within scope. However, if the client's human rights would be (or would be likely to be) breached without legal aid, funding may be available under the 'exceptional case provisions' in section 10. Unfortunately, section 10 funding is rarely granted.

7.1.2 Where the Act refers to 'civil legal services', it means all forms of legal aid are available, Legal Help or Family Help (Lower) for advice and negotiation and Family Help (Higher) and Legal Representation certificates for representation in proceedings. Advice before or outside proceedings is included within the definition of 'civil legal services'. So, advice where the local authority has concerns about the care of a child, which may lead to care proceedings being issued, can be provided under Legal Help/Family Help (Lower).

7.1.3 Legal aid is available in public law CA 1989 cases. Certain parties are entitled to non-means/non-merits tested legal representation for 'special Children Act proceedings' (other than appeal proceedings). This covers any child who is the subject of the proceedings or the parent of such a child or person with parental responsibility for that child within the meaning of the 1989 Act.

7.1.4 It is worth being aware of the guidance as to 'delegated parental responsibility' and when that applies to carers who are not parents as this would enable such persons to be eligible for this form of legal aid) in any of the proceedings below:

(a)   CA 1989, s.31 (a care or supervision order);

(b)   CA 1989, s.43 (a child assessment order);

(c)   CA 1989, s.44 (an emergency protection order);

(d)   CA 1989, s.45 (extension or discharge of an emergency protection order);

(e)   a child in secure accommodation proceedings under CA 1989, s.25.

A parent is entitled to means and merits tested legal aid in these cases but it can be difficult to justify the merits for legal aid as so often the parent is supporting the local authority and so has no separate case to put.

7.1.5   Legal aid is automatically available in the above cases on a non-means/non-merits tested basis (save for parents in secure accommodation cases as noted above) and solicitors are expected to use their 'delegated functions' to grant legal aid so as to start work immediately. There is no justification for delaying the use of delegated functions to grant legal aid in these cases.

7.1.6   It is important to be aware that if the court makes an interim care order of its own motion within private law proceedings the parent is not entitled to non-means and non-merits legal aid (see Civil Legal Aid (Financial Resources and Payment for Services) Regulations 2013, SI 2013/480 Part 2, reg.5), as that only applies if a local authority issues a notice of intention to, or actually issues, care proceedings. That may follow from the making of an interim care order but will be a matter for the local authority. Legal aid may be available on a means and merits tested basis; but as the issue is a matter of private family law, the parent will need to produce prescribed evidence that either he or she is a victim of domestic abuse (see Civil Legal Aid (Procedure) Regulations 2012, SI 2012/3098 Part 4, reg.33) or a child is at risk from an adult who is not the applicant (reg.34).

7.1.7   Legal representation is also available for 'other public law children cases' which are as follows:

(i)   discharge of care order;

(ii)   contact to a child in care;

(iii)   extension of a supervision order;

(iv)   adoption;

(v)   free standing placement order applications;

(vi)   proceedings under the inherent jurisdiction of the High Court in relation to children.

These are subject to the usual means and merits test. If the solicitor seeks legal aid to issue proceedings in one of the categories above then the LAA will need to see that there has been some attempt to resolve matters by negotiation with the local authority before making the application.

7.2   SEPARATE REPRESENTATION

7.2.1   The Legal Aid Agency will accept that there is a conflict of interest between the children and their parents in virtually all the cases above. However, generally it will be expected that the same solicitor will act for all the children if there is more than one child. If acting for an adult party then the solicitor will need to consider whether there is any conflict of interest between them. If the solicitor considers that separate representation is necessary (in relation to any party), this will need to be justified in the application for legal aid. Solicitors need to bear this issue in mind in the course of proceedings as any duplicated costs can be disallowed.

7.3   LEGAL HELP AND FAMILY HELP (LOWER)

7.3.1   Outside court proceedings, there are two types of legal aid available: Legal Help and Family Help (Lower) Public Law. Legal Help is subject to a means test and to the 'sufficient benefit' test:

> it is reasonable for the individual to be provided with help at court having regard to any potential sources of funding for the individual other than under Part 1 of the Act; [and] there is likely to be sufficient benefit to the individual, having regard to all the circumstances of the case, including the circumstances of the individual, to justify the cost of provision of help at court.

> Civil Legal Aid (Merits Criteria) Regulations 2013, reg.33

7.3.2   This is remunerated by way of a fixed fee. Legal Help covers the initial meeting with the client and follow-up correspondence and liaison with the local authority. Advice can be given in relation to child protection conferences but the Legal Aid Agency (LAA) considers that it will only be appropriate to attend these in exceptional circumstances. If the circumstances are considered to justify attendance it is essential that the reasons are fully recorded on file as such attendance may make the fee escape the fixed fee (if it is at least three times that fee) and become payable under hourly rates.

7.3.3   Family Help (Lower) Public Law is non-means/non-merits tested and is available to a parent or person with parental responsibility (but *not* the child), where written notice has been given of intention to issue care or supervision proceedings – namely the letter before proceedings (LbP). Family Help (Lower) here will include the solicitor's attendance at the pre-proceedings meeting (PPM) (see **1.5.1**). Its purpose is to assist parents in the pre-proceedings process of care proceedings in the hope that such proceedings can be avoided. It is essential that a copy of the LbP is kept on the file as proof of eligibility.

7.3.4   Legal Help can be provided to a child client direct where the work is in relation to proceedings in which the child is entitled to begin, prosecute or defend without a next friend or guardian ad litem or there is good reason why a relevant person cannot seek advice on behalf of the child and the child is old enough to give instructions and understands the nature of the work. A child is for these purposes a person under 16 (see the LAA Funding Code: Procedures, para. B4). Solicitors should also be aware that applications may be made on behalf of a child (see the LAA Funding Code: Procedures, para. B5).

7.4   FIXED FEES

7.4.1   In care and supervision cases, once proceedings have commenced, payment under legal aid is by way of fixed fees. These fees vary depending on whether the solicitor is acting for one or more parties, whether the client is a parent, child or joined party and whether the case ends up being heard by a High Court judge or a lower tier judge. Cases can become 'exceptional' and be paid at hourly rates if the fees (not including disbursements or counsel) are more than twice the fixed fee. Such cases will then be the subject of a detailed assessment either by the court or by the LAA. To assist with cash flow, payments on account of costs can be claimed after three months and twice in any one calendar year following the grant of legal aid but will have to be backed up by proof of time undertaken. Payments are up to 75 per cent of the claim. Payment can be claimed in full on account of disbursements at any time.

7.5   HIGH COST CASES

7.5.1   If the total costs of the case including disbursements and counsels' fees (but excluding VAT) will exceed £25,000 then it will be necessary to register the case with the LAA as a Very High Cost Case (VHCC). There is separate important guidance from the LAA about such cases. If the case is not registered then the solicitor will not get paid for anything over £25,000 and this could lead to substantial losses on a case.

7.5.2   On registering a VHCC the funding of the case will change in that the LAA will enter into a separate contract with the solicitor as to how the solicitor is to be paid for the whole case. A separate team at the LAA deals with such cases. LAA will want to have a case plan prepared. There are two models. The first is based on 'events', which are days of hearing or advocates' meeting, and the LAA will pay a set amount for each event. The other model is where the solicitor sets out in detail what work is anticipated to be undertaken to a series of stages (normally hearing dates). The events model is the one which is very much favoured by the LAA and certainly has the significant advantage of simplicity. However, it is for the solicitor to decide which model to use.

7.5.3   There are strict deadlines as to when case plans have to be provided to the LAA and failure to comply with these deadlines can lead to significant problems with real cost implications. Therefore, it is essential that solicitors make themselves very familiar with the guidance published by the LAA on these VHCCs. It can be downloaded from **www.gov.uk/civil-high-cost-cases-family**.

7.6   ADVOCACY

7.6.1   All advocacy in public law proceedings is paid under the Family Advocacy Scheme, a fixed fee scheme with no escape provisions to hourly rates. The advocate must get an Advocacy Attendance form signed by the judge at the conclusion of each hearing. The fee to be claimed will depend on a number of factors, particularly the length of hearings, but it is the same fee whether a solicitor or counsel attends. For these purposes, advocacy includes preparation for advocacy and taking part in advocates' meetings

7.6.2   The Standard Contract (Family Specification) provisions determine what can be claimed in each case and each solicitor must ensure they understand them before embarking on advocacy in these cases.

7.7   FINANCIAL INTEREST

7.7.1   Where the client has (or is likely to have) a financial interest in relation to the costs of the case (e.g. because they have to pay a contribution under a legal aid certificate) solicitors are obliged to provide clients with an estimate of costs, covering profit costs, disbursements and counsels' fees. Clients must also be advised that they have a right to make representations in relation to costs at the end of the case. These costs estimates have to be provided at the start of the case and at regular intervals throughout the case when financial limitations are increased, even if the original costs estimate remains unchanged. Failure to do so can lead to potential difficulties in the solicitor's costs being allowed on a detailed assessment.

7.7.2   However, in a legal aid case where the client is not required to make a contribution and can have no potential costs liability, solicitors do not need to give costs information, e.g. non-means, non-merits tested cases.

7.8 OTHER DUTIES TO THE LAA

7.8.1 Solicitors must ensure that clients are aware there are circumstances in which solicitors' duties to the LAA can override their duty of client confidentiality. For example, the solicitor must report to the LAA if the client wants the case to be conducted unreasonably or at an unjustifiable expense to public funds, or where the solicitor is simply uncertain as to whether it would be reasonable to continue acting. If the solicitor does not make a report and the LAA later decides that they should have done, the LAA may disallow costs incurred after such time as the LAA decides that a report should have been made.

7.8.2 In legal aid proceedings, solicitors are obliged to inform all clients including a child client (who is instructing the solicitor direct rather than through a children's guardian) of their obligations to the LAA. This will include their obligation not to conduct the litigation unreasonably. The solicitor may judge that it is appropriate to adapt the wording of such letters to children as it would be very unusual for the LAA to decide that a child was conducting litigation unreasonably in any non-means and non-merits tested cases. Similarly, solicitors should consider giving their address as the correspondence address for the child client – the solicitor is the child's agent for funding purposes. If a particular legal aid requirement is not going to be met, it is important to note this on the file with reasons, and if in doubt to clarify the situation with the LAA.

7.8.3 Solicitors are reminded of their duty to safeguard public funds and to ensure that the merits criteria applicable to the case remain satisfied, although the criteria applied to 'special Children Act proceedings' are limited. Solicitors should ensure that they file and serve Notice of Issue of a Certificate of Legal Aid and Notice of Discharge of that certificate.

7.8.4 In addition to aspects discussed above, solicitors should be aware of the LAA's Funding Code: Decision-Making Guidance, including the grant of legal representation, related proceedings, and extent of cover. They should also be aware that the children's guardian must look to Cafcass rather than the LAA in the event of a conflict with the child. Professional guardians cannot apply for legal aid.

7.8.5 It is possible for the LAA to discharge a certificate granted on a non-means, non-merits tested basis. Solicitors may consider applying for discharge of a certificate, for example where a client withdraws instructions or where the solicitor believes that the client is causing him or her to conduct a case unreasonably. However, where the client does not seek a change of solicitor, it is advisable to notify the LAA of the situation and to seek clarification of whether the solicitor should remain on the record, in order to avoid delay caused by the parent reappearing at a late stage seeking representation. If a certificate is discharged in special Children Act proceedings for whatever reason the client can always get legal aid again assuming they still fit the criteria for non-means and non-merits tested legal aid but the solicitor cannot use their delegated function and has to apply to the LAA.

7.9 EXPERTS

7.9.1 As a matter of law, solicitors must not instruct experts without leave of the court. The Standard Contract specifically excludes a number of disbursements from all levels of service. Two important ones are set out below but solicitors need to familiarise themselves with all of them to avoid incurring costs which cannot be claimed back:

(i) all costs or expenses of or relating to the residential assessment of a child;

(ii) all costs or expenses of or relating to treatment, therapy, training or other interventions of an educative or rehabilitative nature.

7.9.2 Before an expert can be instructed, the court has to decide that the instruction of an expert is necessary to resolve the proceedings justly. The LAA has set a series of hourly rates it will normally pay experts together with a set of maximum number of hours' work to be undertaken. There is helpful guidance from the LAA as to what will and will not be allowed in its *Guidance on the Remuneration of Expert Witnesses* (2015), which can be found at **www.gov.uk/government/publications**. Solicitors will need to familiarise themselves with the LAA guidance as this guide is not able to cover all aspects of this.

7.9.3 An independent social worker cannot be instructed to act as a guardian due to delay in allocation of a children's guardian by Cafcass, as this falls outside the scope of legal representation. However, an independent social worker may be instructed as an expert (see the 2013 Standard Civil Contract: Specification, para. 7.158). Solicitors have to justify any additional work undertaken due to the lack of a children's guardian.

7.9.4 The *Guidance on the Remuneration of Expert Witnesses* sets out when solicitors may apply for prior authority for disbursements and when they have to apply for prior authority. Solicitors need to be aware that if prior authority is not obtained then they are at risk as to whether the expert's fee will be paid by the LAA at the end of the case. Even if prior authority is obtained, the expert's fee is still subject to assessment by the LAA as to whether their work was undertaken reasonably (i.e. the LAA may still claim that the number of hours claimed was too high for what was actually needed in that particular case even if it is a court assessed bill). Solicitors must take care not to incur costs in respect of legally aided clients that would not be appropriate to privately paying clients, as these will be disallowed on assessment.

7.9.5 Solicitors can claim for a payment on account of a disbursement incurred or to be incurred but need to be aware that the disbursement will still be subject to a detailed assessment at the end of the case and the payment on account does not mean that the disbursement will be allowed following that assessment.

7.9.6 The LAA normally expects that all experts are jointly instructed by all the parties in the case with the costs being shared equally. Solicitors need to be aware that there is joint and several liability for the costs incurred in such situations unless that liability is specifically excluded in the court order directing the expert instruction. If prior authority is being sought it is possible for one solicitor to seek such authority for all the legally aided parties in the case on Form CIV APP8A.

7.10 FURTHER GUIDANCE

7.10.1 Some guidance on the application of legal aid schemes can be found in the Lord Chancellor's guidance on civil legal aid and the Lord Chancellor's guidance on exceptional funding, which can both be downloaded from **www.gov.uk/funding-and-costs-assessment-for-civil-and-crime-matters**.

7.10.2 This is a fast-moving area and solicitors should keep themselves up to date on legal aid as it applies to children matters by checking the website regularly and signing up for the Legal Aid Bulletin. You can subscribe from the Legal Aid Agency page on the Ministry of Justice website: **www.gov.uk/government/organisations/legal-aid-agency**.

Practice Direction 12A – Care, Supervision and Other Part 4 Proceedings: Guide to Case Management

[May 2014]

1 THE KEY STAGES OF THE COURT PROCESS

1.1 The Public Law Outline set out in the Table below contains an outline of:

(1)   the order of the different stages of the process;

(2)   the matters to be considered at the main case management hearings;

(3)   the latest timescales within which the main stages of the process should take place in order to resolve the proceedings within 26 weeks.

1.2 In the Public Law Outline:

(1)   'CMH' means the Case Management Hearing;

(2)   'FCMH' means Further Case Management Hearing;

(3)   'ICO' means interim care order;

(4)   'IRH' means the Issues Resolution Hearing;

(5)   'LA' means the Local Authority which is applying for a care or supervision order or a final order in other Part 4 proceedings;

(6)   'OS' means the Official Solicitor.

1.3 In applying the provisions of FPR Part 12 and the Public Law Outline the court and the parties must also have regard to:

(1)   all other relevant rules and Practice Directions and in particular –

- FPR Part 1 (Overriding Objective);
- FPR Part 4 (General Case Management Powers);
- FPR Part 15 (Representation of Protected Parties) and Practice Direction 15B (Adults Who May Be Protected Parties and Children Who May Become Protected Parties in Family Proceedings);
- FPR Part 18 (Procedure for Other Applications in Proceedings);
- FPR Part 22 (Evidence);
- FPR Part 24 (Witnesses, depositions generally and taking of evidence in Member States of the European Union);
- FPR Part 25 (Experts) and the Experts Practice Directions;
- FPR 27.6 and Practice Direction 27A (Court Bundles);
- FPR 30 (Appeals) and Practice Direction 30A (Appeals);

(2)   the Allocation Rules;

(3)   the Justices' Clerks Rules;

(4)   President's Guidance issued from time to time on –

- Distribution of business of the family court;
- Judicial continuity and deployment;
- Prescribed templates and orders;

(5)   International instruments –

- The Council Regulation (EC) No 2201/2003 (Brussels 2 revised);
- The 1996 Hague Convention;

(6)   Guidance relating to protected parties and others with a disability –

- Protected Parties in Family Proceedings: Checklist For the Appointment of a Litigation Friend (including the Official Solicitor) (published in Family Law (January 2014);
- The Mental Capacity Act 2005 (Transfer of Proceedings) Order 2007 SI 2007/1899, relating to young people over 16 where they are likely to lack decision-making capacity at age 18.

PUBLIC LAW OUTLINE

PRE-PROCEEDINGS

Pre-proceedings Checklist

Annex Documents (the documents specified in the Annex to the Application Form which are to be attached to that form and filed with the court)	Checklist documents (already existing on the LA's files) are –
<ul><li>Social Work Chronology</li><li>Social Work Statement and Genogram</li><li>The current assessments relating to the child and/or the family and friends of the child to which the Social Work Statement refers and on which the LA relies</li><li>Care Plan</li><li>Index of Checklist Documents</li></ul>	(a) Evidential documents including –<ul><li>Previous court orders including foreign orders and judgments/reasons</li><li>Any assessment materials relevant to the key issues including capacity to litigate, section 7 and 37 reports</li><li>Single, joint or inter-agency materials (e.g., health and education/Home Office and Immigration Tribunal documents);</li></ul>(b) Decision-making records including –<ul><li>Records of key discussions with the family</li><li>Key LA minutes and records for the child</li><li>Pre-existing care plans (e.g., child in need plan, looked after</li></ul>

Annex Documents (the documents specified in the Annex to the Application Form which are to be attached to that form and filed with the court)	Checklist documents (already existing on the LA's files) are –
	child plan and child protection plan) • Letters Before Proceedings Only Checklist documents in (a) are to be served with the application form Checklist Documents in (b) are to be disclosed on request by any party Checklist documents are *not* to be – • filed with the court unless the court directs otherwise; and • older than 2 years before the date of issue of the proceedings unless reliance is placed on the same in the LA's evidence

Stage 1 – Issue and Allocation

Day 1 and Day 2 (see interpretation section)

On Day 1 (Day of issue):
- The LA files the Application Form and Annex Documents and sends copies to Cafcass/CAFCASS CYMRU
- The LA notifies the court of the need for an urgent preliminary case management hearing or an urgent contested ICO hearing where this is known or expected
- Court officer issues application

Within a day of issue (Day 2):
- Court considers jurisdiction in a case with an international element
- Court considers initial allocation to specified level of judge, in accordance with the Allocation Rules and any President's Guidance on the distribution of business
- LA serves the Application Form, Annex Documents and evidential Checklist Documents on the parties together with the notice of date and time of CMH and any urgent hearing
- Court gives standard directions on Issue and Allocation including:
  - Checking compliance with Pre-Proceedings Checklist including service of any missing Annex Documents
  - Appointing Children's Guardian (to be allocated by Cafcass/CAFCASS CYMRU)
  - Appointing solicitor for the child only if necessary
  - Appointing (if the person to be appointed consents) a litigation friend for any protected party or any non subject child who is a party, including the OS where appropriate

Day 1 and Day 2 (see interpretation section)
– Identifying whether a request has been made or should be made to a Central Authority or other competent authority in a foreign state or a consular authority in England and Wales in a case with an international element – Filing and service of a LA Case Summary – Filing and service of a Case Analysis by the Children's Guardian – Filing and Serving the Parents' Response – Sending a request for disclosure to, e.g., the police or health service body – Filing and serving an application for permission relating to experts under Part 25 on a date prior to the advocates meeting for the CMH – Directing the solicitor for the child to arrange an advocates' meeting no later than 2 business days before the CMH – Listing the CMH • Court considers any request for an urgent preliminary case management hearing or an urgent contested ICO hearing and where necessary lists the hearing and gives additional directions. • Court officer sends copy Notice of Hearing of the CMH and any urgent hearing by email to Cafcass/ CAFCASS CYMRU.

Stage 2 – Case Management Hearing

Advocates' meeting (including any litigants in person)	Case Management Hearing
No later than 2 business days before CMH (or FCMH if it is necessary)	CMH: Not before day 12 and not later than day 18 A FCMH is to be held only if necessary, it is to be listed as soon as possible and in any event no later than day 25
• Consider information on the Application Form and Annex documents, the LA Case Summary, and the Case Analysis • Identify the parties' positions to be recited in the draft Case Management Order • Identify the parties' positions about jurisdiction, in particular arising out of any international element • If necessary, identify proposed experts and draft questions in accordance with Part 25 and the Experts Practice Directions • Identify any disclosure that in the advocates' views is necessary	• Court gives detailed case management directions, including: – Considering jurisdiction in a case with an international element; – Confirming allocation – Drawing up the timetable for the child and the timetable for the proceedings and considering if an extension is necessary – Identifying additional parties, intervenors and representation (including confirming that Cafcass/CAFCASS CYMRU have allocated a Children's Guardian and that a litigation

Advocates' meeting (including any litigants in person)	Case Management Hearing
• Immediately notify the court of the need for a contested ICO hearing and any issue about allocation • LA advocate to file a draft Case Management Order in prescribed form with court by 11a.m. on the business day before the CMH and/or FCMH	friend is appointed for any protected party or non-subject child) – Giving directions for the determination of any disputed issue about litigation capacity – Identifying the key issues – Identifying the evidence necessary to enable the court to resolve the key issues – Deciding whether there is a real issue about threshold to be resolved – Determining any application made under Part 25 and otherwise ensuring compliance with Part 25 where it is necessary for expert(s) to be instructed – Identifying any necessary disclosure and if appropriate giving directions – Giving directions for any concurrent or proposed placement order proceedings – Ensuring compliance with the court's directions – If a FCMH is necessary, directing an advocates' meeting and Case Analysis if required – Directing filing of any threshold agreement, final evidence and Care Plan and responses to those documents for the IRH – Directing a Case Analysis for the IRH – Directing an advocates' meeting for the IRH – Listing (any FCMH) IRH, Final Hearing (including early Final Hearing) as appropriate – Giving directions for special measures and/or interpreters and intermediaries – Issuing the Case Management Order

Stage 3 – Issues Resolution Hearing

Advocates' meeting (including any litigants in person)	IRH
No later than 7 business days before the IRH	As directed by the court, in accordance with the timetable for the proceedings
<ul><li>Review evidence and the positions of the parties</li><li>Identify the advocates' views of:<ul><li>– the remaining key issues and how the issues may be resolved or narrowed at the IRH including by the making of final orders</li><li>– the further evidence which is required to be heard to enable the key issues to be resolved or narrowed at the IRH</li><li>– the evidence that is relevant and the witnesses that are required at the final hearing</li><li>– the need for a contested hearing and/or time for oral evidence to be given at the IRH</li></ul></li><li>LA advocate to –<ul><li>– notify the court immediately of the outcome of the discussion at the meeting</li><li>– file a draft Case Management Order with the court by 11a.m. on the business day before the IRH</li></ul></li></ul>	<ul><li>Court identifies the key issue(s) (if any) to be determined and the extent to which those issues can be resolved or narrowed at the IRH</li><li>Court considers whether the IRH can be used as a final hearing</li><li>Court resolves or narrows the issues by hearing evidence</li><li>Court identifies the evidence to be heard on the issues which remain to be resolved at the final hearing</li><li>Court gives final case management directions including:<ul><li>– Any extension of the timetable for the proceedings which is necessary</li><li>– Filing of the threshold agreement or a statement of facts/issues remaining to be determined</li><li>– Filing of:<ul><li>Final evidence and Care Plan</li><li>Case Analysis for Final Hearing (if required)</li><li>Witness templates</li><li>Skeleton arguments</li></ul></li><li>– Judicial reading list/reading time, including time estimate and an estimate for judgment writing time</li><li>– Ensuring Compliance with PD27A (the Bundles Practice Direction)</li><li>– Listing the Final Hearing</li></ul></li><li>Court issues Case Management Order</li></ul>

2   FLEXIBLE POWERS OF THE COURT

2.1   Attention is drawn to the flexible powers of the court either following the issue of the application or at any other stage in the proceedings.

2.2   The court may give directions without a hearing including setting a date for the Final Hearing or a period within which the Final Hearing will take place. The steps, which the court will ordinarily take at the various stages of the proceedings provided for in the Public Law Outline, may be taken by the court at another stage in the proceedings if the circumstances of the case merit this approach.

2.3   The flexible powers of the court include the ability for the court to cancel or repeat a particular hearing. For example, if the issue on which the case turns can with reasonable practicability be crystallised and resolved by taking evidence at an IRH then such a flexible approach must be taken in accordance with the overriding objective and to secure compliance with section 1(2) of the 1989 Act and resolving the proceedings within 26 weeks or the period for the time being specified by the court.

2.4   Where a party has requested an urgent hearing a) to enable the court to give immediate directions or orders to facilitate any case management issue which is to be considered at the CMH, or b) to decide whether an ICO is necessary, the court may list such a hearing at any appropriate time before the CMH and give directions for that hearing. It is anticipated that an urgent preliminary case management hearing will only be necessary to consider issues such as jurisdiction, parentage, party status, capacity to litigate, disclosure and whether there is, or should be, a request to a Central Authority or other competent authority in a foreign state or consular authority in England and Wales in an international case. It is not intended that any urgent hearing will delay the CMH.

2.5   Where it is anticipated that oral evidence may be required at the CMH, FCMH or IRH, the court must be notified in accordance with Stages 2 and 3 of the Public Law Outline well in advance and directions sought for the conduct of the hearing.

2.6   It is expected that full case management will take place at the CMH. It follows that the parties must be prepared to deal with all relevant case management issues, as identified in Stage 2 of the Public Law Outline. A FCMH should only be directed where necessary and must not be regarded as a routine step in proceedings.

3   COMPLIANCE WITH PRE-PROCEEDINGS CHECKLIST

3.1   It is recognised that in a small minority of cases the circumstances are such that the safety and welfare of the child may be jeopardised if the start of proceedings is delayed until all of the documents appropriate to the case and referred to in the Pre-Proceedings Checklist are available. The safety and welfare of the child should never be put in jeopardy by delaying issuing proceedings whether because of lack of documentation or otherwise. (Nothing in this Practice Direction affects an application for an emergency protection order under section 44 of the 1989 Act). Also, where an application for an interim order is urgent, then the hearing of that application is *not* expected to be postponed until the Case Management Hearing. The Case Management Hearing is still to be held not before day 12 and not later than day 18 in accordance with the Public Law Outline and guidance in this Practice Direction. If an urgent preliminary Case Management Hearing or an urgent contested ICO hearing is held before the CMH, the court should not dispense with the CMH unless all of the parties have been sufficiently prepared and the court has been able to deal with all case management issues which would have come before it at the CMH.

3.2 The court recognises that preparation may need to be varied to suit the circumstances of the case. In cases where any of the Annex Documents required to be attached to the Application Form are not available at the time of issue of the application, the court will consider making directions on issue about when any missing documentation is to be filed. The expectation is that there must be a good reason why one or more of the documents are not available. Further directions relating to any missing documentation will also be made at the Case Management Hearing.

4   ALLOCATION

4.1 The court considers the allocation of proceedings in accordance with the Allocation Rules and any Guidance issued by the President on distribution of business of the family court. The justices' clerk or assistant justices' clerk (with responsibility for gatekeeping and allocation of proceedings) will discuss initial allocation with a district judge (with responsibility for allocation and gatekeeping of proceedings) as provided for in any Guidance issued by the President on distribution of business of the family court. The expectation is that, wherever possible, any question relating to allocation of the proceedings will be considered at the CMH.

5   THE TIMETABLE FOR THE CHILD AND THE TIMETABLE FOR PROCEEDINGS

5.1 The timetable for the proceedings:

(1) The court will draw up a timetable for the proceedings with a view to disposing of the application –

    (a) without delay; and

    (b) in any event within 26 weeks beginning with the day on which the application was issued in accordance with section 32(1)(a)(ii) of the Children Act 1989.

(2) The court, when drawing up or revising a timetable under paragraph (1), will in particular have regard to –

    (a) the impact which the timetable or any revised timetable would have on the welfare of the child to whom the application relates; and

    (b) the impact which the timetable or any revised timetable would have on the duration and conduct of the proceedings.

5.2 The impact which the timetable for the proceedings, any revision or extension of that timetable would have on the welfare of the child to whom the application relates are matters to which the court is to have particular regard. The court will use the Timetable for the Child to assess the impact of these matters on the welfare of the child and to draw up and revise the timetable for the proceedings.

5.3 The 'Timetable for the Child' is the timetable set by the court which takes into account dates which are important to the child's welfare and development.

5.4 The timetable for the proceedings is set having particular regard to the Timetable for the Child and the Timetable for the Child needs to be reviewed regularly. Where adjustments are made to the Timetable for the Child, the timetable for the proceedings will have to be reviewed consistently with resolving the proceedings within 26 weeks or the period for the time being specified by the court.

5.5   Examples of the dates the court will record and take into account when setting the Timetable for the Child are the dates of:

(1)   any formal review by the Local Authority of the case of a looked after child (within the meaning of section 22(1) of the 1989 Act);

(2)   any significant educational steps, including the child taking up a place at a new school and, where applicable, any review by the Local Authority of a statement of the child's special educational needs;

(3)   any health care steps, including assessment by a paediatrician or other specialist;

(4)   any review of Local Authority plans for the child, including any plans for permanence through adoption, Special Guardianship or placement with parents or relatives;

(5)   any change or proposed change of the child's placement;

(6)   any significant change in the child's social or family circumstances; or

(7)   any timetable for the determination of an issue in a case with an international element.

5.6   To identify the Timetable for the Child, the applicant is required to provide the information needed about the significant steps in the child's life in the Application Form and the Social Work Statement and to update this information regularly taking into account information received from others involved in the child's life such as the parties, members of the child's family, the person who is caring for the child, the children's guardian, the Independent Reviewing Officer, the child's key social worker and any Central Authority or competent authority in a foreign state or a consular authority in England and Wales in a case with an international element.

5.7   Where more than one child is the subject of the proceedings, the court should consider and will set a Timetable for the Child for each child. The children may not all have the same timetable, and the court will consider the appropriate progress of the proceedings in relation to each child.

5.8   Where there are parallel care proceedings and criminal proceedings against a person connected with the child for a serious offence against the child, linked directions hearings should where practicable take place as the case progresses. The timing of the proceedings in a linked care and criminal case should appear in the Timetable for the Child. The time limit of resolving the proceedings within 26 weeks applies unless a longer timetable has been set by the court in order to resolve the proceedings justly in accordance with section 32(1)(a)(ii) and (5) of the 1989 Act. Early disclosure and listing of hearings is necessary in proceedings in a linked care and criminal case.

6   EXTENSIONS TO THE TIMETABLE FOR PROCEEDINGS

6.1   The court is required to draw up a timetable for proceedings with a view to disposing of the application without delay and in any event within 26 weeks. If proceedings can be resolved earlier, then they should be. A standard timetable and process is expected to be followed in respect of the giving of standard directions on issue and allocation and other matters which should be carried out by the court on issue, including setting and giving directions for the Case Management Hearing.

6.2   Having regard to the circumstances of the particular case, the court may consider that it is necessary to extend the time by which the proceedings are to be resolved beyond 26 weeks to enable the court to resolve the proceedings justly (see section 32(5) of the 1989 Act). When making this decision, the court is to take account of the guidance that extensions are not to be granted routinely and are to be seen as requiring specific justification (see section 32(7) of the 1989 Act). The decision and reason(s) for extending a case should be recorded in writing (in the Case Management Order) and orally stated in court, so that all parties are aware of the reasons for delay in the case (see FPR 12.26C). The Case Management Order must contain a record of this information, as well as the impact of the court's decision on the welfare of the child.

6.3   The court may extend the period within which proceedings are intended to be resolved on its own initiative or on application. Applications for an extension should, wherever possible, only be made so that they are considered at any hearing for which a date has been fixed or for which a date is about to be fixed. Where a date for a hearing has been fixed, a party who wishes to make an application at that hearing but does not have sufficient time to file an application notice should as soon as possible inform the court (if possible in writing) and, if possible, the other parties of the nature of the application and the reason for it. The party should then make the application orally at the hearing.

6.4   If the court agrees an extension is necessary, an initial extension to the time limit may be granted for up to eight weeks (or less if directed) in order to resolve the case justly (see section 32(8) of the 1989 Act). If more time is necessary, in order to resolve the proceedings justly, a further extension of up to eight weeks may be agreed by the court. There is no limit on the number of extensions that may be granted in a particular case.

6.5   If the court considers that the timetable for the proceedings will require an extension beyond the next eight week period in order to resolve the proceedings justly, the Case Management Order should:

(1)   state the reason(s) why it is necessary to have a further extension;
(2)   fix the date of the next effective hearing (which might be in a period shorter than a further eight weeks); and
(3)   indicate whether it is appropriate for the next application for an extension of the timetable to be considered on paper.

6.6   The expectation is that, subject to paragraph 6.5, extensions should be considered at a hearing and that a court will not approve proposals for the management of a case under FPR 12.15 where the consequence of those proposals is that the case is unlikely to be resolved within 26 weeks or other period for the time being allowed for resolution of the proceedings. In accordance with FPR 4.1(3)(e), the court may hold a hearing and receive evidence by telephone or by using any other method of direct oral communication. When deciding whether to extend the timetable, the court must have regard to the impact of any ensuing timetable revision on the welfare of the child (see section 32(6) of the 1989 Act).

7   INTERPRETATION

7.1   In this Practice Direction:

'Allocation Rules' mean any rules relating to composition of the court and distribution of business made under section 31D of the Matrimonial and Family Proceedings Act 1984;

'Care Plan' is a separate document from the evidence that is filed by the local authority. It is a 'section 31A plan' referred to in section 31A of the 1989 Act which complies with guidance as to content issued by the Secretary of State;

'Case Analysis' means a written or, if there is insufficient time for a written, an oral outline of the case from the perspective of the child's best interests prepared by the children's guardian or Welsh family proceedings officer for the CMH or FCMH (where one is necessary) and IRH or as otherwise directed by the court, incorporating an analysis of the key issues that need to be resolved in the case including –

(a)   a threshold analysis;

(b)   a case management analysis, including an analysis of the timetable for the proceedings, an analysis of the Timetable for the Child and the evidence which any party proposes is necessary to resolve the issues;

(c)   a parenting capability analysis;

(d)   a child impact analysis, including an analysis of the ascertainable wishes and feelings of the child and the impact on the welfare of the child of any application to adjourn a hearing or extend the timetable for the proceedings;

(e)   an early permanence analysis including an analysis of the proposed placements and contact framework; by reference to a welfare and proportionality analysis.

(f)   whether and if so what communication it is proposed there should be during the proceedings with the child by the court;

'Case Management Order' is the prescribed form of order referred to in any Guidance issued by the President from time to time on prescribed templates and orders;

'Day' means 'business day'. 'Day 1' is the day of issue and 'Day 2' is the next business day following the day of issue of proceedings. 'Day 12', 'Day 18' and 'Day 25' are respectively the 11th, 17th and the 24th business days after the day of issue of proceedings (Day 1). '26 weeks' means 26 calendar weeks beginning on the day of issue of proceedings (Day 1);

'Experts Practice Directions' mean –

(a)   Practice Direction 25A (Experts – Emergencies and Pre-Proceedings Instructions);

(b)   Practice Direction 25B (The Duties of An Expert, The Expert's Report and Arrangements For An Expert To Attend Court);

(c)   Practice Direction 25C (Children's Proceedings – The Use Of Single Joint Experts and The Process Leading to An Expert Being Instructed or Expert Evidence Being Put Before the Court);

(d)   Practice Direction 25E (Discussions Between Experts in Family Proceedings);

'Genogram' means a family tree, setting out in diagrammatic form the child's family and extended family members and their relationship with the child;

'Index of Checklist Documents' means a list of Checklist Documents referred to in the Public Law Outline Pre-Proceedings Checklist which is divided into two parts with Part A being the documents referred to in column 2, paragraph (a) of the Pre-Proceedings Checklist and Part B being those referred to in column 2, paragraph (b) of the Pre-proceedings Checklist;

'International instruments'

'the Council Regulation (EC) No 2201/2003 (Brussels 2 revised)' means Council Regulation (EC) No 2201/2003' of 27 November 2003 on jurisdiction and the recognition and enforcement of judgments in matrimonial matters and in matters of parental responsibility;

'The 1996 Hague Convention' means the Convention on Jurisdiction, Applicable Law, Recognition, Enforcement and Co-operation in Respect of Parental Responsibility and Measures for the Protection of Children;

105

'Justices' Clerks Rules' means any rules made under section 310 of the Matrimonial and Family Proceedings Act 1984 enabling functions of the family court or judge of that court to be carried out by a justices' clerk or assistant to a justices' clerk;

'Letter Before Proceedings' means any letter from the Local Authority containing written notification to the parents and others with parental responsibility for the child of the Local Authority's likely intention to apply to court for a care or supervision order and any related subsequent correspondence confirming the Local Authority's position;

'Local Authority Case Summary' means a document prepared by the Local Authority legal representative for each case management hearing in the form referred to in any Guidance issued by the President from time to time on prescribed templates and orders;

'Parents' Response' means a document from either or both of the parents containing

(a)   in no more than two pages, the parents' response to the Threshold Statement, and
(b)   the parents' placement proposals including the identity and whereabouts of all relatives and friends they propose be considered by the court;
(c)   Information which may be relevant to a person's capacity to litigate including information about any referrals to mental health services and adult services;

'Section 7 report' means any report under section 7 of the 1989 Act;

'Section 37 report' means any report by the Local Authority to the court as a result of a direction under section 37 of the 1989 Act;

'Social Work Chronology' means a schedule containing –

(a)   a succinct summary of the length of involvement of the local authority with the family and in particular with the child;
(b)   a succinct summary of the significant dates and events in the child's life in chronological order, i.e. a running record up to the issue of the proceedings; providing such information under the following headings –

    (i)   serial number;
    (ii)   date;
    (iii)   event-detail;
    (iv)   witness or document reference (where applicable);

'Social Work Statement' means a statement prepared by the Local Authority limited to the following evidence –

Summary

(a)   The order sought;
(b)   Succinct summary of reasons with reference as appropriate to the Welfare Checklist;

Family

(c)   Family members and relationships especially the primary carers and significant adults/other children;
(d)   Genogram;

Threshold

(e)   Precipitating events;
(f)   Background circumstances;

(i)   summary of children's services involvement cross-referenced to the chronology;

(ii)   previous court orders and emergency steps;

(iii) previous assessments;

(g)   Summary of significant harm and or likelihood of significant harm which the LA will seek to establish by evidence or concession;

Parenting capability

(h)   Assessment of child's needs;

(i)   Assessment of parental capability to meet needs;

(j)   Analysis of why there is a gap between parental capability and the child's needs;

(k)   Assessment of other significant adults who may be carers;

Child impact

(l)   Wishes and feelings of the child(ren);

(m)   Timetable for the Child;

(n)   Delay and timetable for the proceedings;

Permanence and contact

(o)   Parallel planning;

(p)   *Realistic* placement options by reference to a welfare and proportionality analysis;

(q)   Contact framework;

Case Management

(r)   Evidence and assessments necessary and outstanding;

(s)   Any information about any person's litigation capacity, mental health issues, disabilities or vulnerabilities that is relevant to their capability to participate in the proceedings; and

(t)   Case management proposals.

'Standard Directions on Issue and Allocation' means directions given by the court on issue and upon allocation in the prescribed form referred to in any Guidance issued by the President from time to time on prescribed templates and orders;

'Threshold Statement' means a written outline by the legal representative of the LA in the application form of the facts which the LA will seek to establish by evidence or concession to satisfy the threshold criteria under s31(2) of the 1989 Act limited to no more than 2 pages;

'Welfare Checklist' means the list of matters which is set out in section 1(3) of the 1989 Act and to which the court is to have particular regard in accordance with section (1)(3) and (4).

Practice Direction 12B – Child Arrangements Programme

[April 2014]

1 WHEN DOES THE CHILD ARRANGEMENTS PROGRAMME APPLY?

1.1 The Child Arrangements Programme (the 'CAP') applies where a dispute arises between separated parents and/or families about arrangements concerning children.

1.2 The CAP is designed to assist families to reach safe and child-focused agreements for their child, where possible out of the court setting. If parents / families are unable to reach agreement, and a court application is made, the CAP encourages swift resolution of the dispute through the court.

1.3 It is well-recognised that negotiated agreements between adults generally enhance long-term co-operation, and are better for the child concerned. Therefore, separated parents and families are strongly encouraged to attempt to resolve their disputes concerning the child outside of the court system. This may also be quicker and cheaper.

2 SIGNPOSTING SERVICES, PARENTING PLANS, AND PUBLIC FUNDING

2.1 **Services**: Where a dispute arises in relation to a child, or children, parents and families are encouraged to obtain advice and support as soon as possible.

2.2 There are many services available for such families, who seek advice about resolving disputes concerning their child.

2.3 The following services are recommended:

(1) For more information about family mediation and to find the nearest mediation service (including those providing a MIAM): **www.familymediationcouncil.org.uk**;

(2) For a Guide about children and the family courts for separating parents (including representing yourself in court): the form 'CB7': **www.cafcass.gov.uk/media/168195/ cb7-eng.pdf**;

(3) For Cafcass (England): **www.cafcass.gov.uk**;

(4) For CAFCASS Cymru (Wales): **www.wales.gov.uk/cafcasscymru**;

(5) To find a legal adviser or family mediator: **http://find-legaladvice.justice.gov.uk**;

(6) To check whether you can get financial help (legal aid) to pay for non-court dispute resolution, and/or advice and representation at court, and to find a legal aid solicitor or mediator: **www.gov.uk/check-legal-aid**;

(7)   For general advice about sorting out arrangements for children, the use of post-separation mediation, and/or going to court: **www.advicenow.org.uk**; **www.advicenow.org.uk/advicenow-guides/family/sortingout-arrangements-for-your-children**;

(8)   For general advice on separation services and options for resolving disputes: **www.sortingoutseparation.org.uk**;

(9)   For general advice about sorting out arrangements for children: **http://theparentconnection.org.uk**;

(10)   For advice about Contact Centres, which are neutral places where children of separated families can enjoy contact with their non-resident parents and sometimes other family members, in a comfortable and safe environment; and information about where they are: **www.naccc.org.uk**;

(11)   For the form to apply for a child arrangements order: **www.gov.uk/looking-after-children-divorce/apply-forcourt-order**;

(12)   For help with taking a case to court without a lawyer, the Personal Support Unit: **http://thepsu.org**;

(13)   For guidance on representing yourself at court, including a list of commonly used terms that you may come across: **www.barcouncil.org.uk/instructing-abarrister/representing-yourself-in-court**;

(14)   For advice about finding and using a family law solicitor see: Law Society **www.lawsociety.org.uk**, and Resolution (family law solicitors): **www.resolution.org.uk**;

(15)   For advice about finding using a family law barrister: see **www.barcouncil.org.uk/about-the-bar/find-a-barrister**, and for arrangements for using a barrister directly see **www.barcouncil.org.uk/instructing-a-barrister/publicaccess**.

2.4   Parenting Plan: A Parenting Plan is widely recognised as being a useful tool for separated parents to identify, agree and set out in writing arrangements for their children; such a plan could appropriately be used as the basis for discussion about a dispute which has arisen. It is likely to be useful in any event for assisting arrangements between separated parents.

2.5   The Parenting Plan should cover all practical aspects of care for the child, and should reflect a shared commitment to the child and his/her future, with particular emphasis on parental communication (learning how to deal with differences), living arrangements, money, religion, education, health care and emotional well-being.

2.6   A Parenting Plan is designed to help separated parents (and their families) to work out the best possible arrangements for the child; the plan should be understood by everyone, including (where the child is of an appropriate age and understanding) the child concerned.

2.7   For help on preparing a Parenting Plan, see:

(1)   Cafcass 'Putting Your Children First: A Guide for Separated Parents' (see also paragraph 4 below);

(2)   A draft of a Parenting Plan for parents or families to complete: **www.cafcass.gov.uk/media/190788/parenting_plan_final_web.pdf**.

2.8   Publicly funded mediation and/or legal advice: If parents need access to mediation, and legal advice in support of that mediation, they may be eligible for public funding. The Legal Aid Agency (LAA) will provide funding for Mediation Information and Assessment Meetings (MIAMs) and family mediation for all those who are eligible:

(1)   Where at least one party is eligible, the LAA will cover the costs of both parties to attend a MIAM to encourage any non-eligible client to find out about the benefits and suitability of mediation without incurring any costs.

(2)   The LAA will provide public funding for eligible parties to participate in family mediation and they may also receive some independent legal advice connected to the mediation process and where a settlement is reached can receive legal assistance to draft and issue proceedings to obtain a consent order.

(3)   Parties may find out if they are likely to be eligible for legal aid at the following link: **www.gov.uk/check-legal-aid**.

(4)   To find the nearest publicly funded mediation service a client can use the search at **familymediationcouncil.org.uk**. Publicly funded legal advisors can be found at: **www.gov.uk/check-legal-aid**.

2.9   Public funding for legal advice and/or representation at court is available in limited circumstances. Further information can be found here: **www.justice.gov.uk/legal-aid-for-private-family-matters**.

3   EXPLANATION OF TERMS

3.1   Some of the terms used in this document, and in the websites referred to above, may not be familiar to those who seek help and support.

3.2   A guide to some of the relevant terms is attached in the Annex at the end of this document.

4   THE CHILD IN THE DISPUTE

4.1   In making any arrangements with respect to a child, the child's welfare must be the highest priority.

4.2   Children and young people should be at the centre of all decision-making. This accords with the Family Justice Young People's Board Charter (**www.cafcass.gov.uk/media/179714/fjypb_national_charter_1013.pdf**).

4.3   The child or young person should feel that their needs, wishes and feelings have been considered in the arrangements which are made for them.

4.4   Children should be involved, to the extent which is appropriate given their age and level of understanding, in making the arrangements which affect them. This is just as relevant where:

(1)   the parties are making arrangements between themselves (which may be recorded in a Parenting Plan),

        as when:
(2)   arrangements are made in the context of dispute resolution outside away from the court,

        and/or
(3)   the court is required to make a decision about the arrangements for the child.

4.5   If an application for a court order has been issued, the judge may want to know the child's view. This may be communicated to the judge in one of a number of ways:

(1)   By a Cafcass officer (in Wales, a Welsh Family Proceedings Officer (WFPO)) providing a report to the court which sets out the child's wishes and feelings;
(2)   By the child being encouraged (by the Cafcass officer or WFPO, or a parent or relative) to write a letter to the court;

(3)   In the limited circumstances described in paragraph 18 below, by the child being a party to the proceedings;

and/or:

(4)   By the judge meeting with the child, in accordance with approved Guidance (currently the FJC Guidelines for Judges Meeting Children subject to Family Proceedings (April 2010)). See **www.judiciary.gov.uk/wp-content/uploads/JCO/Documents/FJC/voc/Guidelines_+Judges_seeing_+Children.pdf**.

5   NON-COURT RESOLUTION OF DISPUTED ARRANGEMENTS FOR CHILDREN

5.1   Dispute resolution services, including mediation, are available to provide opportunities for parents and families to work in a positive and constructive way, and should be actively considered and attempted where it is safe and appropriate to do so. Information about mediation and other non-court dispute resolution is available widely (see 'Signposting Services for Families' – paragraph 2 above).

5.2   It is not expected that those who are the victims of domestic violence should attempt to mediate or otherwise participate in forms of non-court dispute resolution. It is also recognised that drug and/or alcohol misuse and/or mental illness are likely to prevent couples from making safe use of mediation or similar services; these risk factors (which can be discussed at a MIAM – see below, paragraph 5.3) are likely to have an impact on arrangements for the child. Court Orders, including those made by consent, must be scrutinised to ensure that they are safe and take account of any risk factors, in accordance with Practice Direction 12J FPR.

5.3   **Attendance at Mediation Information and Assessment Meeting (MIAM)**: Subject to paragraph 5.6 (below), before making a family application to the court (a 'relevant family application' as defined in paragraph 23 below), the person who is considering making such application must attend a family MIAM. A prospective respondent is expected to attend a MIAM – whether this is a separate MIAM or the same MIAM attended by the prospective applicant. At the MIAM, information will be provided about mediation of disputes of the kind to which the application relates, ways in which the dispute may be resolved otherwise than by the court, and the suitability of mediation (or any other way of resolving the dispute) for trying to resolve the dispute. The mediator will also assess whether there has been, or is a risk of,

(1)   domestic violence, and/or

(2)   harm by a prospective party to a child that would be the subject of the application.

5.4   It is the responsibility of the prospective applicant (or that person's legal representative) to contact a family mediator to arrange attendance at a MIAM.

5.5   Only an authorised family mediator can carry out a MIAM. An authorised family mediator means a mediator who is a member of a mediation organisation affiliated to the Family Mediation Council (and is therefore subject to the Family Mediation Council's Code of Conduct), and is authorised to undertake MIAMs by the professional practice consultant supervising the mediator's practice.

5.6   A prospective applicant is not required to attend a MIAM where one of the circumstances set out in rule 3.8(1) or 3.8(2) FPR applies.

5.7 Information on how to find a family mediator may be obtained from **www.familymediationcouncil.org.uk** website which hosts the 'find a local family mediator' database (see also 'Signposting Services for Families' – paragraph 2 above).

5.8 The prospective applicant (or the prospective applicant's legal representative) should provide the mediator with contact details for the other party or parties to the dispute ('the prospective respondent(s)'), so that the mediator can contact the prospective respondent(s) to discuss their willingness and availability to attend a MIAM.

5.9 The prospective applicant and, where they agree to do so, the prospective respondent(s), should then attend a MIAM arranged by the mediator. If the parties are willing to attend together and where it is assessed by the mediator to be safe, the meeting may be conducted jointly; otherwise, separate meetings will be held.

5.10 The Family Mediation Council sets the requirements for mediators who conduct MIAMs. In summary, a mediator who arranges a MIAM with one or more parties to a dispute should consider any risk factors present and how these should be managed, and should also consider with the party or parties concerned whether public funding may be available to meet the cost of the meeting and any subsequent mediation. Where neither of the parties is eligible for, or wishes to seek, public funding, any charge made by the mediator for the MIAM will be the responsibility of the party or parties attending, in accordance with any agreement made with the mediator.

5.11 Mediation is a confidential process; none of the parties to the mediation may provide information to the court as to the content of any discussions held in mediation and/or the reasons why agreement was not reached. Similarly, the mediator may not provide such information, unless the mediator considers that a safeguarding issue arises.

5.12 However, it is important that the parties, or either of them, introduce at the MIAM (or any subsequent court application) any other evidence of attempts to resolve a dispute and to focus on the needs of the child.

6 RESOLUTION OF DISPUTED ARRANGEMENTS FOR CHILDREN THROUGH THE COURT

6.1 The judge is obliged to consider, at every stage of court proceedings, whether non-court dispute resolution is appropriate.

6.2 The parties should also actively consider non-court dispute resolution even if proceedings are issued and are ongoing.

6.3 If the court considers that another form of dispute resolution is appropriate, the court may direct that the proceedings, or a hearing in the proceedings, be adjourned for such specified period as it considers appropriate:

(1)   to enable the parties to obtain information and advice about non-court dispute resolution; and

(2)   where the parties agree, to enable non-court dispute resolution to take place.

6.4 Where the court adjourns proceedings, it shall give directions about the timing and method by which the parties must tell the court if any of the issues in the proceedings have been resolved.

6.5 It is to be noted that some courts operate an at-court mediation scheme, and at-court MIAMs, with providers contracted to the Legal Aid Agency. Some mediators may prefer to conduct mediation outside of the court premises. A mediation assessment may be possible at court; alternatively, the court may help in making an appointment with a local mediator for a MIAM or for mediation. Information about mediation arrangements should be advertised in the local court.

7 LOCAL GOOD PRACTICE

7.1 The CAP is designed to provide a framework for a consistent approach to the resolution of the issues in private family law in England & Wales.

7.2 Local practices and initiatives can be operated in addition to, and within, the framework

8 APPLICATION TO COURT

8.1 Unless one of the MIAM exemptions applies (see rule 3.8 FPR), an application to court for determination of most issues concerning a child (see the definition of 'relevant family application' in rule 3.6 FPR and paragraphs 11 and 12 of PD3A) can be made only after a MIAM has taken place (at which meeting mediation and other forms of non-court dispute resolution will have been considered). One of the exemptions may be that the case is urgent, in which case see 'Urgent and Without Notice Applications' in paragraph 12 below. The grounds for urgency are defined in rule 3.8(c) FPR.

8.2 The application for a child arrangements order or other Children Act 1989 private law order shall be made on the relevant prescribed form.

8.3 For section 8 Children Act 1989 applications, the applicant will be required, on the form C100, to confirm attendance at a MIAM or specify that an exemption applies *unless* the application is for a consent order, or if the application concerns a child who is the subject of ongoing emergency proceedings, care proceedings or supervision proceedings, or if the child concerned is already the subject of an emergency protection order, care order or supervision order (see paragraphs 11 and 12 of PD3A).

8.4 The relevant part of the form C100 must be completed showing that either:

(1) the applicant has attended a MIAM; or
(2) the applicant has not attended a MIAM and claims one of the exemptions (rule 3.8(1) FPR) – exemptions include (but are not limited to) evidence of domestic violence, child protection concerns, urgency, previous MIAM attendance or exemption; or
(3) an authorised family mediator confirms in the form that he or she is satisfied that

  (a) mediation is not suitable because the respondents is (if more than one respondent, any one of them is) unwilling to attend a MIAM;
  (b) mediation is not suitable as a means of resolving the dispute because the respondent (if more than one, any of them) failed without good reason to attend a MIAM; or
  (c) mediation is otherwise not suitable as a means of resolving the dispute.

8.5 The C100 form may be obtained from the Family Court or from **www.gov.uk**.

8.6   If the parties have previously prepared a Parenting Plan, this shall be attached to the Form C100.

8.7   If possible at the time of issue, and in any event by no later than one working day after issue, or in courts where applications are first considered on paper by no later than two working days after issue, the court shall send or hand to the Applicant the following:

(i)   A copy of the application form C100 (together with the Supplemental Information Form C1A),
(ii)   The Notice of Hearing;
(iii)   The Acknowledgment Form C7;
(iv)   A blank Form C1A, (if required);
(v)   Information leaflets for the parties (which must include the CB7 leaflet)

8.8   Unless the applicant requests to do so, or the court directs the applicant to do so, the Court will serve the respondent(s) with:

(i)   A copy of the application form C100 (together with Supplemental Information Form C1A) (if provided);
(ii)   The Notice of Hearing;
(iii)   The Acknowledgement Form C7;
(iv)   A blank form C1A;
(v)   Information leaflet for the parties (which must include the CB7 leaflet).

8.9   The court shall send to Cafcass / CAFCASS Cymru a copy of the Form C100 (and the form C1A, if supplied), and the C6 Notice of Hearing no later than 2 working days after the date of issue. This will be in electronic format where possible.

8.10   The court shall not send to Cafcass / CAFCASS Cymru any other application under the Children Act 1989, or any other private law application, unless the Court has made a specific direction requesting the assistance of Cafcass/CAFCASS Cymru. Therefore, any application which is not in Form C100 or which does not contain a direction to Cafcass/CAFCASS Cymru will be returned to the court at which the application has been issued.

9   ALLOCATION AND GATEKEEPING

9.1   It is important that the form C100 is fully completed (including the provision of telephone numbers of the relevant parties), otherwise there may be a delay in processing the application; where the form is not fully completed, the court staff may request further information before the application form is accepted for issue.

9.2   The application shall be considered by a nominated Legal Adviser &/or nominated District Judge ('the Gatekeeper(s)') within one working day of the date of receipt in accordance with the appropriate Rules of Procedure.

9.3   An application for a relevant family order shall be allocated to a level of judge in the Family Court in accordance with the Guidance issued by the President on 'Allocation and Gatekeeping for Proceedings under Part II of the Children Act 1989 (Private Law Proceedings)' and the 'Family Court (Composition and Distribution of Business) Rules 2014', together with the Allocation Schedule.

9.4   Gatekeepers shall be able to issue Directions on Issue (on Form CAP01) in the following circumstances:

(1)   where, on the basis of information provided on the application form and any additional information provided on a C1A Supplemental Information Form, the Gatekeeper finds that the exemption from attending a MIAM has not been validly been claimed, the Gatekeeper will direct the applicant, or direct the parties to attend a MIAM before the FHDRA, unless the Gatekeeper considers that in all the circumstances of the case the MIAM requirement should not apply to the application in question; the Gatekeeper will have particular regard to the matters set out in rule 3.10(3) FPR when making this decision;

(2)   where it appears that an urgent issue requires determination, the Gatekeeper may give directions for an accelerated hearing;

(3)   exceptionally, where it appears that directions need to be given for the service and filing of evidence, he/she may give directions for the filing of evidence.

10   JUDICIAL CONTINUITY

10.1   All private law cases will be allocated to a level of judge within the Family Court upon issue.

10.2   Continuity of Judicial involvement in the conduct of proceedings from the FHDRA to the making of a final order should be the objective in all cases.

10.3   Where the case has been allocated to be heard before lay justices, the expectation of judicial continuity should apply where

(1)   There has been a hearing to determine findings of fact,

(2)   A decision yet to be made in the interests of a child by a court depends upon rulings or judicial assessments already made in the proceedings, in which case, wherever possible, the hearing shall be listed before the same lay justices; alternatively, it shall be listed before the same the legal adviser and at least one lay justice (preferably the chairman) to provide that continuity. Where a case is adjourned part-heard the court which resumes the hearing shall, wherever possible, be composed of the same lay justices as dealt with the previous part of the hearing (see rule 8 of the Family Court (Composition and Distribution of Business) Rules 2014).

11   KEY WELFARE PRINCIPLES

11.1   Section 1 of the Children Act 1989 applies to all applications for orders concerning the upbringing of children. This means that:

(1)   the child's welfare is the court's paramount consideration;

(2)   delay is likely to be prejudicial to the welfare of the child, and

(3)   a court order shall not be made unless the court considers that making an order would be better for the child than making no order at all.

11.2   Parties, and the court, must also have regard to the FPR in particular the following:

(1)   FPR Rule 1. The 'overriding objective' will apply, so that the court will deal with a case justly, having regard to the welfare issues involved and specifically will

    (a)   Ensure that the case is dealt with expeditiously and fairly;

    (b)   Deal with the case in ways which are proportionate to the nature, importance and complexity of the issues;

    (c)   Ensure that the parties are on an equal footing;

(d)   Save expense;

(e)   Allot to each case an appropriate share of the court's resources, while taking account of the need to allot resources to other cases.

(2)   Rule 3, and Practice Direction 3A;

(3)   FPR Part 4 'General Case Management Powers';

(4)   FPR Part 15 (Representation of Protected Parties) and Practice Direction 15B (Adults Who May Be Protected Parties and Children Who May Become Protected Parties in Family Proceedings);

(5)   FPR Part 16 (Representation of Children) (and see also paragraph 18 below);

(6)   FPR Part 18 (procedure for Other Applications in proceedings);

(7)   FPR Part 22 (Evidence);

(8)   FPR Part 24 (Witnesses, depositions generally and taking of evidence in Member States of the European Union);

(9)   FPR Part 25 (Experts) and the Experts Practice Directions;

(10)   FPR 27.6 and Practice Direction 27A (Court Bundles).

11.3   Where a fact-finding hearing is required, this shall take place in accordance with revised Practice Direction 12J FPR.

11.4   The court shall exercise its powers flexibly. The flexible powers of the court include the ability for the court to cancel or repeat a particular hearing.

12   URGENT AND WITHOUT NOTICE APPLICATIONS

12.1   **Urgent**: Where an order is sought as a matter of urgency, an application may be made to the Court for an emergency order without the requirement for the Applicant to have attended at a MIAM. The categories of urgent application justifying such an exemption are set out in rule 3.8(c) FPR and include cases in which:

(1)   There is a risk to the life, liberty, or the physical safety of the prospective applicant or his or her family, or his or her home;

(2)   Any delay caused by attending a MIAM would cause:

    (i)   A risk of harm to the child;

    (ii)   A risk of unlawful removal of a child from the United Kingdom or a risk of unlawful retention of a child who is currently outside England and Wales;

    (iii)   A significant risk of a miscarriage of justice;

    (iv)   Unreasonable hardship to the prospective applicant;

    (v)   Irretrievable problems in dealing with the dispute (including the irretrievable loss of significant evidence).

(3)   There is a significant risk that in the period necessary to schedule and attend a MIAM, proceedings relating to the dispute will be brought in another state in which a valid claim to jurisdiction may exist, such that a court in that other State would be seised of the dispute before a court in England and Wales.

12.2   **'Without Notice'**: Applications to court made 'Without Notice' to the respondent(s) shall be allocated in accordance with the Family Court (Composition and Distribution of Business) Rules 2014, and determined by reference to the provisions of Practice Direction 18A, paragraph 5.1, with further regard to the principles set out in Practice Direction 20A, paragraph 4.3-4.5 FPR (noting particularly paragraph 4.3(c)).

12.3   Without Notice Orders should be made only exceptionally, and where:

(1)   If the applicant were to give notice to the respondent(s) this would enable the respondent(s) to take steps to defeat the purpose of the injunction; cases where the application is brought without notice in order to conceal the step from the respondent(s) are very rare indeed; or

(2)   The case is one of exceptional urgency; that is to say, that there has been literally no time to give notice (either by telephone, text or e-mail or otherwise) before the injunction is required to prevent the threatened wrongful act; or

(3)   If the applicant gives notice to the respondent(s), this would be likely to expose the applicant or relevant child to unnecessary risk of physical or emotional harm.

12.4   Any Order which follows an emergency 'without notice' hearing should specify:

(1)   the reason(s) why the order has been made without notice to the respondent(s),

(2)   the outline facts alleged which have been relied upon by the court in making the order, unless the facts are clearly contained in the statement in support; and

(3)   the right of the respondent(s) to apply to vary or discharge the order.

12.5   Gatekeeping decisions: Following any urgent or 'without notice' hearing, unless all issues have been determined or the application has been dismissed without any further directions given, the judge may make gatekeeping decisions, including allocation and venue of future hearing, (and if so, shall notify the Gatekeeping team responsible for the area in which the child resides), or shall refer the application to the relevant Gatekeeping team for a decision on allocation and venue of future hearing; in either event, a copy of the C100 shall be sent to Cafcass for safeguarding checks, and (depending on the Gatekeeping decision) the file shall be sent to the court where future hearings will take place (if at a different court centre from the court where the urgent hearing occurred).

13   SAFEGUARDING

13.1   Where an application is made for a child arrangements order (but not necessarily for specific issue or prohibited steps orders), before the FHDRA (see paragraph 14 below) Cafcass / CAFCASS Cymru shall identify any safety issues by the steps outlined below.

13.2   Such steps shall be confined to matters of safety. The Cafcass Officer or (in Wales) the Welsh Family Proceedings Officer (WFPO) shall not discuss with either party before the FHDRA any matter other than one which relates to safety. The parties will not be invited to talk about other issues, for example relating to the substance of applications or replies or about issues concerning matters of welfare or the prospects of resolution. If such issues are raised by either party, they will be advised that such matters will be deferred to the FHDRA when there is equality between the parties and full discussion can take place which will be a time when any safety issues that have been identified can also be taken into account.

13.3   In order to inform the court of possible risks of harm to the child Cafcass / CAFCASS Cymru will carry out safeguarding enquiries. For all child arrangements orders this will include seeking information from local authorities, and carrying out police checks on the parties. For all other applications received from the court on the form C100, Cafcass / CAFCASS Cymru will carry out a screening process and will undertake those checks if in the professional judgment of the Cafcass officer, or the WFPO in Wales, such checks are necessary.

13.4   Cafcass / CAFCASS Cymru will, if possible, undertake telephone risk identification interviews with the parties and if risks of harm are identified, may invite parties to meet separately with the Cafcass Officer, or WFPO in Wales, before the FHDRA to clarify any safety issue.

13.5   Cafcass / CAFCASS Cymru shall record and outline any safety issues for the court, in the form of a Safeguarding letter (in Wales, this is called a 'Safeguarding report').

13.6   The Cafcass officer, or WFPO, will not initiate contact with the child prior to the FHDRA. If contacted by a child, discussions relating to the issues in the case will be postponed to the day of the hearing or after when the Cafcass officer or WFPO will have more knowledge of the issues.

13.7   Within 17 working days of receipt by Cafcass / CAFCASS Cymru of the application, and at least 3 working days before the hearing, the Cafcass Officer or WFPO shall report to the court, in a Safeguarding letter / report, the outcome of the risk identification work which has been undertaken.

13.8   Further, Cafcass and CAFCASS Cymru are required, under section 16A Children Act 1989, to undertake (and to provide to the court) risk assessments where an officer of the Service ('Cafcass Officer' or WFPO) suspects that a child is at risk of harm.

14   FIRST HEARING DISPUTE RESOLUTION APPOINTMENT (FHDRA)

14.1   The FHDRA may (where time for service on the respondent(s) has been abridged) take place within 4 weeks, but should ordinarily take place in week 5 following the issuing of the application; at the latest it will take place in week 6 following the issuing of the application.

14.2   The respondent(s) shall have at least 10 working days' notice of the hearing where practicable, but the court may abridge this time.

14.3   The respondent(s) should file a response on the Forms C7/C1A no later than 10 working days before the hearing, unless the court has abridged this time.

14.4   Unless the court otherwise directs, any party to proceedings, and any litigation friend of the parties must attend this (and any other) hearing. If a child is a party and represented by a children's guardian, the children's guardian need not attend directions hearings if represented.

14.5   A party may choose to be accompanied at this (or any) hearing by a McKenzie Friend to support them (a McKenzie Friend is someone who can provide moral support at court for the party; take notes; help with case papers; quietly give advice on any aspect of the conduct of the case.) If so, the McKenzie Friend must comply with the relevant Guidance (currently set out in the Practice Guidance: McKenzie Friends (Civil and Family Courts): July 2010: **www.judiciary.gov.uk/Resources/JCO/Documents/Guidance/ mckenzie-friends-practice-guidance-july-2010.pdf**).

14.6   A Cafcass Officer or WFPO shall attend this hearing. A mediator may attend where available.

14.7   The Cafcass Officer or WFPO shall, where practicable, speak separately to each party at court before the hearing in particular where it has not been possible to conduct a risk identification interview with either party.

14.8   The FHDRA provides an opportunity for the parties to be helped to an understanding of the issues which divide them, and to reach agreement. If agreement is reached,

(1)   The Court will be able to make an order (which in many cases will be a final order) reflecting that agreement;

(2)   The Court will assist the parties (so far as it is able) in putting into effect the agreement/order in a co-operative way.

14.9   The FHDRA is not privileged. That is to say that what is said at the FHDRA may be referred to at later court hearings.

14.10   By the time of the hearing, the Court should have the following documents:

(a)   C100 application, and C1A (if any);
(b)   Notice of Hearing;
(c)   C7 response and C1A (if any);
(d)   Cafcass/CAFCASS Cymru safeguarding letter/report.

14.11   At the FHDRA the judge, working with the Cafcass Officer, or WFPO, will seek to assist the parties in conciliation and in resolution of all or any of the issues between them. Any remaining issues will be identified, the Cafcass Officer or WFPO will advise the court of any recommended means of resolving such issues, and directions will be given for the future resolution of such issues. At all times the decisions of the Court and the work of the Cafcass Officer or WFPO will take account of any risk or safeguarding issues that have been identified.

14.12   The court should have information obtained through safeguarding checks carried out by Cafcass / CAFCASS Cymru, to ensure that any agreement between the parties, or any dispute resolution process selected, is in the interests of the child and safe for all concerned.

14.13   The FHDRA will be conducted in the most appropriate way in the interests of the child. In particular the court shall consider the following matters:

● **Safeguarding**, in this respect:

   (a)   The court shall inform the parties of the content of the safeguarding letter/report provided by Cafcass/CAFCASS Cymru, where it has not already been sent by Cafcass/CAFCASS Cymru to the parties, unless it considers that to do so would create a risk of harm to a party or the child. The court may need to consider whether, and if so how, any information contained in the checks should be disclosed to the parties if Cafcass/CAFCASS Cymru have not disclosed the letter/report.

   The court will further consider:
   (b)   Whether a fact finding hearing is needed to determine allegations which are not accepted, and whose resolution is likely to affect the decision of the court.
   (c)   Risk identification followed by active case management including risk assessment, and compliance with the Practice Direction 12J.

   Further:
   (d)   If the safeguarding information is (contrary to the arrangements set out in the CAP) not available at the FHDRA, the court should adjourn the application until the safeguarding checks are available. Interim orders (unless to protect the safety of a child) should not be made in the absence of safeguarding checks.

   And further:
   (e)   Where the court so directs, a safeguarding letter/report ought to be attached to any referral to a supported or supervised child contact centre in the event the court directs supported or supervised contact.

● **MIAM**, specifically:

(a) Whether, if a MIAM exemption has been claimed, the Applicant has validly claimed the exemption;

(b) Whether the Respondent has attended a MIAM;

(c) If the court finds that a MIAM exemption has not been validly claimed the court will direct the applicant or direct the parties to attend a MIAM and if necessary adjourn the proceedings to enable a MIAM to take place, unless the court considers that in all the circumstances of the case, the MIAM requirement should not apply to the application in question; when making the decision the court will have particular regard to the matters contained in rule 3.10(3) FPR.

- **Mediation, At-Court Mediation assessment, and other Dispute Resolution**: allowing the parties the time and opportunity to engage in non-court dispute resolution.

(a) At the FHDRA, the judge will specifically consider whether, and the extent to which, the parties can safely resolve some or all of the issues with the assistance of the Cafcass Officer, WFPO, or a mediator.

(b) There will be, at every FHDRA, a period in which the Cafcass Officer, or WFPO, will seek to conciliate and explore with the parties the resolution of all or some of the issues between them if safe to do so. The procedure to be followed in this connection at the hearing will be determined by local arrangements between the Cafcass manager, or equivalent in Wales, and the Designated Family Judge or the Justices' Clerk where appropriate

The court will further consider:

(c) What is the result of any such meeting at Court?

(d) What other options there are for resolution e.g. may the case be suitable for further intervention by Cafcass/CAFCASS Cymru; Should a referral for mediation be made? Is collaborative law appropriate? Should the parties be advised to complete a Parenting Plan?

(e) Would the parties be assisted by attendance at an Activity Separated Parents Information Programme, (or in Wales, Working Together For Children (WT4C)) or other Activity or intervention, whether by formal statutory provision under section 11 Children Act 1989 or otherwise;

(f) An at-court assessment of the suitability of the parties for mediation.

- **Consent Orders**:

(a) Where agreement is reached at any hearing or submitted in writing to the court, no order will be made without scrutiny by the court.

(b) Where safeguarding checks or risk assessment work remain outstanding, the making of a final order may be deferred for such work. In such circumstances the court shall adjourn the case for no longer than 28 days to a fixed date. A written notification of this work is to be provided by Cafcass/CAFCASS Cymru in the form of an updating Safeguarding letter/report, or if deemed relevant by Cafcass/CAFCASS Cymru, a section 16A risk assessment in accordance with the timescale specified by the court. If satisfactory information is then available, the order may be made at the adjourned hearing in the agreed terms without the need for attendance by the parties. If satisfactory information is not available, the order will not be made, and the case will be adjourned for further consideration with an opportunity for the parties to make further representations

- **Reports**:

(a) Reports may be ordered where there are welfare issues or other specific considerations which should be addressed in a report by Cafcass/CAFCASS Cymru or the Local Authority. Before a report is ordered, the court should consider alternative ways of working with the parties such as are referred to in paragraph 5 ('non-court resolution of disputed arrangements') above.

(b)   If a report is ordered in accordance with section 7 of the Children Act 1989, the Court should direct which specific matters relating to the welfare of the child are to be addressed. Welfare reports will generally only be ordered in cases where there is a dispute as to with whom the child should live, spend time, or otherwise have contact with. A report can also be ordered :

   (i)   If there is an issue concerning the child's wishes, and/or
   (ii)   If there is an alleged risk to the child, and/or
   (iii)   Where information and advice is needed which the court considers to be necessary before a decision can be reached in the case.

(c)   General requests for a report on an application should be avoided; the Court should state on the face of the Order the specific factual and/or other issue which is to be addressed in the focused report.

(d)   In determining whether a request for a report should be directed to the relevant local authority or to Cafcass/CAFCASS Cymru, the court should consider such information as Cafcass/CAFCASS Cymru has provided about the extent and nature of the local authority's current or recent involvement with the subject of the application and the parties, and any relevant protocol between Cafcass and the Association of Directors of Children's Services.

(e)   The court may further consider whether there is a need for an investigation under section 37 Children Act 1989.

(f)   A copy of the Order requesting the report and any relevant court documents are to be sent to Cafcass/CAFCASS Cymru or, in the case of the Local Authority to the Legal Adviser to the Director of the Local Authority Children's Services and, where known, to the allocated social worker by the court forthwith.

(g)   Is any expert evidence required? If so, section 13 Children and Families Act 2014, and Part 25 of the FPR must be complied with. This is the latest point at which consideration should be given to the instruction of an expert in accordance with Rule 25.6(b) of the FPR; the court will need to consider carefully the future conduct of proceedings where the preparation of an expert report is necessary but where the parties are unrepresented and are unable to fund the preparation of such a report.

- **Wishes and feelings of the child**:

(a)   In line with the Family Justice Young People's Board Charter, children and young people should be at the centre of all proceedings.

(b)   The child or young person should feel that their needs, wishes and feelings have been considered in the court process

(c)   Each decision should be assessed on its impact on the child.

(d)   The court must consider the wishes and feelings of the child, ascertainable so far as is possible in light of the child's age and understanding and circumstances. Specifically, the Court should ask:

   (i)   Is the child aware of the proceedings?
   (ii)   Are the wishes and feelings of the child available, and/or to be ascertained (if at all)?
   (iii)   How is the child to be involved in the proceedings, and if so, how; for example, should they meet the judge/lay justices? Should they be encouraged to write to the court, or have their views reported by Cafcass/ CAFCASS Cymru or by a local authority?
   (iv)   Who will inform the child of the outcome of the case, where appropriate?

- **Case Management**:

  (a) What, if any, issues are agreed and what are the key issues to be determined?

  (b) Should the matter be listed for a fact-finding hearing?

  (c) Are there any interim orders which can usefully be made (e.g. indirect, supported or supervised contact) pending Dispute Resolution Appointment or final hearing?

  (d) What directions are required to ensure the application is ready for a Dispute Resolution Appointment or final hearing – statements, reports etc?

  (e) Should the application be listed for a Dispute Resolution Appointment (it is envisaged that most cases will be so listed)?

  (f) Should the application be listed straightaway for a final hearing?

  (g) Judicial continuity should be actively considered (especially if there has been or is to be a fact finding hearing or a contested interim hearing).

- **Allocation**:

  (a) The Allocation decision will be considered by the Court;

  (b) If it is necessary to transfer the case to another court within the DFJ area or another area, or re-allocate it, the court shall state the reasons for transfer/re-allocation, and shall specifically make directions for the next hearing in the court.

- **Order (other than a final order)**: Where no final agreement is reached, and the court is required to give case management directions, the following shall be included on the order [CAP02]:

  (a) The issues about which the parties are agreed;

  (b) The issues that remain to be resolved;

  (c) The steps that are planned to resolve the issues;

  (d) Any interim arrangements pending such resolution, including arrangements for the involvement of children;

  (e) The timetable for such steps and, where this involves further hearings, the date of such hearings;

  (f) A statement as to any facts relating to risk or safety; in so far as they are resolved the result will be stated and, in so far as not resolved, the steps to be taken to resolve them will be stated.

  (g) Whether the parties are to be assisted by participation in mediation, Separated Parents Information Programme, WT4C, or other types of parenting intervention, and to detail any activity directions or conditions imposed by the court;

  (h) The date, time and venue of the next hearing;

  (i) Whether the author of any section 7 report is required to attend the hearing, in order to give oral evidence. A direction for the Cafcass officer or WFPO to attend court will not be made without first considering the reason why attendance is necessary, and upon what issues the Cafcass officer or WFPO will be providing evidence.

  (j) Where both parties are Litigants in Person, the court may direct HMCTS to produce a Litigant in Person bundle;

  (k) The judge will, as far as possible, provide a copy of the order to both parties before they leave the courtroom, and will, if necessary, go through and explain the contents of the order to ensure they are clearly understood by both parties. The parties should know the date, time and venue of any further hearing before they leave the court.

15 TIMETABLE FOR THE CHILD

15.1   Court proceedings should be timetabled so that the dispute can be resolved as soon as safe and possible in the interests of the child.

15.2   The judge shall, at all times during the proceedings, have regard to the impact which the court timetable will have on the welfare and development of the child to whom the application relates. The judge and the parties shall pay particular attention to the child's age, and important landmarks in the immediate life of the child, including:

(a)   the child's birthday;
(b)   the start of nursery/schooling;
(c)   the start/end of a school term/year;
(d)   any proposed change of school; and/or
(e)   any significant change in the child's family, or social, circumstances.

15.3   While it is acknowledged that an interim order may be appropriate at an early stage of court proceedings, cases should not be adjourned for a review (or reviews) of contact or other orders/arrangements, and/or for addendum section 7 report, unless such a hearing is necessary and for a clear purpose that is consistent with the timetable for the child and in the child's best interests.

15.4   When preparing a section 7 report, Cafcass / CAFCASS Cymru (or, where appropriate, the local authority) is encouraged to make recommendations for the stepped phasing-in of child arrangements (i.e. recommendations for the medium and longer term future for the child) insofar as they are able to do so safely in the interests of the child concerned;

15.5   Where active involvement or monitoring is needed, the court may consider making:

(1)   An order under section 11H Children Act 1989 (Monitoring);
(2)   A Family Assistance Order under section 16 Children Act 1989) (in accordance with the Practice Direction 12M FPR, and if all the named adults in the order agree to the making of such an order and if the order is directed to a local authority, the child lives (or will live) within that local authority area or the local authority consents to the making of the order.

16 CAPACITY OF LITIGANTS

16.1   In the event that the judge has concerns about the capacity of a litigant before the court, the judge shall consider:

(1)   the Guidance issued by the Family Justice Council in relation to assessing the capacity of litigants;
(2)   Practice Direction 15B (Adults Who May Be Protected Parties and Children Who May Become Protected Parties In Family Proceedings).

17 EVIDENCE

17.1   No evidence shall be filed in relation to an application until after the FHDRA unless:

(1)   It has been filed in support of a without notice application
(2)   It has been directed by the Court by the Directions on Issue (CAP01);
(3)   It has been directed by the Court for the purposes of determining an interim application.

18   RULE 16.4 CHILDREN'S GUARDIANS

18.1   The Court should be vigilant to identify the cases where a rule 16.4 children's guardian should be appointed. This should be considered initially at the FHDRA.

18.2   Where the court is considering the appointment of a children's guardian from Cafcass/ CAFCASS Cymru, it should first ensure that enquiries have been made of the appropriate Cafcass/CAFCASS Cymru manager in accordance with paragraph 7.4, Part 4 of the Practice Direction 16A. This should either be in writing before the hearing or by way of case discussion with the relevant Cafcass service manager; for cases in Wales, the 'hotline' protocol agreed with CAFCASS Cymru will ensure that such a discussion can take place. The court should consult with Cafcass / CAFCASS Cymru, so as to consider any advice in connection with the prospective appointment, and the timescale involved.

18.3   When the court decides to appoint a children's guardian, consideration should first be given to appointing an Officer of the Service or WFPO. If Cafcass/CAFCASS Cymru is unable to provide a children's guardian without delay, or if there is some other reason why the appointment of a Cafcass officer is not appropriate, the court should (further to rule 16.24 of the FPR) appoint a person other than the Official Solicitor, unless the Official Solicitor expressly consents.

18.4   In considering whether to make such an appointment the Court shall take account of the demands on the resources of Cafcass/CAFCASS Cymru that such an appointment would make. The court should also make clear on the face of any order the purpose of the appointment and the timetable of any work to be undertaken.

19   DISPUTE RESOLUTION APPOINTMENT (DRA)

19.1   The Court shall list the application for a Dispute Resolution Appointment ('DRA') to follow the preparation of section 7 or other expert report, or Separated Parenting Information Programme (SPIP) (or WT4C in Wales), if this is considered likely to be helpful in the interests of the child.

19.2   The author of the section 7 report will only attend this hearing if directed to do so by the Court.

19.3   At the DRA the Court will:

(1)   Identify the key issue(s) (if any) to be determined and the extent to which those issues can be resolved or narrowed at the DRA;
(2)   Consider whether the DRA can be used as a final hearing;
(3)   Resolve or narrow the issues by hearing evidence;
(4)   Identify the evidence to be heard on the issues which remain to be resolved at the final hearing;
(5)   Give final case management directions including:

  (a)   Filing of further evidence;
  (b)   Filing of a statement of facts/issues remaining to be determined;
  (c)   Filing of a witness template and / or skeleton arguments;
  (d)   Ensuring Compliance with Practice Direction 27A (the Bundles Practice Direction);
  (e)   Listing the Final Hearing.

20   FACT-FINDING HEARING

20.1   If the court considers that a fact-finding hearing is necessary it shall conduct that hearing in accordance with revised Practice Direction 12J

21   ENFORCEMENT OF CHILD ARRANGEMENTS

21.1   On any application for enforcement of a child arrangements order, the court shall:

- consider whether the facts relevant to the alleged non-compliance are agreed, or whether it is necessary to conduct a hearing to establish the facts;
- consider the reasons for any non-compliance;
- consider how the wishes and feelings of the child are to be ascertained;
- consider whether advice is required from Cafcass/CAFCASS Cymru on the appropriate way forward;
- assess and manage any risks of making further or other child arrangements order;
- consider whether a SPIP or referral for dispute resolution is appropriate;
- consider whether an enforcement order may be appropriate, and
- consider the welfare checklist.

21.2   The Gatekeepers shall list any application for enforcement of a child arrangements order for hearing, before the previously allocated judge if possible, within 20 working days of issue. Enforcement cases should be concluded without delay.

21.3   An application made within existing proceedings in the family court shall be allocated to the level of judge in accordance with rule 17 of the Family Court (Composition and Distribution of Business) Rules 2014.

21.4   The Gatekeepers shall, if considered necessary, direct that further safeguarding checks are required from Cafcass/CAFCASS Cymru. On any application for enforcement issued more than three months after the order which is the subject of the enforcement, safeguarding checks shall be ordered.

21.5   The court has a wide range of powers in the event of a breach of a child arrangements order without reasonable excuse.

21.6   This range of powers includes (but is not limited to):

(a)   referral of the parents to a SPIP, or in Wales a WT4C, or mediation;
(b)   variation of the child arrangements order (which could include a more defined order and/or reconsidering the contact provision or the living arrangements of the child);
(c)   a contact enforcement order or suspended enforcement order under section 11J Children Act 1989 ('Enforcement order' for unpaid work), (see paragraph 21.7 below);
(d)   an order for compensation for financial loss (under section 11O Children Act 1989);
(e)   committal to prison or
(f)   a fine.

21.7   In the event that the court is considering an enforcement order for alleged non-compliance with a court order (under section 11J Children Act 1989) or considering a Compensation order in respect of financial loss (under section 11O Children Act 1989), the court shall (in the absence of agreement between the parties about the relevant facts) determine the facts in order to establish the cause of the alleged failure to comply.

21.8   Section 11L Children Act 1989 provides that if the court finds that a breach has occurred without reasonable excuse it may order the non-compliant party to undertake unpaid work if that is necessary to secure compliance, and if the effect on the non-compliant party is proportionate to the seriousness of the breach. The court must also consider whether unpaid work is available in the locality and the likely effect on the non-compliant party. It is good practice to ask Cafcass/CAFCASS Cymru to report on the suitability of this order. Section 11L(7) also requires the court to take into account the welfare of the child who is the subject of the order for contact.

22   COURT TIMETABLE

22.1   Working Day 1: Paperwork received. Court office checks whether the revised form C100 has been completed correctly. The application will not be issued unless the form has been completed correctly.

22.2   Working Day 2: Case considered by Gatekeeping team. Case allocated by Gatekeepers in accordance with the President's Guidance on allocation and the Family Court (Composition and Distribution) Rules 2014. The Gatekeeper(s) undertaking allocation to check whether form C100 has been completed. If there has been no MIAM, and there are reasons to believe that the applicant should have attended a MIAM, the Gatekeeping judge can direct that a MIAM should take place before the FHDRA.

22.3   17 working days from the date of its receipt of the application Cafcass/CAFCASS Cymru will provide the safeguarding letter / report to the Court (20 working days in the area of CAFCASS Cymru).

22.4   Week 5 (or latest, week 6): Case listed for FHDRA (before week 5 if requirements of notice have been abridged).

22.5   Thereafter, case may be listed for fact-finding hearing, DRA &/or final hearing.

23   RELEVANT FAMILY APPLICATION (DEFINITION)

23.1   A relevant family application for the purposes of the CAP is an application that:

(1)   Is made to the court in, or to initiate, family proceedings, and
(2)   Is of a description specified in the Family Procedure Rules.

Flowcharts

Public Law Outline 2014 (26 weeks)

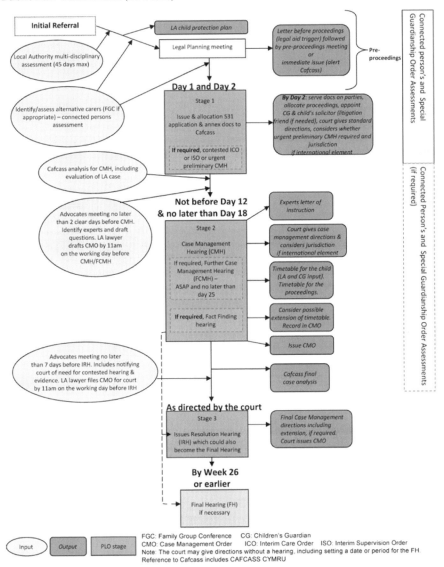

FGC: Family Group Conference   CG: Children's Guardian
CMO: Case Management Order   ICO: Interim Care Order   ISO: Interim Supervision Order
Note: The court may give directions without a hearing, including setting a date or period for the FH.
Reference to Cafcass includes CAFCASS CYMRU

Child Arrangements Programme

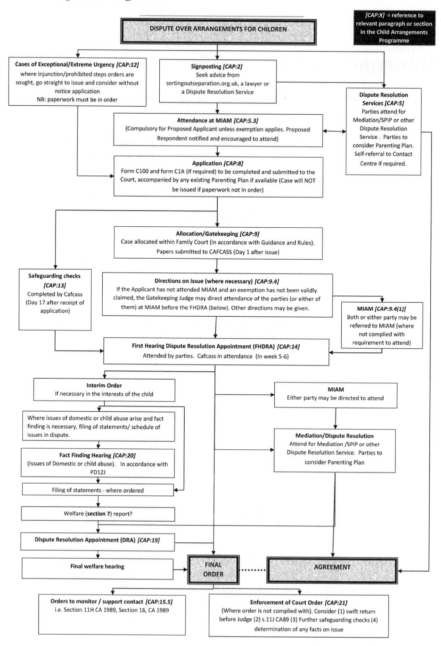

APPENDIX 4

Preparing for Care and Supervision Proceedings

[Care Proceedings Programme, Ministry of Justice, August 2009]

1   INTRODUCTION

1.1   Background to the reforms

Following the Review of the Child Care Proceedings System in England and Wales,[1] reforms to s.31 CA 1989 proceedings were brought into effect in April 2008 by two key documents:

1.   The Practice Direction: Guide to Case Management in Public Law Cases;[2] and
2.   The Children Act 1989 Guidance and Regulations, Volume 1: Court Orders[3] in England, and The Children Act 1989 Guidance and Regulations, Volume 1: Court Orders (Wales)[4] in Wales.

The aim of the reforms can be broadly stated as an intention to make the system for s.31 CA 1989 proceedings more efficient by reducing delay and to improve the outcomes for children and families who may become the subject of court proceedings. The Statutory Guidance focuses on social work undertaken pre-proceedings for two principal reasons. In many cases there will still be an opportunity for the social worker to work with the child and family with a view to avoiding the need for court proceedings. Secondly, work done at these stages can impact on the proceedings (if proceedings are later initiated) and the ability for the proceedings to be conducted as smoothly and expeditiously as possible providing the best possible outcome for the child and his/her family.

1.2   The status of this best practice guide

Ten initiative areas[5] tested elements of the PLO prior to it being finalised. Professionals from those areas were well placed to share information about how their areas were dealing with the

1. Review of the Child Care Proceedings System in England and Wales, Department of Constitutional Affairs, Department for Education and Skills and Welsh Assembly Government (May 2006). Accessible at: **http://www.dca.gov.uk/publications/reports_reviews/childcare_ps.pdf**.
2. The Practice Direction: Guide to Case Management in Public Law Cases, Judiciary of England & Wales and Ministry of Justice (April 2008). Accessible at: **http://www.judiciary.gov.uk/docs/public_law_outline.pdf**.
3. The Children Act 1989 Guidance and Regulations, Volume 1: Court Orders, Department for Children, Schools and Families (April 2008). Accessible at: **http://www.dcsf.gov.uk/localauthorities/_documents/content/childrensactguidance.pdf**.
4. The Children Act 1989 Guidance and Regulations, Volume 1: Court Orders, Welsh Assembly Government and NHS Wales (March 2008). Accessible at: **http://new.wales.gov.uk/dhss/publications/children/guidance/actguidance/courtorderse.pdf?lang=en**.
5. Birmingham, London, Liverpool, Warrington/Chester, Newcastle/Sunderland, Exeter/Plymouth, Leicester, Milton Keynes/Oxford, Swansea, Portsmouth.

reforms 'on the ground'. The Ministry of Justice's Care Proceedings Programme Office[6] held two workshops in July 2008 (Reading and Liverpool). The 'Moving Forward Workshops' brought together professionals from all fields of expertise (HMCS, legal, social work and Cafcass/CAFCASS CYMRU) from the initiative areas. A wealth of information came out of the workshops. We learned about the many examples of good practice, which some areas had already implemented and were working to; many of those ideas have been incorporated into this guide. We also learned of challenges, which some professionals were experiencing. We have sought to bring all that information into this one comprehensive guide to both share the ideas of good practice already operating but also to address and assist with some of the perceived problems.

The guide is not Statutory Guidance: it has no legal status. We have taken careful steps to ensure that various experts in their respective fields reviewed this guide before it was finalised. We hope practitioners may find it a useful additional source of information and explanation but it is no substitute for acting within the statutory framework set out in the Children Act 1989 and the regulations made under Part 3 of the Act and the Statutory Guidance on it.

1.3   Who should read this guide

This guide is written for all professionals who work with or for children and families where s.31 CA 1989 care proceedings are being considered or applied for. In the main those who we hope will find the guide of most use to their work are: LA social workers, LA managers, lawyers for the LA and for parents, Children's Guardians, lawyers for children, HMCS court staff and legal advisers, the judiciary and expert assessors who may be instructed pre-proceedings and within proceedings.

1.4   How to use this guide

This guide is separated into two parts. Chapter 2 covers the pre-proceedings stages up to the point that a s.31 CA 1989 application is issued at court. Chapter 3 looks at the stages from the point that the LA issues a s.31 CA 1989 application through to disposal of the application and conclusion of the proceedings.

Some of the aspects discussed in this guide will be connected or relate to other aspects. We have used cross-referencing where this is the case. The intention of the guide is that it should act as a quick-reference tool to good practice. As the guide has been written to cater for all parties involved in care proceedings readers should gain a better understanding of the roles and responsibilities of other professionals involved . To make the guide as user-friendly as possible the contents identify the paragraphs which are recommended reading for the various professionals involved in s.31 CA 1989 proceedings.

2   PRE-PROCEEDINGS STAGES

2.1   Introduction

In this document the term pre-proceedings is used to indicate the several stages of interaction between the child, family and the LA which occur prior to a court application being issued for a s.31 CA 1989 order. It is straightforward to ascertain the 'end' of pre-proceedings because this will be the date that the application to court is issued. Where the pre-proceedings stages 'begin' however, is less well defined. On the one hand all stages of involvement prior to an application being made could be termed 'pre-proceedings' but for the purposes of the recent reforms the use

---

6. An inter-agency group set up to deliver the recommendations arising from the 2006 Care Review at: **www.justice.gov.uk/guidance/careproceedings.htm**.

of the term pre-proceedings is rather precise. It denotes the stages from the point that the LA is considering making an application to court to protect the child but the risk of harm to the child is manageable if an application is not made immediately. Effectively, the LA's approach will be to further attempt to engage with the parent in order to put an agreement in place which reduces the risk of significant harm to the child to a manageable level at that stage.

The point at which pre-proceedings stages nominally commence in view of the recent reforms is where the legal gateway/planning meeting (section 2.3) has been held and the LA makes the decision to send a Letter before Proceedings (LbP) (section 2.4).

2.2 Social work

Volume 1 of the Children Act Guidance and Regulations is issued under section 7 of the Local Authority Social Services Act 1970. Local Authorities must, in exercising their social services functions, act under this guidance.

The Children Act 1989, the Adoption and Children Act 2002, and the Children Act 2004 combined with Regulations made under those statutes and the Statutory Guidance set out the statutory framework within which social workers should perform functions on behalf of the LA. The Statutory Guidance seeks to provide advice to the LA on relevant matters. In relation to care proceedings the Guidance stipulates the 'matters to be considered by the LA before making an application for a care or supervision order'.[7] The LA has many duties and obligations with which it must comply. The most relevant (at this stage) is the general duty to safeguard and promote the welfare of children in need and 'so far as is consistent with that duty, to promote the upbringing of such children by their families by providing a range and level of services appropriate to those children's needs' (s.17(1) CA 1989).

The original version of Volume 1 was published in 1991. The revised Guidance gives updated advice to LAs on how they should meet their duties. Some key points from the Guidance are:

- That voluntary arrangements for the provision of services should be fully explored together with consideration of potential alternative carers.
- That prior to proceedings, work should be undertaken to explore alternative care solutions for the child, assess the suitability of those arrangements and consider the legal status of those arrangements.

2.3   The Legal Gateway/Planning Meeting

The purpose of a legal gateway or planning meeting is for the LA to seek legal advice about a particular case. These meetings should be attended by the child's social worker and managers together with the lawyer advising the LA. The social work team will usually set out the facts of the case, their concerns and explain what has been done to work with the child and family. The ultimate question will be 'is the threshold criteria met and are court proceedings necessary at this stage?'

In those cases where it is agreed that it will be necessary to initiate Care Proceedings the LA will consider if it is appropriate to write to the parent to inform him or her that an application to court will be made shortly and to explain that he or she should seek legal advice. A template letter can be found at Annex A. There are two important points to note about sending such a letter to the parent:

- This letter is not intended to be a 'LbP' and therefore may not act as the trigger letter for Family Help Lower (level 2) publicly funded advice and assistance (section 2.6.3).

---

7. Statutory Guidance, paras. 3.22-3.33.

However, the parent may still be eligible for means-tested advice under Legal Help (level 1) from a solicitor. Parents should be advised to seek further guidance from a solicitor on this point; and

- It will not be appropriate to send this letter in all cases where immediate issue of proceedings is decided. Whether or not to send the letter requires very careful assessment by the LA. For example, there may be concerns that if a parent knows that the LA is going to apply to court for an order allowing it to remove the child from his or her care, the parent and their children may leave the area.

2.4 The Letter before Proceedings (LbP)

If following a legal gateway/planning meeting it is decided that there is time to work with the family to avoid proceedings, and the short term safety and welfare of the child permits, a LbP should be issued. The LbP allows social workers to structure their work with the child and family and to consider alternative options and services which could be provided to the family. Once the LbP inviting a parent to a Pre-Proceedings Meeting (PPM) is sent out, the LA has an opportunity to work with the family and to explore all options prior to making an application to court. Some LAs have indicated that the use of the LbP has helped to stop the drift in more long-standing cases. We found that many LAs have given lots of time and effort to adjusting the template LbP contained in the Statutory Guidance to their particular areas and we have been informed that generally parents have found the LbP useful as it sets out in one place the LA's concerns.

2.4.1 Ownership

As the LbP is a new stage in the process introduced by the revised Statutory Guidance (SG) we are aware that LAs have varying experiences of its use. The template LbP which is annexed to the SG envisages that the signature carried on the LbP will be that of the social worker's team manager.

The LA should request that their legal department check the contents of this letter to ensure that it includes all information relevant to the grounds for proceedings.

2.4.2 Timing

In deciding the timing about when best to send the LbP, the LA will have first considered and sought legal advice about whether it should make an application to the court (section 2.3). If it makes an 'in principle' decision that it would be appropriate to apply for an order but also concludes that the risk can be managed without an immediate application, the LA is effectively concluding that it can see a window of opportunity to try to continue to work with the family to maintain their children safely with their parents. The LbP should be sent at this point.

Once the LbP is sent the LA should utilise this opportunity to secure a plan or agreement to protect the child safely at home and work towards reducing the risk of significant harm to the child.

Where a local authority judges that there is not a window of opportunity to work with the family to continue to maintain the child at home, given its assessment of the safeguarding concerns in the case, the LA will need to apply immediately to court even on short notice for a s.31 CA 1989 order. Where this is the case LAs should consider using the immediate issue template letter at Annex A.

2.4.3 Contents

The Letter before Proceedings (LbP) is an important letter and should be carefully drafted. It is the trigger for non-means, non-merits tested publicly funded legal advice and assistance under 'Family Help Lower' (also referred to as Level 2 advice) (sections 2.6.2 & 2.6.3). It will be filed with the court, and it needs to be concise, clear and focused. For this reason the template LbP in the Statutory Guidance should be used as the basis for the letter.

It is important that the LbP is understood by the recipient. The template LbP in the Statutory Guidance uses very simple English and is jargon free so that it can be understood by recipients. If applicable it should be translated into the language used by the parent or carer. It is important that there should be no surprises in the LbP. Although the parent should already have had notice or knowledge of the LA's concerns, the purpose of the LbP is to be clear (in one place) about the concerns and what the LA needs to change or improve in order to reduce those concerns. Finally, it acts as formal notification that the parent should seek legal advice, together with a final warning that court proceedings may follow if the situation fails to improve.

The LbP also invites the parent to a Pre-Proceedings Meeting (PPM) to discuss matters and hopefully finalise a plan or agreement. There needs to be sufficient time balanced against risk to the child to allow the recipient of the LbP to actually receive the letter, consider it and to seek advice from a lawyer in advance. Social workers will need to consider these factors when proposing the date and time of the PPM in the LbP.

2.4.4 Plans and Agreements

The Letter before Proceedings will state what concerns need to be addressed by the parent and what support will be provided by the LA to help. These issues will be reflected in the existing child in need/child protection or care plan. The plan may be one of the following formats:

(a) a care plan because the child is looked-after by the LA pursuant to a s.20 CA 1989 agreement; a looked after child's plan can only be amended at a Statutory review at which the parents will (hopefully) be present;

(b) a child protection plan if the child is already the subject of child protection measures;

(c) a Child in Need plan if the child is not looked-after but is deemed to be 'in need' of services pursuant to s.17 CA 1989.

It follows that the LA should update the plan and send it to the parent as a draft plan (ideally with the LbP) which he or she will be asked to agree at the PPM.

The Pre-Proceedings Meeting (PPM) will work best where both the LA and the parent have had a good opportunity to prepare. For the parent this will mean considering the LbP and understanding the plan which he or she is being asked to agree to. The LbP must actively encourage the parent to see a solicitor for advice; ideally he or she will have given instructions and at least sought some brief advice before coming to the PPM with the solicitor. Parents should understand the details of the concerns about the child's developmental needs, including the need for safeguarding and the plan to meet them in order to know what is required of them and how they can fulfil the requirements or discuss the issues if they feel unable to make a meaningful change. Alternatively, they will be in a position to suggest factual corrections or amendments to the proposed plan through the negotiation that will take place during the PPM.

2.4.5 Communicating messages

It is important to be sensitive and careful in communicating messages from the LbP. Nothing in the proposed plan should be new or a surprise to the parent. The concerns will have continuously been referred to during meetings, case conferences, documents or correspondence between the LA and the parent.

- The LA should consider hand delivering the LbP (taking into account if it is safe to do so) so that the social worker can be sure that the LbP was actually delivered.
- The social worker may wish to ask the parent to sign a 'receipt' to evidence delivery of the LbP. Feedback informs us that parents are more likely to attend the PPM where the LA has met the parent to deliver the LbP to reinforce its meaning and purpose.

- If communication is difficult it will be even more important to record on the LA file the methods attempted by the social worker to deliver the letter.
- Where the LbP is being posted then use recorded delivery

The expectation is that the parents will seek legal advice and take the LbP to their solicitor.

The Ministry of Justice's Care Proceedings Programme Office will be issuing in 2009 a written pack for parents to encourage better engagement during the pre-proceedings stages. The material's target audience will be parents who are involved with the LA at the pre-proceedings stages. It is hoped that social workers and lawyers for parents will be able to refer parents to the material to aid their understanding of the pre-proceedings stages. It is intended that the material will be made more widely available within voluntary sector agencies/organisations whose service-user groups include parents involved with the LA in relation to their children.

2.5 The Pre-Proceedings Meeting (PPM)

2.5.1 Timing

The Letter before Proceedings will have stated a date, time and venue for the PPM. Consideration should be given to re-scheduling when requested by the parents so long as this not does affect the child's safety and welfare.

2.5.2 Organisation and co-ordination

Ethos: The aim of the PPM is to reach an agreement on the proposed plan between the family and the LA. Although agreement may not be able to be reached in all cases or about all areas of the plan, a conciliatory approach is encouraged of the participants and their lawyers. It should be noted that the PPM is not intended to be adversarial in nature and therefore it would be unhelpful for any participant to take such an approach. It must be borne in mind that the PPM is a social work led meeting and not a court or tribunal where a judge or arbiter listens to evidence, argument and makes decisions. Neither is the PPM a forum for disputed facts to be determined, such as in a fact finding hearing. If there are disputed facts or issues, the participants can through negotiation agree facts or narrow issues down voluntarily. The PPM will not however, decide on anything which fundamentally remains contested or disputed. No participant should feel pressured to agree to anything that he or she does not want to. Legal advice during the meeting will assist the parent with this. It is vital for the parent to understand that the proposed plan being put forward by the LA warrants careful thought so that the parent is aware of what is likely to happen in the event that an agreement to the plan or amended plan cannot be secured.

Venue of the PPM: We know that in certain familial situations the issue of where the PPM takes place can be 'make or break' in terms of whether the parent will attend and engage in the PPM. The decision regarding venue will be taken by the social worker in conjunction with his or her manager and the person who will chair the PPM. The social worker will be key in influencing this decision – having the most detailed knowledge of the circumstances of the family.

Agenda for the PPM: Many LAs have formulated an outline agenda for use at the PPM. They have found that this is helpful as it formalises the meeting, ensures that everything is covered and demonstrates to the participants that the PPM is of a more serious nature than perhaps other routine meetings between a parent and the LA. Annex C is a list of points/agenda items which may be considered for inclusion in any agenda for such meetings. It remains, of course, for each LA to decide how it wishes to conduct the meetings and whether it chooses to create its own agenda using some or all of the suggestions contained in Annex C.

Engaging the parent: There may be times when a parent will either refuse to attend the PPM or disagree with the proposed plan. This can be a difficult process but there may still be an opportunity to narrow some of the issues. A brief case example is given at the bottom of Annex C.

Minutes of the PPM: It is good practice for minutes to be taken of the PPM and then for those to be approved by the LA and circulated to the parent as quickly as possible. The parent will then have the opportunity to suggest corrections or additions which the LA can then consider. We suggest that the LA adopt a similar practice regarding minutes of the PPM as they will have in place for child protection case/review conferences. Minutes are important for any formal meeting and it is preferable that they are provided in relation to all PPMs.

Communicating plans: The plan and any agreement which has been reached during the meeting will be a material document and it is important that it is accurate, and comprehensive.

2.5.3 Participants

Legal: If parents attend with their lawyer the LA lawyer should also attend.

Wider family members: Should a parent wish to bring a person in a supportive role it is in the discretion of the LA to allow this.

One possible tool that the LA might re-consider at this point is the use of a Family Group Conference/Family meeting which might assist identification of wider family support. However, it must be remembered that the child's welfare is paramount and also that the parents should be central to this process and their agreement obtained at the outset and throughout the process.

Other agencies/organisations: The PPM is not a multi-disciplinary meeting or forum and it is not appropriate for other agencies to attend.

Chairing the PPM: Some LAs have stated that they have not found it helpful for the child's social worker or manager to chair the PPM. Some suggestions on people who might be better suited to chair the PPM are:

- A senior manager from the LA; or
- A contracted person who is suitably qualified akin to an Independent Reviewing Officer.

In either case, it is preferable that the person who does chair should be someone with no prior direct involvement with the child and family and where practicable that this person should chair all the PPMs in that LA. LAs who are operating a system of one nominated person as chair for all meetings are finding this is beneficial to the outcome.

If this person has no prior involvement the chances of a productive meeting increase as the parent will hopefully look to the chair as someone who is fresh to the case, less likely to have preconceived ideas about the child or family, perhaps be more impartial than the child's social worker, and is sufficiently distanced to have a wider perspective on the issues. If the chair is able to gain the trust of the participants in the meeting, the meeting will proceed more effectively.

2.5.4 Attendees with particular needs

Given the nature, sensitivity and seriousness of the issues which fall to be discussed at the PPM it is crucial that the participants understand and are able to follow the discussions.

Some of the issues which come within the remit of the pre-proceedings stages are just as important as some of those that arise within proceedings. Where a person lacks the capacity to follow the litigation within proceedings, it is likely that he or she would also find it difficult to understand everything that is being said and asked of him or her pre-proceedings. Where an informal assessment suggests a parent may struggle to follow the pre-proceedings discussions or otherwise may have a learning disability or mental health problems which affect the parent's ability to follow the issues, then an immediate and urgent referral must be made to the Adults with Learning Disability Team/Community Learning Disability Team (ALDT/CLDT) or LA equivalent. Lord Justice Wall's comments in a recent case have clarified the Court's expectations in this instance:

It is, I think, inevitable that in its pre-proceedings work with a child's family, the local authority will gain information about the capacity of the child's parents. The critical question is what it does with that information, particularly in a case where the social workers form the view that the parent in question may have learning difficulties. (Para. 175.)

At this point, in many cases, the local authority will be working with the child's parents in an attempt to keep the family together. In my judgment, the practical answer in these circumstances is likely to be that the parent in question should be referred to the local authority's adult learning disability team (or its equivalent) for help and advice. If that team thinks that further investigations are required, it can undertake them: it should, moreover, have the necessary contacts and resources to commission a report so that as soon as the pre-proceedings letter is written, and proceedings are issued, the legal advisers for the parent can be in a position, with public funding, to address the question of a litigation friend. It is, I think, important that judgments on capacity are not made by the social workers from the child protection team. (Para. 176.)

In the pre-proceedings phase local authorities should feel free to do whatever is necessary in social work terms to assist parents who may become protected parties. My view, however, is that this is best achieved by members of the adult learning disabilities team who do not have responsibility for the children concerned. (Para. 181.)

P v. Nottingham City Council and the Official Solicitor [2008] EWCA Civ 462

On a practical level ALDT/CLDT must be asked to assess the parent and to make recommendations as to capacity to understand the information being discussed and shared at the pre-proceedings meetings. It may be that the parent can properly engage during pre-proceedings if supported by a social worker from the ALDT/CLDT. Alternatively, a voluntary sector organisation may be able to provide an advocate who is experienced in working with those with learning disability. If those options fail then the LA may wish to consider inviting a close family member or friend to support the parent during the PPM. That however is not ideal. Ultimately, if the social worker or the lawyer for the parent believes that the parent is unable to understand and follow the subject matter properly in order to then give considered instructions to the solicitor, it may be the case that the LA will have to issue an application to court so that the Official Solicitor can be invited to act for the parent within the proceedings.

Language barriers must also be considered where a parent's capacity to understand is clearly limited and the LA should make arrangements for a suitable independent interpreter and not rely on a family member of friend.

2.5.5   Reviewing plans

The objective of the PPM is to:

- Agree a plan; and
- Track and monitor progress to implementing the plan

The plan for the child might be that the child will be accommodated by the local authority. This is a key option for the child even if only as a temporary measure (section 2.8). If it is agreed that the child should be looked-after under s.20 1989 the LA must comply with all statutory duties in relation to looked after children.

Where the child is not a looked-after child because he or she will remain in the care of the family or be subject to a private fostering arrangement between the parent and a third person (such as a family friend or more distant relative) it is likely that the child will remain a child in need for the requisite period. The LA will however be responsible for checking and supervising any private fostering arrangements. If the arrangements are brokered by the LA then the child becomes a looked-after child under a s.23 placement.

2.5.6   Children's participation and the participation of the child

So far as it is reasonably practicable and consistent with the child's welfare, every child should be notified in age appropriate language by the LA that a PPM is to be held, with an explanation that the purpose is to help parents to keep them safe. The child should then be given the chance to make written representations to the PPM. The social worker has an ongoing duty to ascertain the wishes and feelings of the child.[8] The social worker should be in a position to feed those wishes and feelings into the PPM. Acting in the best interests of the child will be the responsibility which pervades everything the social worker does in a particular case. The social worker is therefore in a position to make clear the child's views at the PPM.

Additionally, the LA must decide in each individual case whether to invite the child to the PPM. In considering the matter, there will be a variety of factors which will be taken into account including:

- The child's age;
- The child's level of understanding as to what is involved;
- The child's coping skills; and
- Whether it is appropriate for the child to be present for all or for part of the PPM.

If the child is invited and attends the meeting, the LA should review agenda items, as there may be information that could be difficult for a child to manage within this forum. The social worker should also inform the chair of the PPM that the child will be attending.

If it is felt inappropriate to invite the child to attend the PPM or the child rejects the invitation, the social worker must consider how the child's wishes and feelings could be heard at the PPM.

The LA should ascertain the parent's views towards the child's attendance at the meeting. If the parents oppose the child's attendance at the meeting it must be remembered that the LA does not have parental responsibility at this stage.

If parents do not wish the child to attend, the child should be informed about the LAs complaints procedure. In these circumstances the LA should consider other methods of ensuring that the child's voice is heard, such as:

- the child making written representations for the meeting;
- the social worker having a meeting with the child;
- the child being referred to a local advocacy service able to support the child.

A template letter to the child can be found at Annex B. This should be tailored and adapted where the LA decide to notify a child about the PPM in writing. If the child does not attend the meeting the social worker will explain the plan to the child and take account of their wishes and feelings. As in all issues pre, during and after proceedings there must be a child focused timetable.

2.5.7   The role of lawyers

The role of lawyers in PPMs is to provide impartial legal advice in private to a client if appropriate.

If the lawyer is able to familiarise himself or herself with the relevant papers at the outset this will aid his or her ability to properly advise the client when needed. Lawyers for LAs are likely to first hear about a particular case during the legal gateway/planning meeting. It may however, be some time later when the LA come back to the lawyer for further advice or to ask that the lawyer be present at the PPM. Reading updated social work documents is useful at this point. In relation to lawyers for parents, in some circumstances the lawyer will have been instructed even prior to

---

8. Amendments were made by s.53 CA 2004 to the following sections of CA 1989: s.17(4A), s.47(5A) and s.20(6) (all of which relate to ascertaining wishes and feelings of the child).

the LbP being sent (section 2.6.1). Where this is the case, the lawyer may have already seen documents or will have sought disclosure from the LA. Otherwise the first involvement for the lawyer for the parent will be where the parent brings in the LbP to the first attendance with the solicitor. There may be very little time between instruction of lawyers and the PPM taking place.

2.5.8 *Lawyer for the parent*

If the PPM is to have the best possible chance of resolving issues or identifying an alternative care solution it is vital that both the LA and the parent have appropriate advice from their qualified legal advisors.

2.6 Public funding (Legal Help and Legal Aid)

2.6.1 *Legal Help – public law*

Some parents may have had a lawyer during other stages of their involvement with the LA. In those cases the lawyer will have assessed the client's eligibility for Legal Help (referred to as 'Level 1 Advice'). Unlike Family Help Lower this level of service is means-tested and therefore not all parents will be financially eligible. There is also a merits-test which has a low threshold ('the sufficient benefit test'). This is payable by way of a fixed fee.

2.6.2 *Importance of the LbP*

Each local authority will have sent the parent a Letter before Proceedings (LbP) inviting the recipient of the letter to a meeting to discuss concerns and plans for the child and family. From the moment that the letter is received, the person to whom it is addressed automatically becomes eligible for advice and assistance. It is vital that the LA ensure that the parent receives the LbP (section 2.4). Only then will he or she be able to secure non-means, non-merits tested advice and assistance from a solicitor on this basis; the LbP acting as the trigger for eligibility. The LA are encouraged to enclose with the LbP a list of firms/organisations who do such work and in particular those that have staff who are members of the Solicitors Regulation Authority's (formerly the Law Society) Children Panel.

2.6.3 *Family Help Lower*

Advice and assistance is provided by the legal advisor under a scheme called Family Help Lower (also referred to as 'Level 2 Advice'). This is a form of Controlled Work and therefore it is for the lawyer to assess whether the person seeking assistance is eligible for this level of service. Any parent or person with Parental Responsibility (PR) who receives a LbP is entitled to this level of service; it is non-means and non-merits tested. The parent is free to instruct any firm or organisation which does public funded family work.

    The level of service (Family Help Lower) is remunerated as a standard fee. The LSC has calculated this fee based upon Controlled Legal Representation rates, which are higher than Legal Help and are similarly used in mental health and immigration cases involving priority clients. The LSC has increased the fee so that it currently represents over 7 hours of work.

2.6.4 *Exceptional cases*

There may be cases where the issues are very complex or great in numbers. For example there may be several persons with PR or the LA has had long-standing involvement and so there are many historic but relevant issues and documents or the assisted person (client) has significant learning difficulties or mental health problems. Those circumstances may make taking instructions, advising the client or negotiation on behalf of the client difficult and complicated. Work done under either Legal Help, Family Help Lower (or both levels of service) when compared to hourly rates may exceed the fixed fee. Where the work was justified and the time spent (based on applicable hourly rates) amounts to three times or over the fixed fee the firm/organisation will be able to claim their costs on a full hourly rates basis rather than being restricted to the fixed fee.

2.6.5 Further information

Further information about publicly funded family services can be found on the Legal Service Commission's website: **www.legalservices.gov.uk**.[9] A list of LSC family regional contacts can be found at: **www.legalservices.gov.uk/civil/civil justice_system_initiatives.asp**.

2.7 Assessments

2.7.1 Adapting to change

The assessment of children and their families is a key task for social work professionals. What the reforms do is to focus on purposeful, analytical and evidence based assessments and their importance. The child's allocated social worker is responsible for coordinating the work on that child's case with support from team/service managers and possibly other agencies. The assessment process is discussed in the Statutory Guidance[10] and in Working Together.[11] Assessments, both Initial and Core should be undertaken in accordance with these documents and the detailed guidance set out in the Framework for the Assessment of Children in Need and their Families DH et al (2000). The LA must not work in isolation and it is imperative that the appropriate sharing of information between the professional network continues to take place to ensure that the child's safety and welfare is kept central to the process.

Where cases rely on specialist assessments to inform the assessment which may not be completed within the target time frame, the core assessment should still be completed and should note any timescales agreed with partners who may be undertaking specialist assessments documented.[12] Planning, intervention and urgent work to safeguard the child's welfare will need to continue not withstanding an incomplete or outstanding core assessment.

The core assessment is the means by which LAs gather and analyse information about the child and family as it undertakes its s.47 CA 1989 enquires.[13] It is the process by which evidence is gathered which is important to the LA's case when it applies to court;[14] the LA will file the core assessment record with the court as its primary piece of evidence to support its application. As it is a live document it will continue to be updated during the LA's involvement with the child and it may well evolve as circumstances change and new information about the family is obtained. Assessment is a continuing process and not a single event.

2.7.2 Change of circumstances

It is essential that the extent to which a child is suffering, or is likely to suffer, harm is kept under constant review and that if necessary the matter proceeds immediately to court irrespective of whether or not the LA has completed its preparation or documentation.

Where the LA decides (usually having taken legal advice) that it needs to take steps to protect a child who it considers to be suffering or likely to suffer significant harm, the LA may take

9. A Q&A document is also helpful reading and is accessible at: **http://www.legalservices.gov.uk/docs/cls_main/QandAPublicLawCareProceedings050308.pdf**.
10. Statutory Guidance, paras. 3.12-3.18.
11. Working Together, paras. 5.60-5.67.
12. Statutory Guidance, para. 3.16.
13. Statutory Guidance, para. 3.15.
14. Statutory Guidance, para. 3.16.

immediate protective measures which could include requesting police protection or an application at court for an order. This may be for an emergency protection order (EPO)[15] because the LA believes the child is in imminent danger, or for an interim care or supervision order[16] in order to safeguard the child. It is recognised that in some cases a core assessment will not have been completed or even started at the point that an application is made to the court. Where however, the LA has been involved with a family for some time and/or has already commenced enquiries pursuant to s.47 CA 1989 it should be conducting the enquiries via a core assessment and documenting findings from the assessment process in a core assessment record. Where the core assessment is not available or completed at the time of issue, the LA will inform the court of the reason why it has not been filed and of the expected date of filing. That information should be given at column (d) of Part 1 ('Pre-proceedings checklist') of the Supplementary PLO1 form. See the Practice Direction 10.2 and 10.3 for guidance on compliance with the pre-proceedings checklist.

2.7.3 Specialist assessments (pre-proceedings)

The key question for the LA to ask itself is 'is there an element or aspect of the core assessment process which cannot be completed because specialist expertise is required'.

Specialist assessments are those assessments which the LA believe are required when for example there is a particular aspect of the child's or family's circumstances which require a specialist assessment from a professional other than a social worker such as an adult mental health assessment. The specialist assessment will only address that specific aspect and it will feed into the core assessment.

Where a specialist assessment is thought to be required, the decision to commission such an assessment must be made as soon as possible to avoid introducing unnecessary delay into resolution of the proceedings. Consideration should also be given to the joint instruction of experts. The PPM can be used for this purpose.

Any specialist assessments commissioned pre-proceedings should be presented by the LA in any proceedings, and for that reason it is suggested that the LA consider the requirements of the Experts PD,[17] particularly those that relate to pre-proceedings assessments

2.8 Alternative care for children: Section 20 Children Act 1989 and the function of the Independent Reviewing Officer (IRO)

There will be some circumstances where it will be appropriate for children to be looked after by the local authority following agreement with those who have parental responsibility that this arrangement would be the best way to meet the child's needs. Where the authority provides accommodation for a child under a voluntary agreement, then the LA does not share parental responsibility for the child and the parents may remove the child from the arrangement at any time. The parents' wishes regarding the care of their child must be respected, unless they are putting the child at risk of significant harm, and the parents and the child must be consulted before any decisions are taking that affect their child. Providing services to children in this way will not be appropriate where there are continuing concerns about significant harm to the child.

Children accommodated under s.20 like every other looked after child, must have a care plan based on a comprehensive assessment of their needs, setting out how the authority intends to meet those needs in partnership with the child's parents. This will include detail about how the authority intends to establish legally secure care arrangements for the child (e.g. permanency options might include making arrangements to reunite the child with their birth family or

---

15. Statutory Guidance, paras. 4.25-4.63.
16. Statutory Guidance, paras. 3.44-3.47.
17. **http://www.hmcourts-service.gov.uk/cms/files/Experts-PD-flagB-final-version-14-01-08.pdf**.

planning for the child to be placed in a permanent substitute family or long term foster care). The care plan must be regularly reviewed. Review meetings must be held at minimum statutory intervals – within 28 days of placement, then within 3 months and six monthly thereafter. Reviews must involve the child, their carers and representatives of the local authority responsible for their care, most reviews will also involve other appropriate professionals. The LA must appoint an Independent Reviewing Officer (IRO) to chair reviews.

The IRO's functions are to

a)   Participate in the review of the case of each looked after child
b)   Monitor the authority's functions in respect of the review
c)   Refer a case to Cafcass/CAFCASS CYMRU if the failure to implement the care plan might be considered to breach the child's human rights

Regulations require IROs to fulfil the following responsibilities:

a)   To ensure that the views of children and young people are understood and taken into account (in care planning);
b)   that the person's responsible for implementing any decision taken in consequence of the review are identified; and
c)   that any failure to review the case or to take proper steps (to implement review recommendations) is brought to the attention of person's at an appropriate level of seniority within the responsible authority.

The review meeting is one of the key components within the core processes of working with children and families. The purpose of the review meeting is to consider the plan for the welfare of the child and then to monitor the progress of the plan and make decisions to amend the plan as necessary in light of changed knowledge and circumstances. The appropriate legal status for the child's care must be considered at every review meeting and the review should make recommendations to senior managers in children's services if the child's legal status no longer seems appropriate to the child's needs. For example, where the circumstances of a child accommodated under s.20 have changed such that it may be necessary for the authority to consider making application for a care order to make legally secure plans to meet the child's future needs.

DCSF are currently re-writing all the Children Act 1989 regulations and guidance and the NMS for fostering and adoption services. In addition DCSF will be issuing Strategic Guidance for consultation in October 2009 on a new framework for family and friends care which will contain a model for assessing relative carers.

2.9   Safeguarding and Child Protection

2.9.1   Threshold

S.31 (2) Children Act 1989 sets out the threshold criteria. A court has no power to make a care or supervision order in favour of a local authority unless, as a matter of fact, it is satisfied that:

(a)   the child concerned is suffering, or is likely to suffer, significant harm, and
(b)   that the harm or likelihood of harm is attributable to **either** (i) the care given to a child or likely to be given to him if the order were not made not being what it would be reasonable to expect a parent to give him **or** (ii) the child is beyond parental control

Harm includes impairment from seeing or hearing the ill treatment of another.

The court will only act on evidence and will make findings of fact about whether the child is suffering significant harm. If the LA have reasonable cause to suspect that a child is suffering significant harm they will make, or cause to be made, such enquiries as they consider necessary to enable them to decide whether they should take any action to safeguard or promote a child's welfare. The court has to establish that it is more probable that the fact(s) in question occurred than they did not. Mere suspicions are not sufficient. It has to be shown that the child is or is likely to suffer significant harm, with significant being the key word. The harm has to be due to unreasonable parenting i.e. parents not giving the care it would be reasonable for a parent to give that child.

The threshold is established as a matter of fact on the evidence at the point when protective measures are implemented.

Only once the court is satisfied that this threshold has been established does the court have the power to make a care or supervision order.

Finding that threshold is proven does not mean that the court must automatically make a care order. Once threshold is established, the court will then go on to hear argument and evidence to determine what order is in the best interests of the child having regard to the welfare checklist set out in section 1 of the Children Act 1989. This might be a care or supervision order or, for example where a suitable kinship carer has been identified, it might be a residence order. The final outcome may also be an order of 'No Order' where the court believes that the interests of the child would be best served by no order being made.

The Public Law Outline usually needs to be considered in the context of whether or not there is a need for an order at that stage and the focus should be upon whether the risk is manageable without an order.

2.9.2 Managing significant harm

Managing possible harm to the child whilst working with families is a delicate task which demands careful social work judgement in discussion with line managers. The Statutory Guidance emphasises the importance of taking pre-proceedings steps such as the Pre-Proceedings Meeting which follows the Letter before Proceedings (LbP) and investigating alternative care solutions, it also recognises that there will be some cases where an immediate application to court will be required. The LA may consider that a case may fit into this category and that certain pre-proceedings steps e.g. dispatch of the LbP cannot be complied with because it might place the child at increased risk of harm or fail to stop the child suffering harm. A typical example might be where the social worker considers there is a real risk of a parent absconding with the child if he or she were to become aware that that the LA is considering applying to court. This is entirely a decision for the LA, making a judgement based on its professional experience of child protection and its knowledge of the child and the family.

When the court application is prepared there may be some information or documentation which cannot be submitted with the application such as the LbP or kinship assessments which may not yet be completed. It is again essential to emphasise that if the child is suffering or likely to suffer significant harm and s31 threshold has been established following legal advice, the matter must proceed to court. The supplementary form PLO1 lists the documentation, which should accompany the application form itself. Column (d) on that form allows the Applicant Authority to state any reason why it has not filed any document. In an emergency LAs are not required to provide pre-proceedings documentation on issue but will be required to file it later.

2.10 Working with partner organisations and agencies

2.10.1 Sharing information

Sharing information arising from the PPM is subject to the usual guidance and practice which governs the LA sharing of information. The general position is that 'the consent of children, young people and their parents or caregivers should be obtained when sharing information, unless to do so would place the child at risk of significant harm. Decisions should also be made with their agreement, whenever possible, unless to do so would place the child at risk of significant harm'.[18]

Where consent to sharing information cannot be secured it will generally be safe to share information where this is justified in the public interest. For example, where there is a clear risk of significant harm to a child or adult it will usually be justified to share information so long as sharing that information is in the best interest of the child's safety and welfare. Detailed guidance can be found in 'Information sharing: Practitioners' guide'.[19]

3 MAKING A SECTION 31 CA 1989 APPLICATION

3.1 Preparing an application for court

3.1.1 The forms

Set out below is a list of some of the forms available at the present time with advice on their completion:

- **PLO1 – Application for a care order or supervision order: Supplementary form**. To be filed by the LA with its application. Part 1 is a checklist of the necessary documents. Part 2 is the Record of Case Management Documents filed and to record which case management documents are filed as the case progresses.
- **PLO2 – Local Authority Case Summary**. This standard form should be filed by the LA setting out its position, before the First Appointment (FA), Case Management Conference (CMC) and Issues Resolution Hearing (IRH) and will include details of: proceedings relating to the child, living arrangements, summary of incidents/concerns, key issues in the case and directions for the court to consider.
- **PLO3 – Case Management Order**. This contains standard provisions designed to help the parties, their legal representatives and the court, and has three sections: 1) Preliminary, 2) Order and 3) Recitals. The LA should prepare an initial draft in advance of each advocates' discussion/meeting and share this with all advocates involved in the case, as this document forms the basis of discussions at the advocates' meeting. Following each advocates' discussion/meeting, it is the responsibility of the local authority advocate to file the draft order with the court at least one working day before either the CMC or IRH.
- **PLO4 – Allocation Record and Timetable for the Child**. To be filed by the LA with its application. It sets out an allocation proposal regarding the appropriate tier of court. It will also be used to record the court's allocation decision and reasons. The LA also uses it to provide important dates in the child's life to assist the court set a suitable Timetable for the Child.
- **PLO5 – Standard Directions and allocation on issue of proceedings**
- **PLO6 – Standard Directions and allocation at First Appointment**. Forms PLO 5 and 6 are completed by a judge or legal adviser once an application is lodged at court and at the First Appointment. The court will consider giving standard directions appropriate to each case at Issue and First Appointment stages using these forms

3.1.2 The documentation

All pre-proceedings checklist documents should be filed with the application where available.

---

18. Working Together p. 101.
19. 'Information sharing: Practitioners' guide', HM Government 920020. Accessible at: **www.everychildmatters.gov.uk/_files/ACB1BA35C20D4C42A1FE6F9133A7C614.pdf**.

The documents which the LA are called upon to create specifically for filing with the application are:

1. The Schedule of Proposed Findings;
2. Initial Social Work Statement;
3. Care Plan for each child;
4. The Allocation Record; and
5. Timetable for the Child.

The Public Law Outline is explicit about the required documents that should be filed and issued by the court.

LAs should file and serve under the category of the 'Other relevant reports and records' (see item 7 on form PLO1, Part 1) the child's full birth certificate or relevant ID as this is likely to be required by the court at some stage and therefore would be useful to be filed at the outset.

3.2   Parties with particular needs

In s.31 CA 1989 proceedings where the social worker or any party believes that a parent may not have capacity to conduct the litigation the court can be asked to make a direction inviting the Official Solicitor to act on that person's behalf. It must be considered that appropriate social work expertise within the local authority disability team can be used pre or post proceedings to inform a decision on their client's capacity. The Official Solicitor is a 'litigation friend of last resort' and will only accept that invitation if there is no one else who is willing and suitable to conduct the litigation on the parent's behalf. Invariably in family proceedings it will be difficult to say with any certainty that another family member is suitable because he or she may have a view which is in conflict with the parent or otherwise because he or she is very close to the subject of the litigation so will not be able to present the parent's views properly. It is important that the Official Solicitor is approached as soon as possible if required to assist:

> if all the professionals involved with the proceedings and with the parents, including the judges, solicitors, barristers, advocates, and court staff, are aware of the need from the start of the proceedings to take time to consider the parent and whether the proceedings are proving too much for the parent to fully understand. If at any time there is a genuine concern about the parent's capacity to understand the proceedings and to instruct their solicitor, the parent should be able to ask for, and to receive assistance without being made to feel stigmatised by their disability

> www.officialsolicitor.gov.uk/docs/parentsnetworkarticle.doc

3.3   Advocates' Meetings

3.3.1   Attendees

A Children's Guardian (CG) is a social work professional appointed by a court to independently represent a child subject a care or adoption procedures. They are officers of Cafcass/CAFCASS CYMRU. Children's Guardians and social workers must not attend Advocates' Meetings but they should be notified of the time and date of the meeting and they should be contactable throughout so that counsel may take instructions as necessary.

The Advocates' Meeting should not take place on the morning of the hearing but in accordance with the requirements of the PLO. It is advisable to book the meeting promptly following any previous meeting. When advocates are considering timetabling a meeting, due consideration should be given to utilising telephone or video conferencing where attendance in person is impractical.

It is recognised that it is sometimes unhelpful to a party to have a different advocates representing him or her at various hearings. At times, this can have a bearing on the smooth running of the proceedings. Any client should be free of constraints to choose who he or she wishes to instruct as his or her representative and therefore the Practice Direction (PD) cannot be prescriptive on the issue. Nevertheless the PD does acknowledge the concern and provides a reminder to advocates (for all parties) that the advocate who represents at the final hearing should be the same advocate representing the client at the CMC and IRH. Where this is not possible the PD suggests that an advocate who is familiar with the issues in the case should attend.[20]

3.3.2 Preparation

The aim of the Advocates' Meeting is to facilitate agreement between the parties and narrow the issues in dispute.[21] In order to save valuable court time the Advocates' Meeting also acts as a forum where the draft Case Management Order is discussed and prepared.[22] Meetings will only be productive if all the advocates have prepared what is the background to and the issues in the case, what their respective client seeks to achieve from the proceedings, and up to date instructions from their clients in advance but as close to the Advocates' Meeting as possible.

To aid the smooth running of the Advocates' Meeting the draft Case Management Order should be prepared as an initial draft by the LA in advance of the Advocates' Meeting itself. If this is circulated to the other parties even a day before the Advocates' Meeting is scheduled to take place, it will act as a working document which all can come to the meeting armed with comments on. It will also act as the agenda for the meeting which would be helpful.

If proceedings are to run smoothly and with as little delay as possible, it will be important that all parties comply with the filing of evidence and in time. Where compliance with a particular direction is not looking possible, the relevant party's representative must seek agreement from all the parties for an extension of time or draw the non compliance to the attention of the court.

3.3.3 Drafting the Case Management Order

During the Advocates' Meeting there will be a discussion about the Case Management Order and the Applicant's advocate (usually the LA) will take the lead in preparing or drafting that document together with the other advocates. Ideally matters can be agreed and the Case Management Order can be filed as a single agreed case management tool to assist the judge at the hearing. Where that is not possible the advocates will specify on the Case Management Order (or on a separate document if necessary) the provisions which they agree and disagree.[23] There must be a clear narrative detailing what the LA is asking the court to do, with the CMO fully completed. Detailed standard variable directions are available from the HMCS website to provide assistance on the full and appropriate wording to be used when considering the required directions for the draft case management order.

3.4 Care planning

The plan for the care of the child should be based on findings from the initial and core assessments. It should set out the aims of the plan and intended outcomes for the child, informed by the findings from the assessments ie. The identified developmental needs of the child and the capacity of the parents to respond to the child's needs in the context of their wide family and environmental factors. It will set out clearly what the plan for the child if the Court makes a care order.

---

20. PD, para. 16.
21. PD, para. 3.11.
22. PD, paras. 13.1-13.7.
23. PD, para. 13.5.

In those relatively few cases where the identified permanence option, at the point of the commencement of proceedings, is for the adoption of the child, and where the decision that the child should be placed for adoption has been taken in accordance with the Adoption Agencies Regulations 2005 (SI 2005/384), the local authority must apply for a placement order issued simultaneously with, or as soon as possible after, the issue of the care proceedings.

3.5   Role of the Children's Guardian and the Independent Reviewing Officer

Where possible the Children's Guardian (CG) should meet with the child, where age appropriate, and with other parties in advance of the First Appointment (FA). The Guardian must have read the court papers and provided the required analysis.

The Practice Direction defines Case Analysis & Recommendation (A&R) as being a 'written or oral outline of the case from the child's perspective prepared by the Children's Guardian or other officer…'.[24] A list follows that paragraph of the PD setting out the particular points that the Case A&R should address. It is anticipated that the CG may not always be in a position to file a written Case A&R and this is why the definition allows for an oral outline to be provided by the CG at the FA. Where an oral report is given it is suggested that the child's solicitor takes a note of the oral report and then files it as an agreed note. However, in Wales practice guidance requires that the CG provides an initial analysis in written form at the earliest stage and if feasible by the FA.

In subsequent hearings, the CG should be up to speed and in a position to provide written Case A&R that will be filed by the child's solicitor as per the court's directions.

The child's care plan must be maintained by the local authority and kept under review at the statutory intervals and whenever significant changes are proposed to the plan throughout proceedings. It will be good practice for the Children's Guardian and the IRO to maintain a constructive working relationship throughout proceedings. Both the Children's Guardian and the IRO should be properly informed about the local authority's plans for the child so they are bale to scrutinise these plans to make sure that they are based on good quality assessment so that the plan demonstrates how the child's needs will be met, with the child being provided with the opportunity to be meaningfully involved in planning for their care. The local authority will need to take the views of the IRO on the quality of planning into account in formulating the final care plan to be put to the Court.[25]

Where a child is accommodated by the LA upon issue of proceedings e.g. under s20 of the CA 1989, it is good practice for the LA to serve a copy of the LA Case Summary (form PLO2) together with a copy of the Initial Social Work Statement, Schedule of Proposed Findings, Care Plan and Allocation Record and timetable for the child on the IRO. Additionally the LA should provide the parties and the Children's Guardian with the name and contact details of the IRO together with the dates of any statutory reviews which have been arranged.

At the conclusion of proceedings IROs may well have an important role in ensuring that the implications of the agreed care plan are understood by all professionals, cares and family members, as there will no longer be any oversight by the Court of the care planning process. In particular, the IRO will have a role in enabling the child to understand their plan and to participate in future care planning.

---

24. PD, para. 25(8).
25. The Children and Young person Act includes provision which significantly strengthens the IRO function. In future each looked after child must have their own personal named IRO; the IRO will be responsible for monitoring the quality of the local authority's care planning function; and ensure that in every care plan due consideration has been given to the child's wishes and feelings.

3.6 Issues Resolution Hearings and Final Hearings

The purpose of the Issues Resolution Hearing (IRH) is to narrow the issues in so far as to conclude proceedings if possible.

There is some concern amongst professionals that a final hearing is only listed by the court at the IRH. This seems to have given rise to some anxiety about the List Office's ability to secure a date in the court diary for a final hearing soon after the IRH. Where the court is able to do this, some are worried that there will not be an opportunity to give adequate notice to experts and that this may also cause difficulty for the consistency of advocates.

The Practice Direction itself does not require final hearings to only be listed at the IRH. The PD states that at the Case Management Conference (CMC) the court will set a date for the IRH and 'if necessary, specify a period within which the Final Hearing of the application is to take place unless a date has already been set'.[26] Rather than taking a prescriptive approach the PD is flexible about the listing of final hearings leaving it for the court to decide when it lists the final hearing and in accordance with its case management functions. The Timetable for the Child will greatly influence how the court manages its case especially in regard to the listing of hearings.

3.7 Collective participation and co-operation

All professionals involved in public law proceedings will work together with the court to assist achievement of the overriding objective. The parties have a duty to do this, which is enshrined in the PD.[27]

It is also emphasised[28] that the parties and their representatives should co-operate with the court in case management. Furthermore, the parties and representatives should monitor compliance (generally) with the Court's directions and inform the court or court officer about any failure to comply with a direction of the court or any other delay within the proceedings[29]. A number of courts have a case progression officer (CPO) who should be the first point of contact with regard to Public Law cases.

3.8 The nature of the Public Law Outline

The purpose of the PLO is to reduce delay in these important proceedings concerning the short and long-term placement future of children. It has had to be robust in order to achieve its objectives and to secure outcomes for children and families involved within the target timeframe set by the Timetable for the Child (which is one of the case management tools).[30] It should be borne in mind that the PD does acknowledge that the court has flexible powers. At any stage in the proceedings the court may exercise those powers.[31]

The expectations[32] are that the proceedings should be conducted using the Case Management Tools and Documentation and determined in accordance with the stages in the Timetable for the Child (together with the timeframes indicated for the various stages within the PLO). It is however, acknowledged that the child's welfare in some cases may require a more tailored approach; possibly one that does not fall firmly within the stages and expectations of the PLO. In those cases it will be for the court to determine the appropriate case management directions and timetable[33] but the court must record on the face of any order its reasons for departing from the

26. PD, para. 14.5(2).
27. PD, para 2.3.
28. PD, para 5.4.
29. PD, para5.5.
30. PD, paras 3.2-3.4.
31. PD, paras 17.1-17.3.
32. PD, para. 4.1.
33. PD, para. 4.2.

PLO's general approach. This aids the parties' understanding of why the court is managing its case in the way it is and it also protects the court itself from any potential criticism for departing from the PLO's expectations.

ANNEX A: IMMEDIATE ISSUE LETTER (TEMPLATE)

SENT BY [RECORDED DELIVERY/BY HAND]

Office Address
Contact
Direct line

My ref
Fax
E-mail
Date

Dear [parent and/or full name(s) of all people with parental responsibility]

Re: [insert name of Local Authority] CONCERNS ABOUT [insert name(s) of child]
    I am writing as you were told I would, when you spoke to [name of social worker] on [insert date of last interaction]. As you are aware [name of Local Authority] is extremely worried about your care of [name(s) of child/ren]. We told you about these main concerns in [reference to the Letter before Proceedings/PPM/child protection case conference/any social work meetings].
    We have tried to work with you to help you improve your care of [name(s) of child/ren] but unfortunately things have not changed. We are writing to tell you again that we will be going to court to try and make sure [name of child] is safe. You will soon receive a copy of our application to the court and other important documents, which set out the key issues.
    We would urge you, if you have not done so already, to get advice from a solicitor. We have sent with this letter a list of local solicitors who specialise in work with children and families. They are not part of Children's Services (Social Services).

Yours sincerely

[name]
Team Manager
Local office/service

cc. Social Worker [name]
Local Authority in house Legal Team

Enc. List of Law Society Children Panel Solicitors

ANNEX B: LETTER NOTIFYING A CHILD ABOUT A PRE-PROCEEDINGS MEETING (TEMPLATE)

Delivered by Hand

Office Address
Contact
Direct line

My ref
Fax
E-mail
Date

Dear [name]

As you know, there have been some concerns about how your parents/carers [delete as appropriate and/or name] have been looking after you.

Although we have been trying hard to sort out these problems, unfortunately, at the moment, we are still worried that you may be at risk of harm.

Our next step therefore is to hold a 'pre-proceedings meeting'. At that meeting we will try to agree a plan with your parents/carers about what needs to be done to deal with our worries about you.

If we cannot sort things with your parents/carers at this meeting, it may mean that our only option is to go to court. Hopefully this will not happen but if it does, you will be given plenty of information about what happens and your role in it all.

I am now writing to invite you to attend the pre-proceedings meeting which is being held on [date] at [time] at [venue]. This will give you the chance to tell the meeting about your thoughts, wishes and feelings. If you would rather not attend the meeting, that is fine. You can always put your thoughts in writing if that is easier.

I shall be present at the meeting, with my manager, [name] and our legal advisor. Your parents have of course been invited and may have their lawyer with them.

I shall call you soon to check if you would like to attend all or part of the meeting. It may be that you would like an adult (who should be unconnected to the family) to support you during the meeting.

Alternatively, I may be able to arrange for an advocate to attend the meeting with you. An advocate's job is to make sure that a young person's views are heard, either through speaking for a young person or helping a young person speak for him or herself. Please let me know if you would like any more information on this and you can telephone me on [. . .].

If you have any questions or worries please contact me on the above number.

Yours sincerely

Social Worker [name]
Local office/service

ANNEX C: LIST OF POTENTIAL AGENDA ITEMS FOR A PRE-PROCEEDINGS MEETING

- Introductions
- Setting out any special requirements (interpreter, sign language interpreter, presence of an advocate)
- Outline the purpose of the meeting and establish ground rules and specify roles
- Outline duty of the LA to protect children, duty (where possible) to promote the child living with the family, balance of that against need to protect and promote welfare of the child. Explaining why it may be that a court application is necessary but that the LA hopes that the meeting may avoid the need for that
- Explain the concerns of the LA and referencing the LbP
- Initial views and opinions of the parent and specifying or clarifying any areas of agreement and disagreement
- Discuss what can be done to help improve the child's situation on the part of the parent including any assessment outcomes and gaps identified

- Discuss what services have been be provided to the family by the LA and can be provided to help i.e. promoting the idea of collaborative working between family and the LA in the best interests of the child
- Discuss the outcome of the Family Group Conference/Family meeting
- Identification of alternative carers (this will be a revisit to the concept as it will have been discussed previously within the assessment process)
- Lead into a discussion of the proposed plan for the child including the need for any further assessments (the auspices of that plan i.e. Child in Need plan or Child Protection Plan)
- Break away for both parent and the LA to take advice from their respective lawyers
- Initial views from parent as to their thoughts on the plan/agreement
- Reconvene for focused discussion on the plan. Can an agreement be reached on the plan/agreement as it stands in draft or can revisions/amendments be agreed now to avoid proceedings
- If no agreement can be reached such that the LA believes it will have to issue an application with the court consider scope for discussion as to any issues which may be resolved now.

Brief case example: mother abuses alcohol and her partner is abusive to her. Both elements raise safeguarding concerns. At the PPM the plan is that mother should (1) agree to cease excessive drinking and agree to attend a community drugs and alcohol programme; and (2) agree to her partner moving out of the family home and to seek assistance from domestic abuse support group/project to support mother with skills/knowledge to leave a violent relationship and to avoid entering into similar relationships in the future. Mother agrees to do (1) but not to do (2). Mother provides details for the first time of alternative carers but refuses to agree to information being disclosed to those persons. The LA decides that it will need to seek an interim care order to safeguard the child. Although proceedings have not been avoided, one crucial issue has (potentially) been resolved and the LA will now be able to press ahead with consideration of alternative carers whilst not disclosing information which the mother has not consented to.

APPENDIX 5

Practice Direction 25C – Children Proceedings: the Use of Single Joint Experts and the Process Leading to an Expert Being Instructed or Expert Evidence Being Put Before the Court

[April 2014]

1 SCOPE OF THIS PRACTICE DIRECTION

1.1 This Practice Direction applies to children proceedings and contains guidance on –

(a) the use of single joint experts;

(b) how to prepare for the hearing at which the court will consider whether to give permission for an expert to be instructed, a child to be medically or psychiatrically examined or otherwise assessed for the purposes of provision of expert evidence in the proceedings or for putting expert evidence (in any form) before the court including –

    (i) preliminary enquiries of experts;

    (ii) the content of an application for the court's permission in addition to matters mentioned in FPR25.7;

    (iii) matters to be set out in the draft order to be attached to the application for permission; and

(c) the letter of instruction to the expert.

1.2 'Children proceedings' includes proceedings under Schedule 1 to the 1989 Act as those proceedings are proceedings which relate wholly or mainly to the maintenance or upbringing of a minor referred to in FPR25.2(1).

2 SINGLE JOINT EXPERTS

2.1 Section 13(1),(3) and (5) of the 2014 Act applies to a single joint expert ('SJE') in addition to an expert instructed by one party. This means that the court's permission is required to put expert evidence from an SJE (in any form) before the court section 13(5) of the 2014 Act. The court's permission is also required to instruct an SJE and for a child to be medically or psychiatrically examined or otherwise assessed for the purposes of provision of evidence from an SJE substitute section 13(1) and (3) of the 2014 Act. Wherever possible, expert evidence should be obtained from an SJE instructed by both or all the parties. To that end, a party wishing to instruct an expert should as soon as possible after the start of the proceedings first give the other party or parties a list of the names of one or more experts in the relevant speciality whom they consider suitable to be instructed.

151

2.2 Within 5 business days after receipt of the list of proposed experts, the other party or parties should indicate any objection to one or more of the named experts and, if so, supply the name(s) of one or more experts whom they consider suitable.

2.3 Each party should disclose whether they have already consulted any of the proposed experts about the issue(s) in question.

2.4 Where the parties cannot agree on the identity of the expert, each party should think carefully before seeking the permission of the court to instruct their own expert because of the costs implications. Disagreements about the use and identity of an expert may be better managed by the court in the context of the application for the court's permission to instruct the expert and for directions for the use of an SJE (see paragraph 2.6 below).

Instructing separate experts

2.5 If the parties seek the permission of the court to instruct separate experts –

(a)   they should agree in advance that the reports will be disclosed; and
(b)   the instructions to each expert should comply, so far as appropriate, with paragraphs 4.1 and 6.1 below (Letter of instruction).

Where two or more parties wish to instruct an SJE

2.6 If two or more parties wish to instruct an SJE, before applying to the court for permission and directions for the use of an SJE, the parties should –

(a)   so far as appropriate, comply with the guidance in paragraphs 3.2 (Preliminary enquiries of the expert) and paragraphs 3.10 and 3.11 below;
(b)   receive the expert's confirmation in response to preliminary enquiries referred to in paragraph 8.1 of Practice Direction 25B;
(c)   have agreed in what proportion the SJE's fee is to be shared between them (at least in the first instance) and when it is to be paid; and
(d)   if applicable, have obtained agreement for public funding.

2.7 The instructions to the SJE should comply, so far as appropriate, with paragraphs 4.1 and 6.1 below (Letter of instruction).

3   PREPARATION FOR THE PERMISSION HEARING

3.1 Paragraphs 3.2 to 3.11 give guidance on how to prepare for the hearing at which the court will consider whether to give permission for an expert to be instructed, a child to be examined or otherwise assessed or expert evidence to be put before the court. The purpose of the preparation is to ensure that the court has the information required to enable it to exercise its powers under section 13(1), (3), (5) and (7) of the 2014 Act and FPR 25.5.

Preliminary enquiries of the expert

3.2 In good time for the information requested to be available for the hearing at which the court will consider whether to give permission for an expert to be instructed, a child to be examined or otherwise assessed or expert evidence to be put before the court or for the advocates' meeting or discussion where one takes place before that hearing, the party or parties intending to instruct the expert shall approach the expert with the following information –

(a)   the nature of the proceedings and the issues likely to require determination by the court;

(b)   the issues in the proceedings to which the expert evidence is to relate;

(c)   the questions about which the expert is to be asked to give an opinion (including any ethnic, cultural, religious or linguistic contexts) and which relate to the issues in the case;

(d)   the date when the court is to be asked to give permission for the instruction (or if – unusually – permission has already been given, the date and details of that permission);

(e)   whether permission is to be asked of the court for the instruction of another expert in the same or any related field (that is, to give an opinion on the same or related questions);

(f)   the volume of reading which the expert will need to undertake;

(g)   whether or not permission has been applied for or given for the expert to examine the child;

(h)   whether or not it will be necessary for the expert to conduct interviews – and, if so, with whom;

(i)   the likely timetable of legal and social work steps;

(j)   in care and supervision proceedings, any dates in the Timetable for the Child which would be relevant to the proposed timetable for the assessment;

(k)   when the expert's report is likely to be required;

(l)   whether and, if so, what date has been fixed by the court for any hearing at which the expert may be required to give evidence (in particular the Final Hearing); and whether it may be possible for the expert to give evidence by telephone conference or video link: see paragraphs 10.1 and 10.2 (Arrangements for experts to give evidence) of Practice Direction 25B;

(m)   the possibility of making, through their instructing solicitors, representations to the court about being named or otherwise identified in any public judgment given by the court;

(n)   whether the instructing party has public funding and the legal aid rates of payment which are applicable.

Confidentiality of children proceedings and making preliminary enquiries of an expert

3.3   For the purposes of the law of contempt of court, information relating to children proceedings (whether or not contained in a document filed with the court or recorded in any form) may be communicated only to an expert whose instruction by a party has been permitted by the court (see FPR 12.73(1)(a)(vii) and 14.14(c)(vii)) as children proceedings are confidential.

3.4   Before permission is obtained from the court to instruct an expert in children proceedings, the party seeking permission needs to make the enquiries of the expert referred to above in order to provide the court with information to enable it to decide whether to give permission. In practice, enquiries may need to be made of more than one expert for this purpose. This will in turn require each expert to be given sufficient information about the case to decide whether or not he or she is in a position to accept instructions. Such preliminary enquiries, and the disclosure of information about the case which is a necessary part of such enquiries, will not require the court's permission and will not amount to a contempt of court.

Expert's response to preliminary enquiries

3.5   In good time for the hearing at which the court will consider whether to give permission for an expert to be instructed, a child to be examined or otherwise assessed or expert evidence to be put before the court, the party or parties intending to instruct the expert must obtain the confirmations from the expert referred to in paragraph 8.1 of Practice Direction 25B. These confirmations include that the work is within the expert's expertise, the expert is available to do the work within the relevant timescale and the expert's costs.

3.6 Where the parties cannot agree who should be the single joint expert before the hearing at which the court will consider whether to give permission for an expert to be instructed, a child to be examined or otherwise assessed or expert evidence to be put before the court, they should obtain the above confirmations in respect of all experts whom they intend to put to the court for the purposes of FPR 25.11(2)(a) as candidates for the appointment.

The application for the court's permission mentioned in section 13(1), (3) and (5) of the 2014 Act

Timing and oral applications for the court's permission mentioned in section 13(1), (3) and (5) of the 2014 Act

3.7 An application for the court's permission for an expert to be instructed, a child to be examined or otherwise assessed or expert evidence to be put before the court should be made as soon as it becomes apparent that it is necessary to make it. FPR 25.6 makes provision about the time by which applications for the court's permission should be made.

3.8 Applications should, wherever possible, be made so that they are considered at any directions hearing or other hearing for which a date has been fixed or for which a date is about to be fixed. It should be noted that one application notice can be used by a party to make more than one application for an order or direction at a hearing held during the course of proceedings. An application for the court's permission for an expert to be instructed, a child to be examined or otherwise assessed or expert evidence to be put before the court may therefore be included in an application notice requesting other orders to be made at such a hearing.

3.9 Where a date for a hearing has been fixed, a party who wishes to make an application at that hearing but does not have sufficient time to file an application notice should as soon as possible inform the court (if possible in writing) and, if possible, the other parties of the nature of the application and the reason for it. The party should provide the court and the other party with as much as possible of the information referred to in FPR 25.7 and paragraph 3.10 below. That party should then make the application orally at the hearing. An oral application of this kind should be the exception and reserved for genuine cases where circumstances are such that it has only become apparent shortly before the hearing that an expert opinion is necessary.

The application

3.10 In addition to the matters specified in FPR 25.7(2)(a)and (3), an application for the court's permission for an expert to be instructed, a child to be examined or otherwise assessed or expert evidence to be put before the court, must state –

(a)   the discipline, qualifications and expertise of the expert (by way of C.V. where possible);

(b)   the expert's availability to undertake the work;

(c)   the timetable for the report;

(d)   the responsibility for instruction;

(e)   whether the expert evidence can properly be obtained by only one party (for example, on behalf of the child);

(f)   why the expert evidence proposed cannot properly be given by an officer of the service,

Welsh family proceedings officer or the local authority (social services undertaking a core assessment) in accordance with their respective statutory duties or any other party to the proceedings or an expert already instructed in the proceedings;

(g)   the likely cost of the report on an hourly or other charging basis;

(h)   the proposed apportionment (at least in the first instance) of any jointly instructed expert's fee; when it is to be paid; and, if applicable, whether public funding has been approved.

The terms of the draft order to be attached to the application for the court's permission

3.11   FPR 25.7(2)(b) provides that a draft of the order giving the court's permission as mentioned in section 13(1), (3) and (5) of the 2014 Act is to be attached to the application for the court's permission. That draft order must set out the following matters –

(a)   the issues in the proceedings to which the expert evidence is to relate and which the court is to identify;

(b)   the questions relating to the issues in the case which the expert is to answer and which the court is to approve ensuring that they –

    (i)   are within the ambit of the expert's area of expertise;

    (ii)   do not contain unnecessary or irrelevant detail;

    (iii)   are kept to a manageable number and are clear, focused and direct;

(c)   the party who is responsible for drafting the letter of instruction and providing the documents to the expert;

(d)   the timetable within which the report is to be prepared, filed and served;

(e)   the disclosure of the report to the parties and to any other expert;

(f)   the organisation of, preparation for and conduct of any experts' discussion (see Practice Direction 25E – Discussions between Experts in Family Proceedings);

(g)   the preparation of a statement of agreement and disagreement by the experts following an experts' discussion;

(h)   making available to the court at an early opportunity the expert reports in electronic form;

(i)   the attendance of the expert at court to give oral evidence (alternatively, the expert giving his or her evidence in writing or remotely by video link), whether at or for the Final Hearing or another hearing; unless agreement about the opinions given by the expert is reached at or before the Issues Resolution Hearing ('IRH') or, if no IRH is to be held, by a date specified by the court prior to the hearing at which the expert is to give oral evidence.

4 LETTER OF INSTRUCTION

4.1   The party responsible for instructing the expert shall prepare (in agreement with the other parties where appropriate), a letter of instruction to the expert and shall –

(a)   set out the context in which the expert's opinion is sought (including any ethnic, cultural, religious or linguistic contexts);

(b)   set out the questions approved by the court and which the expert is required to answer and any other linked questions ensuring that they –

    (i)   are within the ambit of the expert's area of expertise;

    (ii)   do not contain unnecessary or irrelevant detail;

    (iii)   are kept to a manageable number and are clear, focused and direct; and

    (iv)   reflect what the expert has been requested to do by the court

(Annex A to this Practice Direction sets out suggested questions in letters of instruction to (1) child mental health professionals or paediatricians, and (2) adult psychiatrists and applied psychologists, in Children Act 1989 proceedings);

(c)   list the documentation provided,or provide for the expert an indexed and paginated bundle which shall include–

    (i)   an agreed list of essential reading; and

    (ii)   a copy of this Practice Direction and Practice Directions 25B and E and where appropriate Practice Direction 15B;

(d)   identify any materials provided to the expert which have not been produced either as original medical (or other professional) records or in response to an instruction from a party, and state the source of that material (such materials may contain an assumption as to the standard of proof, the admissibility or otherwise of hearsay evidence, and other important procedural and substantive questions relating to the different purposes of other enquiries, for example, criminal or disciplinary proceedings);

(e)   identify all requests to third parties for disclosure and their responses in order to avoid partial disclosure, which tends only to prove a case rather than give full and frank information;

(f)   identify the relevant people concerned with the proceedings (for example, the treating clinicians) and inform the expert of his or her right to talk to them provided that an accurate record is made of the discussions;

(g)   identify any other expert instructed in the proceedings and advise the expert of their right to talk to the other experts provided that an accurate record is made of the discussions;

(h)   subject to any public funding requirement for prior authority, define the contractual basis upon which the expert is retained and in particular the funding mechanism including how much the expert will be paid (an hourly rate and overall estimate should already have been obtained), when the expert will be paid, and what limitation there might be on the amount the expert can charge for the work which they will have to do. In cases where the parties are publicly funded, there may also be a brief explanation of the costs and expenses excluded from public funding by Funding Code criterion 1.3 and the detailed assessment process.

5   ADULT WHO IS A PROTECTED PARTY

5.1   Where the adult is a protected party, that party's representative shall be involved in any instruction of an expert, including the instruction of an expert to assess whether the adult, although a protected party, is competent to give evidence (see Practice Direction 15B – Adults Who May Be Protected Parties and Children Who May Become Protected Parties in Family Proceedings).

6   ASKING THE COURT TO SETTLE THE LETTER OF INSTRUCTION TO A SINGLE JOINT EXPERT

6.1   Where possible, the written request for the court to consider the letter of instruction referred to in rule 25.12(2) should be set out in an e-mail to the court and copied by e-mail to the other instructing parties. The request should be sent to the relevant court or (by prior arrangement only) directly to the judge dealing with the proceedings. Where a legal adviser has been appointed as the case manager, the request should also be sent to the appointed legal adviser. The court will settle the letter of instruction, usually without a hearing to avoid delay; and will send (where practicable, by e-mail) the settled letter to the lead solicitor for transmission forthwith to the expert, and copy it to the other instructing parties for information.

ANNEX A

(drafted by the Family Justice Council)

Suggested questions in letters of instruction to child mental health professional or paediatrician in Children Act 1989 proceedings

A   The Child(ren)

1.   Please describe the child(ren)'s current health, development and functioning (according to your area of expertise), and identify the nature of any significant changes which have occurred

- Behavioural
- Emotional
- Attachment organisation
- Social/peer/sibling relationships
- Cognitive/educational
- Physical
  - Growth, eating, sleep
  - Non-organic physical problems (including wetting and soiling)
  - Injuries
  - Paediatric conditions

2.   Please comment on the likely explanation for/aetiology of the child(ren)'s problems/difficulties/injuries

- History/experiences (including intrauterine influences, and abuse and neglect)
- Genetic/innate/developmental difficulties
- Paediatric/psychiatric disorders

3.   Please provide a prognosis and risk if difficulties not addressed above.
4.   Please describe the child(ren)'s needs in the light of the above

- Nature of care-giving
- Education
- Treatment

in the short and long term (subject, where appropriate, to further assessment later).

B   The parents/primary carers

5.   Please describe the factors and mechanisms which would explain the parents' (or primary carers) harmful or neglectful interactions with the child(ren) (if relevant).
6.   What interventions have been tried and what has been the result?
7.   Please assess the ability of the parents or primary carers to fulfil the child(ren)'s identified needs now.
8.   What other assessments of the parents or primary carers are indicated?

- Adult mental health assessment
- Forensic risk assessment
- Physical assessment
- Cognitive assessment

9.   What, if anything, is needed to assist the parents or primary carers now, within the child(ren)'s timescales and what is the prognosis for change?

- Parenting work
- Support
- Treatment/therapy

C ALTERNATIVES

10.   Please consider the alternative possibilities for the fulfilment of the child(ren)'s needs

- What sort of placement
- Contact arrangements

Please consider the advantages, disadvantages and implications of each for the child(ren).

Suggested questions in letters of instruction to adult psychiatrists and applied psychologists in Children Act 1989 proceedings

1.   Does the parent/adult have – whether in his/her history or presentation – a mental illness/disorder (including substance abuse) or other psychological/emotional difficulty and, if so, what is the diagnosis?
2.   How do any/all of the above (and their current treatment if applicable) affect his/her functioning, including interpersonal relationships?
3.   If the answer to Q1 is yes, are there any features of either the mental illness or psychological/emotional difficulty or personality disorder which could be associated with risk to others, based on the available evidence base (whether published studies or evidence from clinical experience)?
4.   What are the experiences/antecedents/aetiology which would explain his/her difficulties, if any, (taking into account any available evidence base or other clinical experience)?
5.   What treatment is indicated, what is its nature and the likely duration?
6.   What is his/her capacity to engage in/partake of the treatment/therapy?
7.   Are you able to indicate the prognosis for, time scales for achieving, and likely durability of, change?
8.   What other factors might indicate positive change?

(It is assumed that this opinion will be based on collateral information as well as interviewing the adult).

APPENDIX 6

Official Solicitor's Litigation Friend Checklist

PROTECTED PARTIES IN FAMILY PROCEEDINGS

Checklist for the appointment of a litigation friend (including the Official Solicitor)

This checklist is to be completed where there is reason to believe that a party or prospective party to proceedings ('PP') lacks capacity (within the meaning of the Mental Capacity Act 2005) to conduct the proceedings. It should be completed by PP's legal representative or, if none, any person (including a local authority) able to provide the relevant information.

Name of party	. . . .		
Describe briefly the reasons for believing that PP lacks capacity to conduct the proceedings			
. . . .			
Evidence and finding as to capacity			
Has the court made a finding that PP lacks capacity to conduct the proceedings	Yes	No	
(if so, give date and attach a copy of the order)	Date		
Has an assessment of capacity been obtained?	Yes	No	
If so, give the date of the assessment, the name and occupation/professional qualification of the author and a concise summary of the conclusion. *A copy should be attached if available.*			
. . . .			
Has PP been informed of the assessment?	Yes	No	
Does PP accept the assessment?	Yes	No	
Has PP been informed of the effect and consequences of the assessment and of being a protected party?	Yes	No	

If there is no assessment of capacity, what, if any, evidence is relied on to determine the question of capacity?		
. . . .		
If an assessment is to be carried out, who is to make the arrangements and when?		
. . . .		
Litigation friend		
Have enquiries been made as to whether any person other than the OS is suitable and willing to act as litigation friend?	Yes	No
If so, is there any such person suitable and willing to act?	Yes	No
If yes, state name, address and relationship, if any, to PP		
. . . .		
If no enquiries have been made, give reasons and state when and how any enquiries are to be made.		
. . . .		
Funding		
Has a public-funding certificate been granted to PP	Yes	No
If not, is PP eligible for public-funding?		
(a) without assessment of merit or means	Yes (a)	No
(b) subject to merit and/or means	Yes (b)	No
If no, how is security for costs to be provided to the Official Solicitor or other litigation friend (*eg PP's funds, with CoP authority if required, or undertaking by another party*)		
. . . .		
Information for the Official Solicitor (where invited to consent) Have the following been provided to the OS?		
• a copy of any court order or finding relating to capacity or the appointment of a litigation friend	Yes	No

• a copy of any assessment of capacity *(including any letter of instruction)*	Yes	No
• the information set out in this form (to be given in writing and including any relevant attendance note)	Yes	No

If the OS consents to act as litigation friend for PP, who is to provide the case papers to him?

. . . .

. . . .

. . . .

This form has been completed by:
Name:
Position:
Address/phone/e-mail:

On [date]:

Further information

- For further information about the appointment of the Official Solicitor, reference should be made to the *Practice Note: Official Solicitor: Appointment in Family Proceedings and Proceedings under the Inherent Jurisdiction in relation to Adults (March 2013).*
- For the procedure in relation to protected parties, see the Family Procedure Rules 2010, Part 15 and Practice Directions 15A and 15B

Contacting the Official Solicitor

To discuss any question in relation to the appointment of the OS in a particular case, contact may be made on:
020 3681 2755 (for public law children proceedings)
020 3681 2754 (for all private law family proceedings, including divorce, civil partnership and proceedings under the Family Law Act 1996)

APPENDIX 7

Practice Note – The Official Solicitor: Appointment in Family Proceedings

1   INTRODUCTION

1. This Practice Note replaces the Practice Note dated 2 April 2001 issued by the Official Solicitor.

2. It concerns:

   (a) the appointment of the Official Solicitor as 'litigation friend' of a 'protected party' or child in family proceedings or where the Family Division of the High Court is being invited to exercise its inherent jurisdiction in relation to a vulnerable adult;[1]

   (b) requests by the court to the Official Solicitor to conduct *Harbin* v *Masterman*[2] enquiries; and

   (c) requests by the court to the Official Solicitor to act as, or appoint counsel to act as, an advocate to the court.[3]

   The Note is intended to be helpful guidance, but is always subject to legislation including the Rules of Court, to Practice Directions, and to case law.

3. For the avoidance of doubt, the Children and Family Court Advisory and Support Service (CAFCASS) has responsibilities in relation to a child in family proceedings in which their welfare is or may be in question (Criminal Justice and Court Services Act 2000, section 12). Since 1 April 2001 the Official Solicitor has not represented a child who is the subject of family proceedings (other than in very exceptional circumstances or where a transfer to the Court of Protection is being considered see paragraph 7 below). In cases of doubt or difficulty, staff of the Official Solicitor's office will liaise with staff of CAFCASS Legal Services to avoid duplication and ensure the most suitable arrangements are made.

Children and Protected Parties who require a litigation friend in proceedings

4. Adults: a 'protected party' requires a litigation friend. In family proceedings this requirement appears in Part 15 of the Family Procedure Rules 2010 (FPR 2010) and in proceedings in the Family Division of the High Court of Justice under the court's inherent jurisdiction it appears in Part 21 of the Civil Procedure Rules 1998 (CPR 1998). In family proceedings, a 'protected party' means a party, or an intended party, who lacks capacity (within the meaning of the Mental Capacity Act 2005) to conduct

---

1. In this context a 'vulnerable adult' is a person who has mental capacity in respect of the decisions in question but who lacks litigation capacity.
2. [1896] 1 Ch 351.
3. Pursuant to the Memorandum 'Requests for the appointment of an advocate to the court' of the Attorney General and the Lord Chief Justice of 19 December 2001.

the proceedings: FPR 2010, rule 2.3; and in proceedings under the inherent jurisdiction the expression has the same meaning: CPR 1998, rule 21.2. The following should be noted:

(a) there must be undisputed evidence that the party, or intended party, lacks capacity to conduct the proceedings;

(b) that evidence, and what flows from the party, or intended party, being a protected party, should have been disclosed to, and carefully explained to, the party or intended party;

(c) the party, or intended party, is entitled to dispute an opinion that they lack litigation capacity and there may be cases where the party's, or intended party's, capacity to conduct the proceedings is the subject of dispute between competent experts. In either case a formal finding by the court under FPR 2010, rule 2.3, or CPR 1998, rule 21.2 is required.

5. Non-subject child: a child whose own welfare is not the subject of family proceedings may nevertheless be a party. The most common examples are:

(a) a child who is also the parent of a child, and who is a respondent to a Children Act 1989 or Adoption and Children Act 2002 application;

(b) a child who wishes to make an application for a Children Act 1989 order naming another child (typically a contact order naming a sibling);

(c) a child witness to some disputed factual issue in a children case and who may require intervenor status;

(d) a child party to an application for a declaration of status under Part III of the Family Law Act 1986;

(e) a child intervenor in financial remedy proceedings;

(f) a child applicant for, or respondent to, an application for an order under Part IV (Family Homes and Domestic Violence) or Part 4A (Forced Marriage) of the Family Law Act 1996.

6. FPR 2010 Part 16 makes provision for the representation of children. Rule 16.6 sets out the circumstances in which a child does not need a children's guardian or litigation friend. Any child party to proceedings under the Children Act 1989, Part 4A Family Law Act 1996, applications in adoption, placement and related proceedings, or proceedings relating to the exercise of the court's inherent jurisdiction with respect to children may rely on the provisions of rule 16.6.

7. Children aged 16-17 years: the Mental Capacity Act 2005 (Transfer of Proceedings) Order 2007 (SI 2007/1899) makes provision for the transfer of proceedings from the Court of Protection to a court having jurisdiction under the Children Act 1989. The Order also makes provision for the transfer of the whole or part of the proceedings from a court having jurisdiction under the Children Act 1989 to the Court of Protection where it considers that in all circumstances, it is just and convenient to transfer the proceedings. Article 3(3) of the Order lists those factors to which the court must have regard when making a determination about transfer either on an application or of its own initiative. Court of Protection proceedings are not family proceedings and therefore transfer of proceedings into the Court of Protection will mean that any involvement by CAFCASS in those proceedings will end.

8. The Court of Protection Rules 2007 apply to proceedings in the Court of Protection. Rule 141 (4)-(6) of those Rules make provision for a child to be permitted to conduct proceedings in the Court of Protection without a litigation friend. However if the child is 'P' within the meaning of rule 6 of the Court of Protection Rules 2007 reference should be made to rule 141(1) and rule 147 of those Rules in relation to the appointment of a litigation friend.

The role of a litigation friend

9.   The case law and the Rules provide that a litigation friend must fairly and competently conduct the proceedings in the protected party's or child's best interests, and must have no interest in the proceedings adverse to that of the protected party or child. The procedure and basis for the appointment of a litigation friend and the duty of a litigation friend are contained in Part 15 (Representation of Protected Parties) FPR 2010 and Part 16 (Representation of Children and Reports in Proceedings Involving Children) FPR 2010 and the associated Practice Directions.

The Official Solicitor's criteria for consenting to act as litigation friend

10.   The Official Solicitor is the litigation friend of last resort. No person, including the Official Solicitor, can be appointed to act as litigation friend without their consent. The Official Solicitor will not accept appointment where there is another person who is suitable and willing to act as litigation friend. The Official Solicitor's criteria for consenting to act as litigation friend are:

     (a)   in the case of an adult that the party or intended party is a protected party;[4]
     (b)   there is security for the costs of legal representation of the protected party which the Official Solicitor considers satisfactory. Sources of security may be

          (i)   the Legal Aid Agency where the protected party or child is eligible for public funding;
          (ii)   the protected party's or child's own funds where they have financial capacity or where they do not where the Court of Protection has given him authority to recover the costs from the adult's or child's funds;
          (iii)   an undertaking from another party to pay his costs;

     (c)   the case is a last resort case.

Invitations to the Official Solicitor: new cases

11.   Solicitors who have been consulted by a child or a protected party (or by someone acting on their behalf, or concerned about their interests) should write to the Official Solicitor setting out the background to the proposed case and explaining the basis on which the Official Solicitor's criteria for acting are met.

Invitations to the Official Solicitor: pending proceedings

12.   Where a case is already before the court, an order inviting the Official Solicitor to act should be expressed as being made subject to his consent. The Official Solicitor aims to provide an initial response to any invitation within 10 working days. But he cannot consent to act unless and until he is satisfied both that his criteria are met and that he has a member of his staff to whom the case can be allocated as the case's case manager. So from time to time there will be a waiting list of cases which meet the Official Solicitor's acceptance criteria but in respect of which, because he has no case manager available to take the case, he cannot accept appointment as litigation friend. Save in exceptional circumstances, cases will be accepted in strict chronological order starting with the earliest placed on the waiting list of cases which have met the criteria for acceptance.

---

4. The Official Solicitor is able to provide a pro forma certificate of capacity to conduct proceedings and notes for guidance.

What constitutes exceptional circumstances will be fact specific; the decision to expedite acceptance of a case is one for the Official Solicitor.

13.   To enable the Official Solicitor to consider the invitation to him to act, he should be provided with the following as soon as possible:

(a)   the sealed court order inviting him to act as litigation friend (with a note of the reasons approved by the Judge if appropriate);

(b)   a copy of the letter of instruction to the expert by which an opinion was sought as to the party's capacity to conduct the proceedings whether in the form of the Official Solicitor's certificate of capacity to conduct the proceedings or otherwise;

(c)   (adult party) the opinion on capacity (the Official Solicitor's pro forma certificate of capacity to conduct proceedings may be requested from his office for the purpose of obtaining an opinion);

(d)   confirmation that there is satisfactory security for the costs of legal representation (including any relevant supporting documents); it is a matter for the Official Solicitor whether the proposed security for costs is satisfactory;

(e)   confirmation that there is no other person suitable and willing to act as litigation friend (including the enquiries made to this end);

(f)   the court file (provision of the court file may not be necessary if the court directs a party to provide a full indexed copy of the bundle to the Official Solicitor on a timely basis).

Litigants in person

14.   If one or more parties is or are litigants in person, and there is reason to believe that any litigant in person may lack capacity to conduct the proceedings, the court will need to consider, and if necessary give directions as to:

(a)   who is to arrange for the assessment of capacity to conduct the proceedings;

(b)   how the cost of that assessment is to be funded;

(c)   how any invitation to act as litigation friend is to be made to either any suitable and willing person or the Official Solicitor so as to provide him with the documents and information (including information to enable him to make the enquiries necessary to establish whether or not there is funding available;

(d)   any resulting timetabling and, where the Official Solicitor is being invited to be litigation friend, having regard to the Official Solicitor's need to investigate whether his acceptance criteria are met, the need for him to have a case manager available to deal with the case and the possibility that an application to the Court of Protection (for authority to pay the costs out of the protected party's or child's funds) may be necessary.

15.   The Official Solicitor will notify the court in the event he expects a delay in accepting appointment either because it is not evident that his criteria are met or for any other reason. The court may wish to consider:

(a)   making enquiries of the parties as to the steps being taken by them to establish that the Official Solicitor's criteria for acting are met in the particular case;

(b)   whether directions should be made to ensure that such enquiries are progressed on a timely basis;

(c)   fixing a further directions appointment.

16.   If, at any time, another litigation friend is appointed before the Official Solicitor is in a position to accept the invitation to him to act, the Official Solicitor should be notified without delay.

Where the Official Solicitor has accepted appointment as litigation friend

17.   Once the Official Solicitor is able to accept appointment as litigation friend he will need time to prepare the case on behalf of the protected party or child and may wish to make submissions about any substantive hearing date.

18.   To avoid unnecessary delay in progression of the case, he will require from the solicitors he appoints for the protected party or child:

(a)   a reading list identifying the material which the solicitors considers will assist by way of introduction to the case in obtaining an overview of the issues from the perspective of the protected party or child;

(b)   a summary of the background to the proceedings, of any major steps that have occurred within the proceedings, and identification of the issues in the proceedings;

(c)   advice as to the steps the Official Solicitor should now take in the proceedings on behalf of the protected party or child;

(d)   copies of all notes of attendance on the protected party or child so that the Official Solicitor is properly informed as to the views and wishes expressed by the protected party or child to date;

(e)   confirmation of the protected party's or child's present ascertainable views and wishes in relation to the proceedings.

Advising the court: *Harbin* v *Masterman* enquiries and Advocate to the Court

19.   Where the Official Solicitor is invited, with his consent, to conduct enquiries under *Harbin* v *Masterman* and it appears to the Official Solicitor that any public body wishes to seek the assistance of the court but is unwilling to carry out the enquiries itself, the Official Solicitor may seek an undertaking from that public body to indemnify him in respect of his costs of carrying out those enquiries.

20.   As noted at paragraph 2(c) above, the Official Solicitor may be invited, with his consent, to act or instruct counsel as a friend of the court (advocate to the court) if it appears to the court that such an invitation is more appropriately addressed to him rather than (or in addition to) CAFCASS Legal Services or to the Attorney-General.

Contacting the Official Solicitor

21.   It may be helpful to discuss the question of appointment with the Official Solicitor or one of his staff by telephoning 020 7911 7127 (family litigation) or 020 7911 7233 (divorce litigation), in particular:

(a)   if in doubt about whether his criteria for acting are met, or

(b)   to request a copy of the Official Solicitor's pro forma certificate of capacity to conduct proceedings and notes for guidance.

The Official Solicitor's certificate of capacity to conduct proceedings, a sample letter of instruction, other precedent documents and further guidance in relation to the appointment of the Official Solicitor are also available at **www.justice.gov.uk** (follow the links to the Official Solicitor).

22.   Enquiries about the appointment of the Official Solicitor as litigation friend should be addressed:

(a)   (in divorce and financial remedy proceedings) to the Divisional Manager, Divorce Litigation;

(b)   (in children proceedings or proceedings under Part IV Family Law Act 1996) to the Divisional Manager, Family Litigation;.

All other enquiries should be addressed to a family lawyer.

The contact details are:

81 Chancery Lane,
London WC2A 1DD.

DX 0012 London Chancery Lane
Fax: 020 7911 7105
Email address: enquiries@offsol.gsi.gov.uk

March 2013
Alastair Pitblado
Official Solicitor

APPENDIX 8

Practice Guidance – Transparency in the Family Courts: Publication of Judgments

THE PURPOSE OF THIS GUIDANCE

1   This Guidance (together with similar Guidance issued at the same time for the Court of Protection) is intended to bring about an immediate and significant change in practice in relation to the publication of judgments in family courts and the Court of Protection.

2   In both courts there is a need for greater transparency in order to improve public understanding of the court process and confidence in the court system. At present too few judgments are made available to the public, which has a legitimate interest in being able to read what is being done by the judges in its name. The Guidance will have the effect of increasing the number of judgments available for publication (even if they will often need to be published in appropriately anonymised form).

3   In July 2011 Sir Nicholas Wall P issued, jointly with Bob Satchwell, Executive Director of the Society of Editors, a paper, The Family Courts: Media Access & Reporting (Media Access & Reporting), setting out a statement of the current state of the law. In their preface they recognised that the debate on increased transparency and public confidence in the family courts would move forward and that future consideration of this difficult and sensitive area would need to include the questions of access to and reporting of proceedings by the media, whilst maintaining the privacy of the families involved. The paper is to be found at: **www.judiciary.gov.uk/Resources/ JCO/Documents/Guidance/family-courtsmedia-july2011.pdf**.

4   In April 2013 I issued a statement, View from the President's Chambers: the Process of Reform, [2013] Fam Law 548, in which I identified transparency as one of the three strands in the reforms which the family justice system is currently undergoing. I said:

> I am determined to take steps to improve access to and reporting of family proceedings. I am determined that the new Family Court should not be saddled, as the family courts are at present, with the charge that we are a system of secret and unaccountable justice. Work, commenced by my predecessor, is well underway. I hope to be in a position to make important announcements in the near future.

5   That applies just as much to the issue of transparency in the Court of Protection.

6   Very similar issues arise in both the Family Court (as it will be from April 2014) and the Court of Protection in relation to the need to protect the personal privacy of children and vulnerable adults. The applicable rules differ, however, and this is something that needs attention. My starting point is that so far as possible the same rules and principles should apply in both the family courts (in due course the Family Court) and the Court of Protection.

7   I propose to adopt an incremental approach. Initially I am issuing this Guidance. This will be followed by further Guidance and in due course more formal Practice Directions and changes to the Rules (the Court of Protection Rules 2007 and the Family Procedure Rules 2010). Changes to primary legislation are unlikely in the near future.

8   As provided in paragraph 14 below, this Guidance applies only to judgments delivered by certain judges. In due course, following the introduction of the Family Court, consideration will be given to extending it to judgments delivered by other judges (including lay justices).

The legal framework

9   The effect of section 12 of the Administration of Justice Act 1960 is that it is a contempt of court to publish a judgment in a family court case involving children unless either the judgment has been delivered in public or, where delivered in private, the judge has authorised publication. In the latter case, the judge normally gives permission for the judgment to be published on condition that the published version protects the anonymity of the children and members of their family.

10   In every case the terms on which publication is permitted are a matter for the judge and will be set out by the judge in a rubric at the start of the judgment.

11   The normal terms as described in paragraph 9 may be appropriate in a case where no-one wishes to discuss the proceedings otherwise than anonymously. But they may be inappropriate, for example, where parents who have been exonerated in care proceedings wish to discuss their experiences in public, identifying themselves and making use of the judgment. Equally, they may be inappropriate in cases where findings have been made against a person and someone else contends and/or the judge concludes that it is in the public interest for that person to be identified in any published version of the judgment.

12   If any party wishes to identify himself or herself, or any other party or person, as being a person referred to in any published version of the judgment, their remedy is to seek an order of the court and a suitable modification of the rubric: Media Access & Reporting, para 82; *Re RB (Adult) (No 4)* [2011] EWHC 3017 (Fam), [2012] 1 FLR 466, paras [17], [19].

13   Nothing in this Guidance affects the exercise by the judge in any particular case of whatever powers would otherwise be available to regulate the publication of material relating to the proceedings. For example, where a judgment is likely to be used in a way that would defeat the purpose of any anonymisation, it is open to the judge to refuse to publish the judgment or to make an order restricting its use.

Guidance

14   This Guidance takes effect from 3 February 2014. It applies

(i)   in the family courts (and in due course in the Family Court), to judgments delivered by Circuit Judges, High Court Judges and persons sitting as judges of the High Court; and

(ii)   to all judgments delivered by High Court Judges (and persons sitting as judges of the High Court) exercising the inherent jurisdiction to make orders in respect of children and incapacitated or vulnerable adults.

15   The following paragraphs of this Guidance distinguish between two classes of judgment:

(i)   those that the judge must ordinarily allow to be published (paragraphs 16 and 17); and
(ii)   those that may be published (paragraph 18).

16   Permission to publish a judgment should always be given whenever the judge concludes that publication would be in the public interest and whether or not a request has been made by a party or the media.

17   Where a judgment relates to matters set out in Schedule 1 or 2 below and a written judgment already exists in a publishable form or the judge has already ordered that the judgment be transcribed, the starting point is that permission should be given for the judgment to be published unless there are compelling reasons why the judgment should not be published.

SCHEDULE 1

In the family courts (and in due course in the Family Court), including in proceedings under the inherent jurisdiction of the High Court relating to children, judgments arising from:

(i)   a substantial contested fact-finding hearing at which serious allegations, for example allegations of significant physical, emotional or sexual harm, have been determined;

(ii)   the making or refusal of a final care order or supervision order under Part 4 of the Children Act 1989, or any order for the discharge of any such order, except where the order is made with the consent of all participating parties;

(iii)   the making or refusal of a placement order or adoption order under the Adoption and Children Act 2002, or any order for the discharge of any such order, except where the order is made with the consent of all participating parties;

(iv)   the making or refusal of any declaration or order authorising a deprivation of liberty, including an order for a secure accommodation order under section 25 of the Children Act 1989;

(v)   any application for an order involving the giving or withholding of serious medical treatment;

(vi)   any application for an order involving a restraint on publication of information relating to the proceedings.

SCHEDULE 2

In proceedings under the inherent jurisdiction of the High Court relating to incapacitated or vulnerable adults, judgments arising from:

(i)   any application for a declaration or order involving a deprivation or possible deprivation of liberty;

(ii)   any application for an order involving the giving or withholding of serious medical treatment;

(iii)   any application for an order that an incapacitated or vulnerable adult be moved into or out of a residential establishment or other institution;

(iv)   any application for a declaration as to capacity to marry or to consent to sexual relations;

(v)   any application for an order involving a restraint on publication of information relating to the proceedings.

18   In all other cases, the starting point is that permission may be given for the judgment to be published whenever a party or an accredited member of the media applies for an order permitting publication, and the judge concludes that permission for the judgment to be published should be given.

19   In deciding whether and if so when to publish a judgment, the judge shall have regard to all the circumstances, the rights arising under any relevant provision of the European Convention on Human Rights, including Articles 6 (right to a fair hearing), 8 (respect for private and family life) and 10 (freedom of expression), and the effect of publication upon any current or potential criminal proceedings.

20   In all cases where a judge gives permission for a judgment to be published:

(i)   public authorities and expert witnesses should be named in the judgment approved for publication, unless there are compelling reasons why they should not be so named;

(ii)   the children who are the subject of the proceedings in the family courts, and other members of their family, and the person who is the subject of proceedings under the inherent jurisdiction of the High Court relating to incapacitated or vulnerable adults, and other members of their family, should not normally be named in the judgment approved for publication unless the judge otherwise orders;

(iii)   anonymity in the judgment as published should not normally extend beyond protecting the privacy of the children and adults who are the subject of the proceedings and other members of their families, unless there are compelling reasons to do so.

21   Unless the judgment is already in anonymised form or the judge otherwise orders, any necessary anonymisation of the judgment shall be carried out, in the case of judgments being published pursuant to paragraphs 16 and 17 above, by the solicitor for the applicant in the proceedings and, in the case of a judgment being published pursuant to paragraph 18 above, by the solicitor for the party or person applying for publication of the judgment. The anonymised version of the judgment must be submitted to the judge within a period specified by the judge for approval. The version approved for publication will contain such rubric as the judge specifies. Unless the rubric specified by the judge provides expressly to the contrary every published judgment shall be deemed to contain the following rubric:

> This judgment was delivered in private. The judge has given leave for this version of the judgment to be published on condition that (irrespective of what is contained in the judgment) in any published version of the judgment the anonymity of the children and members of their family must be strictly preserved. All persons, including representatives of the media, must ensure that this condition is strictly complied with. Failure to do so will be a contempt of court.

22   The judge will need to consider who should be ordered to bear the cost of transcribing the judgment. Unless the judge otherwise orders:

(i)   in cases falling under paragraph 16 the cost of transcribing the judgment is to be at public expense;

(ii)   subject to (i), in cases falling under paragraph 17 the cost of transcribing the judgment shall be borne equally by the parties to the proceedings;

(iii)   in cases falling under paragraph 18, the cost of transcribing the judgment shall be borne by the party or person applying for publication of the judgment.

23   In all cases where permission is given for a judgment to be published, the version of the judgment approved for publication shall be made available, upon payment of any appropriate charge that may be required, to any person who requests a copy. Where a judgment to which paragraph 16 or 17 applies is approved for publication, it shall as soon as reasonably practicable be placed by the court on the BAILII website. Where a judgment to which paragraph 18 applies is approved for publication, the judge shall consider whether it should be placed on the BAILII website and, if so, it shall as soon as reasonably practicable be placed by the court on the BAILII website.

APPENDIX 9

Arrangements for Handling Child Care Cases

[Association of Council Secretaries and Solicitors and Solicitors in Local Government Child Care Law Joint Liaison Group, March 2004]

In October 1990, the Child Care Law Joint Liaison Group offered guidance to local authorities in the conduct of child care cases on behalf of social services departments. Following the implementation of the Children Act 1989, the guidance was revised in 1995 and 2000 to take into account changes in legal practice.

Following the advent of the Protocol for Judicial Case Management in Public Law Children Act Cases[1] in June 2003 the CCLJLG have considered it appropriate to review the guidance again to ensure that it is keeping pace with, not only developments in the approaches taken by the courts in respect of Children Act applications, but also developments in the structure of local authorities.

The following is therefore offered as guidance for best practice in the conduct of child care law cases on behalf of social services departments and should be read in conjunction with Good Practice in Child Care Cases. A Guide for Solicitors Acting in Public Law Children Act Proceedings Including Cases Involving Adoption, the Law Society Good Practice Guide published in March 2004.[2]

1. THE PROVISION OF LEGAL SERVICES FOR SOCIAL SERVICES

1.1 The provision of legal services for social services will vary from authority to authority. It is not the purpose of this guidance to suggest that any one structure is more effective than another, but it is suggested that the following principles should always be adhered to.

1.2 Arrangements for the delivery of legal services in respect of child care cases will usually be handled within a local authority's own legal department, using in-house lawyers. Some authorities may contract the work out entirely by competitive tender.

1.3 Because local authority legal departments are not in a position to turn work away as in private practice, it may be necessary to use specialist counsel/private sector lawyers to assist in work load peaks.

1.4 In the event of work going out to private practice, the local authority will need to ensure that the standard of work carried out by the firm in question meets the authority's own quality standards for the provision of legal services. It is therefore advisable for the Head of Legal

---

1. Protocol for Judicial Case Management in Public Law Children Act Cases 2003 Lord Chancellor's Department, London The Stationery Office.
2. Good Practice in Child Care Cases 2004. The Law Society with the Association of Lawyers for Children, the Child Care Law Joint Liaison Group and the Solicitors Family Law Association London, London, The Law Society.

Services to take steps to identify firms operating at an appropriate quality level. For example, if the local authority in-house team is working to the Lexcel standard, it is desirable to ensure that private practice agents operate the same standard. In any event, a private practice solicitor handling child care cases on behalf of a local authority should be expected to comply with appropriate provisions in this guidance.

1.5　Whilst it is not possible to specify a figure, it is considered that Authorities should aim to keep the conduct of at least 75% of cases 'in-house' to avoid prejudicing the appropriate control advocated by this guidance.

1.6　A situation whereby a social services department was free to choose private solicitors or the in-house legal department or place cases directly with private solicitors would not satisfy this guidance.

1.7　Similarly, a situation in which solicitors are based in Social Services Departments directly responsible to the Director of Social Services is considered to be prejudicial to the operation of best practice as set out in these guidelines.

1.8　If work is placed with a private practitioner, the solicitor with the conduct of the case should be a member of the Law Society Children Panel.

2.　THE IN-HOUSE TEAM

2.1　Many local authorities now require lawyers to specialise entirely in providing legal advice and assistance to the social services department. Although child care is usually a dominant area of work conducted by such lawyers, it is important to recognise that the lawyers in such specialist teams are required to deal with other complex areas of work on behalf of their social services departments. For example, this may include work in relation to the following areas: -

- Care standards
- Complaints procedures
- Access to records/data protection and access to information
- Adoption panels and the local authority adoption agency
- Work for the local education authority
- Community care
- Mental health
- The elderly and vulnerable adults
- Criminal injuries compensation
- Advice to members
- Crime and disorder
- Human rights
- Judicial review
- Partnership working
- Children's services policy matters
- Asylum and immigration

2.2　The legal services team needs to be in a position to be able to offer comprehensive advice upon children law and policy matters. This includes work dealt with within each Area Child Protection Committee administered in accordance with the 'Working Together to Safeguard

Children' guidelines.[3] Members of the local authority legal services may be involved in the work of that Committee.[4] The Authority should recognise the contribution to its work by local authority lawyers, which will include participating in the training of multi-agency staff. Given the time that this can entail, it is considered that this responsibility should be included in the appropriate person's job description.

2.3   The implementation of the Children Act brought together the judiciary, the court administration and other agencies involved in children matters. This is achieved through the Family Court Business Committee and the Family Court/User Forum. An experienced and senior child care lawyer should be members of these Committees, which have an important impact upon how each local authority will present its cases to the court. As above, each authority should recognise the time required to contribute to these Committees by including the responsibility in relevant job descriptions.

2.4   Local authorities should also encourage their more experienced child care lawyers to belong to special interest groups and the representative groups in the field of child care law.

2.5   The legal department of a local authority responsible for social services legal work should include at least one senior solicitor or barrister preferably having a senior management role in the authority who specialises in, and has a considerable experience of, child care legal work on a day to day basis. All such work shall be under the general direction of that lawyer, who shall decide (subject to consultation where necessary with the Head of Service) upon the allocation of Court proceedings to solicitors or other suitably trained or qualified staff where appropriate.

2.6   To ensure the proper conduct of proceedings, the Head of Service should allocate sufficient resources and enlist sufficiently trained staff to:

- Ensure scrutiny of the local authority's case and proper conduct in accordance with the terms of the Protocol.
- Safeguard the integrity of the local authority before the court e.g. ensure through appropriate preparation and presentation that all relevant information is before the court and other parties.
- Appropriately secure the transfer of cases to a higher court.
- Ensure timetable requirements are met.
- Ensure Cases and caseload are monitored.
- Ensure production of properly prepared bundles and other documentation required for court.

2.7   Proceedings in child care cases should not be initiated without legal advice.

2.8   No lawyer should represent a local authority in opposed child care proceedings unless he/she has an up to date working knowledge of child care law, has received appropriate training in those areas not covered by experience in practice, and, has recent significant practical experience of conducting child care proceedings. It is desirable for all local authority child care lawyers to seek accreditation to the Law Society Children Panel and this objective should be promoted by the Head of Service.

3. Department of Health Home Office, Department for Education and Employment 1999. Can be found on **www.the-stationary-office.couk/dob/worktog/worktog.htm**.
4. Working Together to Safeguard Children – para 4.12.

2.9 Although continuity of representation in a child care case is important it may nevertheless be necessary at different stages in the process for the case to be handled by different members of staff with appropriate knowledge of child care law and practice. However, there must be a designated child care lawyer for the case who will take primary responsibility for crucial parts of the process and oversee the conduct of the case through the court. It is the designated lawyer's responsibility to ensure the terms of the Protocol are complied with, as far as possible.

2.10 The Head of Service should establish and keep under review arrangements for ensuring that staff handling child care proceedings receive supervision according to the level of experience and appropriate training, including continuing professional development, both in child care law and advocacy. When a service is dependent on locums particular attention should be paid to these matters. Where appropriate arrangements should be in place for each child care lawyer to have access to a mentor.

2.11 The local authority providing legal services to Social Services should ensure that resources are available to enable proper management information to be compiled for the benefit of its own social services functions and for other interested bodies. (for example the Family Court Business Committee). This will normally require provision of a computerised system to comply with Law Society Practice Management standards. An appropriate officer should be made responsible for ensuring that appropriate management information is compiled from the resources available.

3. RELATIONSHIP WITH 'CLIENT'

3.1 The child care lawyer's client is the local authority, but the day to day working relationship is with the Director of Social Services, acting through managers and social workers.

3.2 Any decision to take legal proceedings on behalf of a local authority should be taken at an appropriate level, on the basis of delegated powers within the authority. Requests to take proceedings in relation to children are made by the Social Services Department.

3.3 Special care should be taken when a decision is required regarding instigation of statutory proceedings in respect of a child. Decisions about the welfare and protection of a child should be taken within the Social Services Department, which is where the necessary expertise to conduct assessments and care planning is to be found. Lawyers do not have social work training and should not take decisions on matters within the province of the Social Services Department.

3.4 Although advice might be given concerning potential difficulties in taking a case to court, an unequivocal request to take proceedings by the Social Services Department should very rarely be refused. If there is a dispute between the client department and the lawyer, this should be resolved at senior management level.

3.5 In addition to the above, there are further expectations with regard to decisions about whether or not the local authority should take care proceedings and the Judicial Case Management Protocol sets out clearly the evidence and documentation that must be available at the outset of proceedings.

3.6   Department of Health Guidance – Volume 1 Court Orders[5] – advises that before proceeding with an application, the Local Authority Social Services Department should always seek legal advice (preferably within the context of the multi disciplinary, multi agency case conference)[6] on:

(a)   Whether, in the circumstances of the case and having regard to the Section 1(3) checklist (the welfare checklist), the court is likely to be satisfied; first, that the Section 31(2) criteria are satisfied (threshold for significant harm) and that an order should be made under the Section 1(5) test (no order principle);

(b)   The implications of another party to the proceedings opposing the application and applying for a Section 8 order instead;

(c)   Whether the application falls within criteria of transfer of cases to a higher court and whether representations about this should be made;

(d)   Whether the court should be asked for an interim care or supervision order, the desired length of the initial interim order and what directions should be sought;

(e)   The matters to be provided for in the Authority's advance statement of case including copies of witness statements that can be made available and a broad outline of the Authority's plans for the child;

(f)   Notification and other procedural requirements and matters likely to be considered at directions appointments;

(g)   Whether the Court is likely to consider that in all the circumstances of the case a Children's Guardian does not need to be appointed;

(h)   Whether use of a residence order linked with a supervision order would be an appropriate alternative to a care order

3.7   An analysis of the steps involved in making a decision about whether or not a child should be made subject to care proceedings and the subsequent conduct of these proceedings reveals a complex process requiring a harmonious interface between lawyer and social worker. Their respective roles are significantly different, but when it comes to making a decision, there will be similar factors for both to consider, albeit from different perspectives. Working relationships on the conduct of child care cases may be greatly assisted by the agreement of a protocol between Social Services and Legal Departments.

3.8   Child care lawyers should create and maintain a professional relationship with the Authority and its Social Services Department which will preserve fully their independent judgement. Care must be taken to ensure that a lawyer does not become so involved in a case that his/her personal emotions adversely effect his/her judgement and independence.

3.9   In particular, lawyers have an overriding duty as Officers of the Court to ensure that all cases are dealt with correctly, and that where and when necessary matters are returned to the Court. The Court may at any time make an order that a party pay the whole or any part of the costs of any other party. In children cases it is unusual to order costs, unless the conduct of a party has been reprehensible or beyond the band of what was reasonable.[7]

5. Department of Health, 1991 London HMSO.
6. In practice many local authorities find that the advice is more appropriately given in another forum, such as social services planning or legal gatekeeping meeting.
7. *Re G (a minor) (Wardship:Costs)* [1982] 2 All ER 32, [1982] 1WLR 438; *Re B (Costs)* [1999] 2 FLR 221, CA. *Bolton Metropolitan Borough Council v B and H* [1990] FCR 57 [1989] 2 FLR 349; *Re M (Local Authority's costs)* [1995] 1 FCR 649, [1995] 1 FLR 533; *Re G (costs: child case)* [1999] 3 FCR 463.

4.   THE CONDUCT OF CHILD CARE CASES

4.1   This section deals with the duties placed upon child care lawyers in conducting child care cases.

4.2   Cases will be allocated to a lawyer with appropriate expertise for the complexity of the case. The lawyer must be capable of advising the appropriate social services officers (and where necessary other officers) on all aspects of an allocated matter.

4.3   All child care lawyers should be able to seek appropriate supervision and support from their manager and colleagues when they require it. All child care lawyers should be able to recognise and report difficulties to their manager who, if appropriate will then be responsible for advising and/or reallocating the case to a more experienced lawyer as appropriate.

4.4   The lawyer appointed to deal with the case will ensure that the social workers and other professionals involved with the child and his/her family are informed of the lawyer's involvement and all other relevant details.

4.5   The child care lawyer is responsible for ensuring the integrity of the local authority's case before the court. All relevant information should be shared with the court and other parties.[8] The lawyer must ensure that the principle that the welfare of the child is paramount must be reflected in the conduct of the case itself. All child care cases should be approached in a non-adversarial manner and all lawyers have a duty to promote this in the interests of children.

4.6   Lawyers who have other responsibilities or roles in addition to their child care duties must endeavour to ensure that these other duties do not adversely affect or delay the performance of their child care work. The Head of Service and designated managers must ensure that the lawyer is able to discharge this responsibility.

4.7   All local authority child care lawyers should have access to the 'Reporting to Court under the Children Act' handbook[9] and adhere to the guidance set out in chapter 4 'The local authority legal adviser'. They should also have access to the Protocol for Judicial Case Management in Public Law Children Act Cases.

4.8   Child care lawyers shall at all times ensure that in all child care cases, and bearing in mind that proceedings are part of the continuing relationship with the family:

(a)   Work to achieve a constructive solution to the child's best interests with the minimum of acrimony and if possible, without prejudicing the child's interests, avoiding adversarial battles in court.

(b)   Ensure that all parties are treated with respect and that all matters are dealt with in as courteous and relaxed a manner as possible.

4.9   The lawyer's legal duty to the court and the paramount interests of the child transcend all duties to the Social Services Department and/or the client authority.

4.10   Lawyers should ensure that full co-operation is given to the Children's Guardian in the performance of his/her duties. Such co-operation shall include full access to the appropriate Social Services case files.

---

8. *Vernon v Bosley (No 2)* [1997] 3 WLR 683, [1998] 2 FLR 304 (CA) R, *Re (Care: Disclosure: Nature of Proceedings)* 2002 1 FLR 755.
9. Plontikoff and Wollfson Department of Health London The Stationery Office 1996.

4.11   All child care proceedings shall be dealt with expeditiously and correctly and in accordance with the Protocol. The lawyer with conduct of a case must comply with directions made by the court, particularly with regard to the Court timetable.

4.12   The lawyer with responsibility for the case should keep social workers and other professionals as appropriate, informed of the state/stage of the proceedings and the reasons for and implications of any changes in plan or delays.

4.13   Lawyers are responsible for keeping abreast of guidance given by the High Court on the conduct of child cases and adherence to the Protocol. Each case should be conducted in compliance with the Protocol and any other guidance offered by the High Court and the Department for Education and Skills. The Head of Service should ensure sufficient funds are made available for the cost of a subscription to either the Family Law Reports[10] or the Family Court Reporter.[11] Suitable practitioners' encyclopaedias should also be made available with a subscription to an updating service.[12] There is also much to be gained by access to CD-ROMs and internet facilities.

4.14   All correspondence in child care cases should be given the appropriate priority and copies sent to the social workers and/or others as necessary.

4.15   Child care lawyers must receive adequate training with regards to the provisions of Human Rights legislation and the United Nations Convention on the Rights of the Child and have up to date resources available on this matter.

5.   THE USE OF EXPERTS

5.1   The lawyer with conduct of a case is responsible for ensuring appropriate liaison with expert witnesses. The requirements of the Protocol and Guidance, offered by the High Court on the use of expert witnesses should be adhered to at all times.

5.2   The use of experts in care proceedings can often lead to delay for the child and expense for the local authority. It is advisable for the Head of Service to agree a protocol with the Social Services Department for the instruction and funding of experts. It is essential that all local authority child care lawyers are aware of the authority's policy and that there is a consistency of approach across the office. It is advisable too that a protocol is agreed with the health agencies in order to ensure professional witnesses from health care are available to advise and assist the local authority where appropriate.

6.   THE USE OF COUNSEL

6.1   The Head of Service should determine, in consultation with the Director of Social Services, the general policy with regard to the instruction of counsel. This will normally allow for lawyers to instruct counsel on their own authority in most cases, but perhaps identify cases where consultation with the Director of Social Services should occur first e.g. where it is proposed to instruct a QC; or in a case of extraordinary length and/or complexity. Where counsel

---

10. Jordan Publishing Ltd.
11. Butterworths.
12. For example, 'Children Law and Practice' Hershman McFarlane; Family Law Jordan Publishing Ltd; 'Clarke Hall and Morrison on Children' Butterworths.

are involved, they must be adequately instructed. Briefs to counsel must include all material information, which will need to be considered by the court.

6.2   If the case is placed with counsel, they should have appropriate expertise in child care law and the requirements of the Protocol.

7.   ATTENDANCE OF THE LOCAL AUTHORITY LAWYER AT CHILD PROTECTION CONFERENCES AND PLANNING MEETINGS

7.1   Child protection procedures including the conduct of the child protection conference are the responsibility of local Area Child Protection Committees acting in accordance with the Department of Health guidance contained in 'Working Together to Safeguard Children'. As stated above, no legal proceedings should be initiated unless legal advice has been given and there should be sufficient legal staff available to advise child protection conferences or other formal planning meetings, as required.

7.2   The Law Society has issued guidance on the conduct of solicitors at child protection conferences. Child care lawyers must read and observe those guidelines. In particular, it should be noted, from the guidelines that:

(a)   Although not a member, the local authority lawyer is part of the conference and lawyers acting for other parties cannot object to the lawyer being present, even if their clients are there and they themselves are unable to attend.

(b)   Social Services departments and the Chairperson must be aware of the role of Lawyers for parents and other significant adults and family members in the conference.

(c)   Where other parties (normally parents) are present, the local authority lawyer should not use their ability to attend without the other party's lawyer being present, to unfair advantage.

(d)   The local authority lawyer should at all times maintain their objectivity with regard to the case and if they are to be the advocate, their standing as an objective advocate before the court. The lawyer should take heed of the Law Society guidance which requires judgement to be made by the lawyer as to times where it may be appropriate to leave the child protection conference when unrepresented parents are present. As an objective advocate, it is one thing to be told of what has transpired at a meeting, it is another to witness what has transpired oneself.

(e)   If the local authority lawyer is present at a child protection conference and inadvertently hears from parents or other parties, information that would constitute an unfair advantage in subsequent proceedings before the court then the lawyer should ensure that another lawyer undertakes the relevant advocacy.

This guidance cannot establish absolute rules to be followed in all circumstances. It is a statement of principles, objectives and guidance designed to assist child care lawyers in local government service achieve their goal of ensuring that children's interests are based on appropriate advice and are properly represented in legal proceedings. Cases may arise where the law or the lawyer's professional duties require action which may not adhere to the guidance. In such circumstances those legal or professional obligations will take precedence over the guidance.

8. OUT OF HOURS ADVICE

Recommendation 36 of the Victoria Climbie Inquiry Report[13] states that 'no emergency action – on a case concerning an allegation of deliberate harm to a child should be taken without first obtaining legal advice. Local Authorities must ensure that such legal advice is available 24 hours a day'. In Keeping Children Safe: The Government's Response to the Victoria Climbie Inquiry Report and Joint Chief Inspectors' Report Safeguarding Children (2003)[14] the Government made clear that 'legal advice should always be sought when time allows'. Accordingly, it is advisable that the Head of Service ensure, that appropriate arrangements are in place in order to ensure access to out of hours legal advice.

13. 2003 **www.victoria-climbie-inquiry.org.uk**.
14. Keeping Children Safe The Government's Response to the Victoria Climbie Inquiry Report and Joint Inspector's Report Safeguarding Children 2003 London DfES, DOH HO.

APPENDIX 10

Useful contacts and websites

ADDRESSES

Association of Child Abuse Lawyers (ACAL)

PO Box 974A
Surbiton KT1 9XF
Tel: 020 8390 4701
Email: info@childabuselawyers.com
www.childabuselawyers.com

The Association of Directors of Children's Services (ADCS) Ltd

Piccadilly House
49 Piccadilly
Manchester M1 2AP
Tel: 0161 826 9484
Email: info@adcs.org.uk
www.adcs.org.uk

Association of Lawyers for Children (ALC)

PO Box 283
East Molesey
Surrey KT8 0WH
Tel/Fax: 020 8224 7071
Email: admin@alc.org.uk
www.alc.org.uk

Cafcass National Office

3rd Floor
21 Bloomsbury Street
London WC1B 3HF
Tel: 0300 456 4000
Email: webenquiries@cafcass.gsi.gov.uk
www.cafcass.gov.uk

Childline

NSPCC Weston House
42 Curtain Road
London EC2A 3NH
Tel: 0800 1111

Child Maintenance Options

Tel: 0800 988 0988 (Mon–Fri 8 am to 8 pm, Sat 9 am to 4 pm)
www.cmoptions.org.uk

Citizens' Advice

Myddleton House
115–123 Pentonville Road
London N1 9LZ
Tel: 020 7833 2181
www.citizensadvice.org.uk

Family and Childcare Trust

The Bridge,
81 Southwark Bridge Road
London SE1 0NQ
Reception: 020 7940 7510
Email: info@familyandchildcaretrust.org
www.familyandchildcaretrust.org

Family Justice Council

Office of the President of the Family Division
WG62 Royal Courts of Justice
Strand
London WC2A 2LL
Tel: 020 7947 7333/7974

Email: fjc@courtservice.gsi.gov.uk
www.judiciary.gov.uk/related-offices-and-bodies/advisory-bodies/fjc/

Law Society of England and Wales

113 Chancery Lane
London WC2A 1PL
Tel: 020 7242 1222
DX: 56 London/Chancery Lane
www.lawsociety.org.uk

Practice Advice Service (matters of legal practice and procedure)
Tel: 020 7320 5675
Email: practiceadvice@lawsociety.org.uk

Children Law Accreditation Scheme
Email: accreditation@lawsociety.org.uk
Tel. 020 7320 5797

Information Commissioner's Office (ICO)

Information Commissioner's Office
Wycliffe House Water Lane
Wilmslow
Cheshire SK9 5AF
Tel: 0303 123 1113
Email: casework@ico.org.uk
www.ico.org.uk

Legal Aid Agency (LAA)

Legal Aid Agency
Unit B8 Berkley Way
Viking Business Park
Jarrow
South Tyneside NE31 1SF
Email: contactcivil@legalaid.gsi.gov.uk
DX: 742350 JARROW

Civil Legal Advice (CLA)

Telephone: 0345 345 4 345
Minicom: 0345 609 6677

Online Support
020 3334 6664

National Association of Child Contact Centres (NACCC)

1 Heritage Mews
High Pavement
Nottingham NG1 1HN
Tel: 0845 4500 280/0115 948 4557
Email: contact@naccc.org.uk
www.naccc.org.uk

National Association of Guardian ad Litems and Reporting Officers (NAGALRO)

PO Box 264
Esher
Surrey KT10 0WA
Tel: 01372 818504
Fax: 01372 818505
Email: nagalro@globalnet.co.uk
www.nagalro.com

Official Solicitor and Public Trustee

Victory House
30–34 Kingsway
London WC2B 6EX
Tel: 020 7911 7127
Email: enquiries@offsol.gsi.gov.uk
www.gov.uk/government/organisations/official-solicitor-and-public-trustee

Solicitors Regulation Authority

Professional Ethics (issues of professional conduct)

The Cube
199 Wharfside Street
Birmingham
B1 1RN
Tel: 0370 606 2577
www.sra.org.uk

Resolution

PO Box 302
Orpington
Kent BR6 8QX
Tel: 020 3195 2469 / 020 3195 0190
DX: 154460 Petts Wood 3
Email: info@resolution.org.uk
www.resolution.org.uk

USEFUL WEBSITES

Action for Children: www.actionforchildren.org.uk
Advocate's Gateway: www.theadvocatesgateway.org
A National Voice: www.anationalvoice.org
Barnado's: www.barnardos.org.uk
British Association for Adoption and Fostering: www.baaf.org.uk
Cafcass: www.cafcass.gov.uk
Catch 22: www.catch-22.org.uk
Children's Commissioner for England: www.childrenscommissioner.gov.uk
Children's Commissioner for Wales: www.childcom.org.uk
Children's Rights Alliance for England: www.crae.org.uk
Children's Society: www.childrenssociety.org.uk
Coram: www.coram.org.uk
Coram Children's Legal Centre: www.childrenslegalcentre.com
Coram Voice: www.coramvoice.org.uk/
Courts & Tribunals Service: www.hmcourts-service.gov.uk
Department of Health: www.dh.gov.uk
Family Procedure Rules/Practice Directions: www.justice.gov.uk/courts/procedure-rules/
   family
Family Rights Group: www.frg.org.uk
Fostering Network: www.fostering.net
Howard League: www.howardleague.org
Judiciary: www.judiciary.gov.uk
Lawyers in Local Government Child Care Lawyers Group:
   www.lawyersinlocalgovernment.org.uks
Legal Aid Agency: www.gov.uk/government/organisations/legal-aid-agency
MIND: www.mind.org.uk
Ministry of Justice: www.justice.gov.uk
NAGALRO: www.nagalro.com
National Autistic Society: www.autism.org.uk
National Youth Advocacy Service: www.nyas.net
NSPCC: www.nspcc.org.uk
Office of the High Commissioner for Human Rights: www.ohchr.org
Refugee Council: www.refugeecouncil.org.uk
Who Cares Trust: www.thewhocarestrust.org.uk

Index